Contributions to Economics

More information about this series at
http://www.springer.com/series/1262

Stefania P.S. Rossi • Roberto Malavasi
Editors

Financial Crisis, Bank Behaviour and Credit Crunch

 Springer

Editors
Stefania P.S. Rossi
Department of Economics and Business
University of Cagliari
Cagliari
Italy

Roberto Malavasi
Department of Economics and Business
University of Cagliari
Cagliari
Italy

ISSN 1431-1933   ISSN 2197-7178   (electronic)
Contributions to Economics
ISBN 978-3-319-17412-9   ISBN 978-3-319-17413-6   (eBook)
DOI 10.1007/978-3-319-17413-6

Library of Congress Control Number: 2015946596

Springer Cham Heidelberg New York Dordrecht London

Printed on acid-free paper

Springer International Publishing AG Switzerland is part of Springer Science+Business Media (www.springer.com)

For my lovely Ludovica who joined me at the conference.

Stefania

Preface

A liquidity shortage, beginning in late 2007, sparked a series of events that resulted in the collapse of large financial institutions and dramatic downturns in key stock markets. The crisis played a significant role in determining extensive failures of economic activities, declines in consumer demand and wealth, and a severe recession in many areas of the globalised world.

Even more depressing consequences were avoided owing to exceptional interventions by monetary authorities and governments, which directly supported the financial markets with bailout policies and massive injections of liquidity. These interventions resulted in further important consequences, with the ex ante distortion of incentives—leading intermediaries to choose arrangements with excessive illiquidity and thereby increasing financial fragility—being the most important.

The European sovereign-debt crisis that spread out later in time is a further result of the global financial crisis. This second wave of crisis hit government bond markets and triggered a further slowdown in economic growth in Eurozone countries, especially those struggling with structural weaknesses such as high public debt and low rates of growth.

From the financial industry perspective, the worsening of sovereign ratings heavily affected banks' balance sheets. Risks linked to bank funding rose systemically, leading to heavy restrictions in credit supply (credit crunch). In addition to the worsening of credit access conditions, firms' less-than-expected returns put pressure on credit quality, implying a sudden increase in impaired loans. The banks' financial structure was deeply stressed and subject to substantial adjustments.

Along with the evolution of the global financial crisis, the recognition of bank fragility has led to several structural regulatory reforms aimed at reducing the bank risk profile and probability of future systemic bank failure.

To discuss these issues, a conference was held in Cagliari in July 2014 that brought contributions from leading scholars in the field. This book, organised into four parts, collects some of the papers selected for the conference.

The first part of the book, *Genesis and Evolution of the Global Financial Crisis*, presents two points of view regarding the economic background behind the origin and the late developments of the crisis. According to Hieronymi, the absence of a global rule-based international monetary order since the early 1970s has led to the growing domination of short-term market-driven "global finance" in the world economy and to recurring major financial crises, including the near worldwide financial collapse in 2008. This absence was also largely responsible for the gradual slowdown of economic growth in the OECD countries during the last 40 years. Moro argues that the cause of the European financial crisis is rooted in the imbalances of European Monetary Union (EMU) countries' balance of payments, where the TARGET2 payment system became crucial. Additionally, the interactions between sovereign problems and banking distress, which led to the severe economic slowdown in Europe, are also regarded as the main source of the fragmentation of Eurozone financial markets.

The second part of this book, *Bank Opportunistic Behaviour and Structural Reforms*, investigates whether policies implemented by governments and monetary authorities to countervail the most negative effects of the financial crisis have produced opportunistic conduct (*moral hazard*) or changes in banks' behaviour. Additionally, some structural reforms and regulatory measures are also debated in this section. Mattana and Rossi devise an empirical model to investigate the extent to which large banks may have taken advantage of moral hazard behaviour in the form of *too big to fail*, during the first wave of the global financial crisis (2007–2009). The authors, by employing a large sample of European banks, are able to detect a form of opportunistic conduct in the European banking system. Duran and Lozano-Vivas examine the moral hazard problem in the form of risk shifting that emerged in relation to the safety net and regulation for the European and the US banking systems. The authors provide a synthesis of the incentive scheme underlying risk shifting and discuss a method to study this form of moral hazard empirically. Several main questions are addressed in the paper. Do banks engage in risk shifting? What is the type of risk shifting present in a banking system, if any? What are the variables that incentivise or create disincentives for risk shifting? The results seem to support the presence of moral hazard behaviour in both the European and US banking systems. Molyneux offers an interesting point of view on the measures able to reduce the likelihood of systemic bank failure. The author provides a description of the European banking system's features along with a brief analysis of structural regulatory reforms aimed at reducing the negative effects of opportunistic conduct (too-big-to-fail guarantees) and other forms of taxpayer support for the banking system. Finally, the issue of banks turning into public utilities is discussed.

The third part of this book, *Bank Regulation, Credit Access and Bank Performance*, collects papers that address the effects of the change in bank regulation on bank lending, bank risk, and bank profit profile throughout the global financial crisis. Moreover, the issues of the formal credit access of female and male firms, as well as the quality of management on bank performance, are also investigated in this section. Within this context, Mascia, Keasey, and Vallascas aim to verify whether throughout this period of financial distress banks implementing Basel II reduced corporate lending growth more than banks adopting the first of the Basel Accords. Furthermore, the paper also tests whether Basel II affects the growth of corporate credit differently according to bank size. Brogi and Langone provide further empirical evidence on the relevant topic of bank regulation. The authors investigate the effects of the Basel III regulation on banks' equity risk for a sample of large European listed banks (those under ECB supervision) for the period 2007–2013. Their findings indicate that better capitalised banks are perceived as less risky by the market and therefore shareholders require a lower return on equity. Galli and Rossi, following some critical issues of the credit access literature, discuss whether there is gender discrimination in formal credit markets in 11 European countries over the period 2009–2013. They also consider in the analysis some banking features as well as social and institutional indicators that may affect women's access to credit. Nguyen, Hagendorff, and Eshraghi conclude this section by offering an interesting perspective on the performance of credit institutions by looking at the value of human capital in the banking industry. This chapter provides insights on policymakers charged with ensuring the competency of executives in banking.

The fourth part of this book, *Credit Crunch: Regional Issues*, aims to investigate the dynamic features of the credit demand and supply during the 2008–2013 crisis and the modifications in the financial structures of small and medium firms. In this regard, the Italian and regional Sardinian cases are discussed. Malavasi investigates the financial structure of the Italian firms that unlike those of other European countries are characterised by a peculiar fragility due to their lower capitalisation and higher leverage. In particular, the chapter provides readers with some answers to two crucial questions: what are the best solutions to rebalance the financial structure of Italian firms, and how should banks refinance firms providing them with the necessary period to settle finances? Lo Cascio and Aliano empirically address the issue of the credit crunch at regional level, by defining the potential demand for credit in certain sectors of the regional Sardinian economy along with the actual credit supply. The analysis, based on macro and micro data for the period 2002–2013, employs different statistical approaches and provides some empirical evidence for bank credit strategies. In the last chapter of this part, Riccio analyses the credit crunch issue by examining the effects of changes in civil and fiscal law made in Italy since 2012 with the aim to facilitate direct access to the debt capital market by unlisted companies in Italy.

Acknowledgements

The papers collected in this book have been discussed in several seminars and presented at the International Workshop "Financial crisis and Credit crunch: micro and macroeconomic implications" held at the Department of Economics and Business, University of Cagliari, Italy, on 4 July 2014. The conference was organised at the end of the first year of the research project "The Global Financial crisis and the credit crunch—Policy implications". We gratefully acknowledge research grants from the Autonomous Region of Sardinia, *Legge Regionale 2007, N. 7* [Grant Number CRP-59890, year 2012]. In addition to the authors of the book chapters, we thank Danilo V. Mascia and Paolo Mattana for their contribution to the research project. A special thanks goes to Vincenzo Rundeddu for assistance in the preparation of this book.

Cagliari   Stefania P.S. Rossi
Spring 2015   Roberto Malavasi

Contents

Part I
Genesis and Evolution of the Global Financial Crisis

The Crisis of International Finance, the Eurozone and Economic Growth

Otto Hieronymi

Abstract This chapter considers the 2008 international financial crisis, the Eurozone and economic growth in a long term perspective. This systemic crisis has been the most severe among the recurring crises that have marked the "age of global finance" which had begun with the destruction of Bretton Woods. The current crisis led to a world-wide, near-meltdown of the financial and banking system, to the debt crisis and the Eurozone crisis. Contrary to the 1930s the worst has been avoided thanks to bold innovation and the successful cooperation among central banks, national governments and international organizations, and due to the break with policy orthodoxy. Yet, many of the excesses of globalization and of global finance still have to be corrected. Today, the world has to face the tasks of ending the artificially low (and even negative) interest rates and returning to a more market-conform interest rate structure without new financial turbulences as well as of overcoming the vicious circle of excessive debt and stagnation or slow growth. Both Europe and the world would be much worse off without the Euro. Strengthening the Eurozone requires cooperation, discipline and solidarity, not the creation of a European "super state". In the long term, in order to restore sustained growth, social progress and economic and monetary stability, we also need a new rule-based global international monetary order. It is the responsibility of the main pillars of the liberal and democratic world economic order, Europe, the United States and Japan, to take the initiative and lead it to success.

1 Introduction

This chapter argues that the relationship between the 2008 crisis of the international financial markets, the Eurozone and economic growth has to be considered in a long term perspective. The crisis that broke into the open with the collapse of the investment bank, Lehman Brothers, in September 2008, and subsequently led to the "debt crisis" and to the "Eurozone crisis", which is far from over, has been the

O. Hieronymi (✉)
Webster University, Geneva, Switzerland
e-mail: hieronymi@webster.ch

© Springer International Publishing Switzerland 2016
S.P.S. Rossi, R. Malavasi (eds.), *Financial Crisis, Bank Behaviour and Credit Crunch*, Contributions to Economics, DOI 10.1007/978-3-319-17413-6_1

3

most severe among the recurring crises that marked the period since the destruction of Bretton Woods.

The deliberate decision in the 1970s by the leading OECD countries not to create a new rule-based international monetary order to replace Bretton Woods was at the origin of the growing excesses of the emerging world of "global finance". In 2008 began a systemic crisis that had been predicted by many observers for several years. The crisis of 2008 was also the crisis of the new theories and policies that had made these excesses possible.

Beside this introduction and the brief conclusions at the end, this chapter is organized in several sections, around five interdependent themes. The second section starts out with a reminder of how much national and international officials, together with the leaders of banks and other financial institutions have to be blamed for the outbreak and the extent of the latest (as well as the earlier) crises. However, their dramatic awakening to the magnitude of the threat and the dramatic shift in policies and activism helped avert an even more drastic outcome. We are, however, still in "uncharted waters" and the world economy operates in "crisis mode". The third section deals with the impact of the growing weight of short-term finance in all economic, political and social decisions. The emergence of world-wide, fully-integrated "24-h financial markets" was in sharp contrast with the systematic narrowing of the responsibilities and tools of national governments and central banks for maintaining financial, monetary and economic stability. Section 4 addresses the issue of growth. The international financial crises that have been succeeding one after the other since the 1970s have had a negative impact on the actual and on the potential rate of growth of the Western advanced economies. Faced with the debt problem and the high level of unemployment, governments and central banks should realize that "austerity" as such is not the solution. In Sect. 5 the crisis of economic theory and of economic methods is discussed. One of the positive impacts of the financial crisis is that there is a revival of the debate on key issues of theory and method and an active search for more effective policy models. In this search for new approaches a better understanding of the original post-war "social-market economy", a most successful experience that combined growth and stability with spreading prosperity and social progress, could be helpful both for policy makers and for academic economists. In Sect. 6 the importance of the Euro for Europe and for the world economy is emphasized. The Euro by itself, however, is not sufficient. As the lack of a global international monetary order was one of the long-term causes of the international financial crises, there is an urgent need to develop the concept, to negotiate and to implement a new global international monetary order.

2   The Crisis Is Not Over

2.1   *The New Activism of Governments and Central Banks*

The leaders of the OECD countries have to be commended for having worked hard and shown courage in taking bold initiatives to avoid a collapse of the international financial and monetary system in the wake of the "sub-prime crisis" and of the "international debt and Euro-zone crises". They deserve this recognition, the same way they deserve the blame for the policies and short-sightedness that led the world, to borrow the term used by one of the leading actors, "to the brink" (Paulson 2010).

At the level of the authorities, the most radical and most extensive changes occurred in the leading Western Central Banks: the Federal Reserve, the European Central Bank, the Bank of England, the Bank of Japan and the Swiss National Bank.[1]

From the early 1970s on there had been a gradual narrowing down of the mandate of the central banks, simultaneously with the growth and expansion of global finance and with the rising monetary and financial instability and fluctuations in the world economy. The risks inherent in this dichotomy were obvious from the start and were regularly pointed out from the 1970s onward (Hieronymi 1980, 1998, 2009a, b). There was, however, no interest in the central banks, in the academic community or in the International Monetary Fund for these critical minority views.

Once the 2008 crisis broke into the open, the US Federal Reserve and other leading central banks radically shifted their position and went out of their way to provide liquidity to the financial system. They adopted a broad range of bold, flexible unorthodox policies to help shore up the banking system. These measures included pushing interest rates to their lowest level ever.

The European Central Bank, which has a narrower legal mandate than the Federal Reserve or the Bank of England, started more cautiously its rescue program for the financial and banking system. Its initial caution was also due to the differences in the economic situation and policy preferences among the member countries of the EMU, in particular Germany, on the one hand, and the countries with higher deficits and accumulated debts, on the other hand.

However, once the extent of the crisis became evident, the ECB also engaged in trying to deal with the crisis and its consequences (European Central Bank 2015b). One of its implicit but important objectives has been to help counteract the pro-cyclical fiscal posture of many European governments, one that was and

---

[1] In 2011 the Swiss National Bank, in order to protect the Swiss currency from a systematic overvaluation and a resulting downward pressure on the economy announced a policy of maintaining the Swiss Franc exchange rate at $1 \ \text{€} = \text{SwFr.} \ 1.20$ through systematic supply of Swiss francs on the currency markets against foreign currencies, primarily Euros. As a result Swiss official reserve holdings increased by a factor of five. This policy was abandoned in January 2015, partly because of the ECB's (undeclared but obvious) policy to put a downward pressure on the Euro in the currency markets. The Swiss National Bank's announcement led to a 20 % overvaluation of the Swiss currency (Swiss National Bank 2015).

continues to be advocated by the European Commission and the "stability hawks" in Germany and some of the other EU Member Countries.

2.2 The ECB, "Quantitative Easing" and the Revival of the "Liquidity Trap"

"Quantitative easing" is one of the central banks' "unorthodox" instruments. It consists of buying financial assets and expanding the monetary base in order to stimulate lending to the private and public sectors. According to President Draghi the ECB aims not only to avoid a deflation but to stimulate inflation. The famous 2 % annual average inflation rate, which had been originally considered as "acceptable", became a target to aim for (European Central Bank 2015a).

Faced with continued sluggish credit demand in the Euro area, in January 2015 the ECB finally also announced the start of a "quantitative easing" program. In this it was following the example of the Bank of Japan, the Federal Reserve and the Bank of England. The adoption of the "quantitative easing" program was opposed by the Bundesbank and by the German Federal Government but approved by a large majority of the ECB Governing Council. The central question about "quantitative easing" in the short term is whether it will succeed in inducing the expansion of credit to the economy and to offset the negative impact of the pro-cyclical fiscal squeeze.

Another major preoccupation has to do with the long-term consequences of the artificially low interest rates and the difficulties that will arise in the longer term during the transition to more market conform (positive) interest rates (Sinn 2014). According to Koo (2015) "many market participants and policymakers are unable to distinguish between the lender-side problem of a financial crisis, where monetary policy is still effective and needed, and the borrower side problem, where monetary policy is ineffective". Richard Koo, like Nobel-Prize Winner Paul Krugman also invokes the "return of the threat of the 'liquidity trap'" (Krugman 2010): "The liquidity trap—that awkward condition in which monetary policy loses its grip because the nominal interest rate is essentially zero, in which the quantity of money becomes irrelevant because money and bonds are essentially perfect substitutes—played a central role in the early years of macroeconomics as a discipline" (Krugman 1998).

3   The Origins and Nature of the International Monetary and Financial Crisis

3.1   Global Finance and the Origins of the Current Systemic Crisis

The crisis that broke fully into the open in September 2008, causing a near melt-down of the global financial system, has been a truly systemic crisis: it is the most severe one in the series of recurring crises since the breakdown of Bretton Woods and the beginning of the "age of global finance" more than 40 years ago.

The absence of a global international monetary order since the 1970s has been one of the principal causes of these crises. The contrast between the lack of a universal rule-based international monetary order and an increasingly short-term market-driven "global finance", has also been partly responsible for the gradual slowdown of economic growth in the OECD countries.

3.2   The Growing Weight of Finance

In fact, the last 40 years have witnessed the emergence of "global finance". Ever since the early 1970s "finance" began to overtake the "real economy" as the main focus of interest of economists and governments. From the end of the War through the end of the 1960s, "stability" was the principal concern when it came to finance and monetary issues and conditions. This world, this set of priorities came to an end in the early 1970s.

The age of global finance, following the breakdown of the Bretton Woods order, started with a "big bang" of inflation, currency devaluations and the deepening of the psychological and actual gap between "virtuous" and "inflationary" countries. The enormous expansion of short-term international capital movements created a built-in deflationary bias in the new "non-system".

Under flexible exchange rates, the distinction between "virtuous" and "profli-gate" governments had even more to do with the perception of their fiscal policies by the "markets" than under Bretton Woods: these perceptions would affect expectations of inflation and of exchange rate movements. Thus, countries with an image of "weakness" in order to live down their reputation had to adopt even more restrictive policies than "strong" countries.

3.3 Global Finance and the Slowdown in the Western Community

Globalization and the opening of markets to competition and the free flow of technology and capital brought overall benefits to the world economy, including the highly developed OECD economies. However, the age of "global finance" witnessed a gradual slowdown in the rate of growth in the OECD countries. Also, under "global finance" the gap in wealth and income between a small increasingly prosperous minority and the majority of the population widened significantly. Social and professional insecurity and marginalization, and especially youth unemployment along with ostentatious displays of wealth, became the hallmarks of contemporary capitalism in many countries.

3.4 Advantages and Shortcomings of Global Finance

"Global finance", one of the key manifestations of globalization, no doubt had and still has advantages. However, the serious drawbacks and the growing risks that were inherent in the increasingly extreme form that it was assuming should have been recognized and corrected well before the outbreak of the Lehman Brothers crisis in 2008.[2]

On the positive side, it should be remembered that finance is an essential conduit among local, national, and world-wide economic actors. With an increasingly open and integrated economy, finance had to catch up with the "real side of the economy". An argument in favour of global finance has been that it promotes the better utilization and remuneration of savings and facilitates the integration and growth of the world economy. It also increases the possibilities of catching-up for emerging economies. Global finance is meant to increase the freedom of choice for citizens and to set "market discipline" against reckless national policies. Integration into international financial markets is expected to provide access to sources of finance at competitive rates for companies, households as well governments.

However, global finance has serious actual or potentially negative consequences. These included: (1) increased vulnerability and fragility, (2) artificial wealth creation and asset destruction; (3) transmission of fluctuations and lack of transparency and artificial risk creation; (4) amplification of disequilibria ("overshooting"); (5) over-compensation of the financial sector at the expense of the "real" economy; (6) a growing gap between the "strong" and the "weak", between "winners" and "losers" at all levels; (7) excessive capital flows; (8) financial engineering and armies of speculators turning all assets and decisions across borders, sectors and markets into comparable "units" (and "derivatives") and "tradable" book entries;

---

[2] On the nature and risks of "global finance" and the responsibilities of governments and of the corporate sector (Hieronymi 2009a, b).

(9) economic, monetary and financial forecasting reflecting less and less an analytical or practical understanding of the economic and business realities, becoming the hunting ground of "mathematical wizards" and "data mining"; and (10) the drastic shortening of the time horizon of all economic, monetary, financial and political perspectives and decisions with short-termism becoming the rule across the world economy.

3.5 The New "Asset-Based" Economic, Financial and Social Order

Increasing the size of the "property-owning" middle class was a legitimate objective of the liberal (or neo-liberal) revival. This concept served multiple objectives: increasing the interest and understanding of the middle class in the market economy, providing new sources of financing both for the private and the public sector, and reducing the reliance of current and future generations on wage income and public transfers, and increasing the share of earnings from capital in household incomes. It also helped to break the power of organized labour. (An extreme example of this approach was the trial balloon coming from the Administration of George W. Bush to shift the American Social Security system to "stock-market type" financing). This transformation also fitted into the general trend of financial deregulation and liberalization, and the shift from traditional (relationship) banking to financial engineering and "market-based" intermediation between savers and investors.

Increased competition and the globalization of the financial sector were meant to serve savers (and the new class of middle class actors on stock exchanges and other securities markets) by offering lower transaction costs, a constantly growing number of market instruments and a (guaranteed) high return on their savings, without risk for the principal. The income of savers and the security of their savings were to be assured by the growing army of "financial experts" who would manage to navigate in the vast range of potential financial assets to provide the highest return and lowest risk for the lenders. In fact, the distance between the actual "lenders" (savers) and "borrowers" (investors) became greater and greater and the role of the "traders" determinant. As a general rule, the return on savings (on "investments") was expected to include not only dividend and interest payments (as well as direct or implicit rental payments) but an increase in the real value of assets: asset prices were expected to exceed the inflation rate and often by a significant margin.[3]

The goal of creating a large property-owning middle class was and remains a legitimate objective. However, some of the policies and developments adopted in the name of these objectives have also created some serious problems and were

---

[3] On the issue of asset price inflation and deflation and on asset value destruction see Hieronymi (1998) and Koo (2009).

among the causes of the world-wide crisis of the financial system and of the challenges still facing the world economy.

3.6   Asset-Price Inflation and Deflation

For many years there was a dichotomy between the concern of both policy makers (governments and central banks and international organizations) and of theorists for price inflation (and in particular consumer price inflation), and their general ignoring of asset price inflation (and the risks of asset price deflation) (see Hieronymi 1998).

The often massive upward and downward overshooting of asset price levels was considered a marginal issue for the advocates of the theories of "efficient markets" and "rational expectations". The herd instinct prevailing on financial markets tended to drive asset prices well above their underlying long-term value. It has taken constantly increasing volumes of trading in order to find favourable asset price differences. It was paradoxical that while, according to the dominant doctrine, "global finance" meant a more efficient service for the real economy, the "financial sector's" share in total (and highly paid) employment and in the share of total income increased significantly.

As mentioned above, it is argued that global finance has contributed to the growing income and wealth divide between a very small minority and a large and growing majority of society in both rich and poorer countries. This socially and economically undesirable, and even dangerous trend was probably reinforced by the unequal access of individuals and families with lower incomes and lower accumulated capital compared to those who have the means and the information to benefit from the ups and downs of the financial markets.

Asset price inflation, i.e., the rise of the market price of financial and other assets beyond their productivity and replacement cost, corrected for the general inflation rate, is a phenomenon of creating value out of nothing. George Soros, who in recent years has been very critical of the shortcomings of the contemporary financial system, maintains nevertheless that there is nothing inherently wrong when trading and speculation drive up the price of financial assets, thereby increasing the total wealth of the community (and in particular of the winners in this process).

While asset price inflation is considered an acceptable part of the system (a typical case is the housing market where it is a common assumption that a correct return on the initial investment can be assured only through the future inflation of prices beyond the general level of inflation), so-called "bubbles" are phenomena that should if possible be avoided. "Bubbles" are situations when "asset-price inflation" gets out of hand.

The reverse phenomenon to "asset-price inflation" (and to "bubbles") can be called "asset-price deflation". This is the situation when a decline in asset prices not only leads to a correction by eliminating "excess value" resulting from "asset-price inflation", but when it destroys economically otherwise useful assets. These reversals can hit hard savers, small and large companies as well as banks and other financial institutions that hold these assets either as a collateral or as their own investments or reserves (Hieronymi and Stephanou 2013).

The concept developed by the Japanese economist Richard Koo from the 1990s onward (see, e.g., Koo 2009) under the terms "balance-sheet recession" or "balance-sheet depression" deals essentially with this phenomenon. "Balance-sheet recession" refers to the behaviour of potential investors and potential borrowers under the impact of the loss of the value of their assets, especially when these assets had been acquired through borrowing. The gap that opens up between assets and liabilities—the value of assets declines while the value of debts remains the same (or can even rise)—acts as a major break on spending (Koo 2011).

4 Austerity Is Not the Solution

A sharp and sudden recession, with negative growth rates in many countries was an immediate consequence of the 2008 crisis. The so-called "Eurozone crisis" created a second wave of recession. The gap between the 2006 real GDP levels and the post 2010 levels were larger than the decline in output in the wake of the oil crisis of the 1970s. In the case of some of the crisis countries this gap has continued to increase until very recently. Even more important than the gap between the 2006–07 and the 2014 actual levels of GDP has been the difference between the current levels of GDP and the levels it would have reached in the absence of the "Great Recession" of recent years.

Rapid and concerted fiscal and monetary policy reaction helped prevent the Great Recession from turning into a new Great Depression. However, there are many signs that the Great Recession (and some of the policies adopted in its wake) have had a lasting negative effect on the potential rate of growth of the OECD countries. This has been the most pronounced in those countries that can least afford it: the crisis countries. The high level of unemployment and in particular among young people and first-time job seekers is an especially worrying phenomenon.

4.1 The Need to Return to Sustained Growth

The vicious circle of asset destruction, recession, unemployment and restrictive fiscal measures, the targeting of "non-productive" social support payments, have led to a new wave of poverty and marginalization of millions of people, on a scale that has been unknown at least in Europe since the 1930s and 1940s. The systematic closing of hospitals, of cutting back and ending unemployment payments, the expulsion of people from even modest apartments in the name of "dealing with the debt problem" have created a climate of hopelessness that is not tempered by any feelings of solidarity and sympathy in the official international rhetoric.

Continuously repeated slogans about the necessity of "fiscal rigour, increased mobility, eliminating wasteful spending and employment in the public sector—read health, culture and education—of downsizing and outsourcing production across the private sector" have led to an atmosphere of doom and resignation not only in families, among individuals of all ages but also among potential investors and innovators.

Without a return to growth the strong countries will also discover that the siren songs of "austerity" are leading down the wrong path: towards stagnation and decline and towards future political and social tensions and financial crises. By now, both the OECD[4] and the International Monetary Fund have been expressing increasing concern about the loss of momentum of the Western advanced economies and the long-term impact of such a development for the world economy as a whole (International Monetary Fund 2014).

The return of a wide-spread perception and reality of two groups of economies in Europe and among the OECD countries: the "successful ones" and the "unsuccessful (or even failed) ones", with a growing marginalization of these latter, should be recognized not as a distant but as a very imminent threat. Such a perception and reality would not only strengthen the defensive (and protectionist) reactions of the "losers", but also the arrogance and the fortress mentality of the "winners"—of losers and winners in a "competition" that serves no one's interest, (a "competition" that could undermine the very foundations of the democratic and liberal international order).

Slow growth and stagnation and a further decline in the actual and potential rate of growth will increase the absolute and the relative weight of both the public and private debt burden (Piketty 2013). Declaring total or partial bankruptcy and/or debt forgiveness are no real solutions: they would create renewed asset destruction and increase the defensive attitude of banks and savers alike. The artificial stimulation of price inflation, in order to ease the debt burden would not be a more realistic solution to the debt problem, than the idea that the debt burden can be reduced through pro-cyclical fiscal policies that perpetuate high unemployment and discourage investments or through social policies that lead to humanitarian emergencies.[5]

---

[4] See for example the "Editorial" of the Chief Economist of the OECD entitled "Avoiding the low-growth trap" in the organization's 2014 Going for Growth report (OECD 2014).

[5] The substantive text of the "fiscal compact", which has been the mantra of mindless fiscal tightening in the OECD countries, especially in Berlin and Brussels in recent years, starts with the following command: "the budgetary position of the general government of a Contracting Party shall be balanced or in surplus" (Article 3). For the classic German "fiscal hawk" arguments see for example: German Council of Economic Experts (Sachverständigenrat) (2014), and Burret and Schnellenbach (2013).

5 The Demise of Dominant Doctrines

The years 2007–08 were also marked by the outbreak of a sudden and profound crisis of the dominant orthodoxy. Financial and monetary policy-making in the leading OECD countries (with the United States the prime example), as well as the prevailing theories, have been shown to have lacked common sense and sound judgement. They extolled the allegedly limitless possibilities of financial engineering and legerdemain to create wealth out of thin air. Their promoters, who had become more and more arrogant and short-sighted, bear a large part for the near over-night collapse of the world's banking and financial system (Keeley and Patrick 2010).

Ever since the 1970s it has been clear that the new dominant doctrines, from monetarism and floating exchange rates to the unlimited faith in the virtues of financial engineering, in rational expectations and "efficient markets", did not provide a realistic and robust theoretical basis for understanding the working of the modern economy and for prudent and reliable economic and monetary rules and policies.

By the 1990s it was evident that the pendulum of theory had swung too far again (Hieronymi 1998): the theorists and practitioners of the new dominant doctrines refused to see the systemic crises that were looming on the horizon. As a result they were also unprepared to deal with their potential consequences and how to shift to better domestic and international economic and monetary models, once these crises were to occur. It is surprising how much the tenants of the dominant doctrines tended to consider the international financial crises which recurred regularly since the 1970s as essentially "regional" phenomena, with no real systemic origins and implications.

5.1 The Crisis in Method and Theory

For well over 200 years by now economists have been trying increasingly to bridge the gap between the "particular" and the "general" through a recourse to mathematical abstraction, to the point that by today there is barely any reflection of economic reality in "academic" papers and discourse. This also means that fewer policy makers and business leaders are able to read and understand "economic theory". This trend has been complemented by the growing use of statistics (in fact statistical estimates) of more and more facets of economic and social phenomena, and the use of statistical theorems and of high-speed software and hardware to try to understand, compare and predict what are considered relevant aspects of the economy ("key variables").

The two trends although related are far from identical. The first one, the use of mathematical reasoning, allows a virtually limitless range of "logical" explanations of the working of the "economy": from its smallest details to its most aggregated expression. The second one, the analysis and the "mining" of increasing masses of data, provides a detailed or global "quantitative" view, with less and less emphasis on theoretical understanding.

The evolution of the international monetary and financial systems since the 1970s and in particular since the breaking into the open of the world-wide monetary and financial crisis in 2007–08, also revealed the problems and limits inherent in these two trends of specialization in the economic profession. The period since 2007–08 has witnessed a profound crisis both of abstract theories and of sophisticated quantitative methods. This crisis of economic science parallels the crisis of public policy making and business decision making. Today there is no consensus about the optimal model or about the way we should define one.

Today we have no generally accepted "growth theory", no reliable "monetary theory" and no "international monetary theory" to speak of, no consensus on a balanced approach to globalization, no consensus on a balanced approach to competition, efficiency and social progress and no common fiscal theory. "Balance-of-payments theory", which used to be one of the centrepieces of economic theory and economic policy has been virtually eliminated both from the policies and the theories of the advanced liberal market economies. This was especially true for American economists and policy makers (both the Federal Reserve and the Treasury denied the relevance of the US balance of payments for American monetary or fiscal policies (see Lamfalussy 1987).

The growth of the relative weight of the financial sector was not a sign of greater efficiency but of reduced effective contribution to economic performance. At the same time, there is no question that increasingly "finance" has become a "factor of production" distinct from "capital" in the narrow sense (Hieronymi 2009a). Among the missing pieces are the links between "money" (and monetary policy and money supply), finance (and credit supply and demand) and the "real" economy (growth and employment). In the same category are the issues of "risk" and "prudent financial" practices and the very nature and structure of financial markets. One of the most controversial and widely discussed issues is the relationship between public finance, financial risk and stability and economic growth. Government-issued IOUs ("government bonds") used to be considered the very symbol of financial trust. Today they are at the centre of the crisis and of theoretical and policy controversies.

The growing recognition in recent years of the shortcomings of the orthodoxy prevailing until 2008 by some of their most vocal exponents and practitioners especially in central banks has been a major positive development.[6] This radical shift of perception can be illustrated by the case of Martin Wolf, Chief Economics Commentator of the *Financial Times*. In 2004 Wolf a prolific, articulate and

---

[6] "In the wake of the crisis, one of the most remarkable changes in the banking system and in the world of financial markets is the belated recognition that a new approach is necessary and extensive reforms of the international banking system must occur. There is a sudden and universal consensus that central banks and governments now have a new and increased level of responsibility towards making the financial system work" (Hieronymi 2009b).

widely-read economist published a powerful treatise on globalization: *Why Globalization Works, The Case for the Global Market Economy*. Exactly 10 years later he wrote an equally voluminous analysis on the shortcomings of unbridled globalization and the risks involved in the excessive weight of finance: *The Shifts and the Shocks: What We have Learned and Still Have to Learn from the Financial Crisis* (Wolf 2004, 2014).

5.2 Germany, Europe and the Model of the "Social Market Economy"

The original German post-war model of the "social market economy" was probably the most successful approach to combining the goal of economic growth and prosperity with social progress and monetary and financial stability: "The concept of the social market economy implied a rejection both of the ultra-liberalism of the old Manchester school and of collectivist planning and of government control and economic nationalism. The model of the social market economy aimed at reconciling the freedom and efficiency of the market economy with equity and social progress and solidarity" (Hieronymi 2005). "Austerity for the sake of austerity" was not part of the core concept and had been explicitly rejected by one of the founders of this school of thought (Röpke 1951).

Germany, the policies advocated by the German government and the "German model" have been at the centre of the European and international debate about the future of the Euro Zone ever since the outbreak of the Euro crisis. Germany's insistence on austerity and more austerity even in the face of massive unemployment is one of the main threats for the future of the Euro and of the European economy as a whole. While there are also many who argue that Germany would be much weaker without investing in solidarity with the rest of Europe (Fischer 2014) their arguments are ignored the way the warnings about the risks of unbridled finance had been ignored in the 1990s (Fratzscher 2014).

Although the Lisbon Treaty includes the development of the social market economy among the European Union's key objectives[7] most people outside Germany have only limited knowledge of this concept. Yet, the original model of the "social market economy" could be the best common basis for the "structural reforms" demanded from the crisis countries and for the European Union as a whole. For this to happen the legendary objective and slogan of the late Ludwig Erhard: "Wohlstand für Alle", "Prosperity for All", would have to be readopted and implemented (Erhard 1957, 2009; Hieronymi 2002).

---

[7] "The Union shall work for a Europe of sustainable development based on balanced economic growth, a *social market economy*, highly competitive and aiming at full employment and social progress..." Article I-3/3: The Union's Objectives, emphasis added (Hieronymi 2005).

6 The World Needs the Euro and a New Global International Monetary Order

The future of the Eurozone is among the principal economic and political issues not only for its members and for the European Union, but also for the Western Community and the world economy as a whole. The project of the European Monetary Union and of the Euro helped bring closer the economies and economic policy making of the "old" members of the European Union, and it also helped define the framework for its enlargement towards the East. Although the enlargement process was rightly criticized as having been overly lengthy and bureaucratic, the prospect of membership in the EMU in the long term helped the transformation of the former Communist economies into competitive open market economies.

The EMU was beneficial to Italy, Spain, Ireland, Portugal and also Greece, despite the fact that these countries had become victims of the boundless faith in the power of unbridled "global finance" to bring about economic convergence. It should also be remembered that Germany was among the principal beneficiaries of the EMU. Monetary union helped anchor more solidly the newly reunited Germany in the European and Western political system (Dyson and Featherstone 1999). It allowed Germany to pass through the fiscally difficult and onerous process of unification that involved enormous annual transfer payments for two decades, without too much external stress and risks of financial instability.

Strengthening the Euro does not require the creation of a centralized European super-State. It requires, however, to quote Mario Draghi, a common will "among its members to come together to solve common problems when it matter(s) most (European Central Bank 2015a)". The same common will and determination are required from the members of the broader Western community of democracies to undertake the long-overdue reform of the international monetary system (Hieronymi 2009a, b).

7 Conclusions

The conclusions of the present chapter can be summarized in the following points: (1) with respect to international finance, it is important to redefine its role and to limit the scope and the impact of asset price inflation and deflation on the real economy and on the distribution of income within and among countries; (2) sustained economic growth across the OECD area is an essential condition for overcoming the impact of the financial crisis and the consequences of the anti-crisis emergency fiscal and monetary measures; (3) it is essential to avoid the breakup of the Eurozone, but this does not require a centralized European super State or the unrelenting squeezing of the economies of the "crisis countries"; (4) finally, in order to reach these goals it is important to achieve closer cooperation and solidarity between Europe, Japan and the United States, and to start building a more stable rule-based international monetary order.

Among the greatest advantages of a free society and a free economy is not that they are free of faults and errors: it is their ability to learn from the errors and faults of the past and to correct policies and institutions. Without the ability to learn and to adjust, free society could not survive. Today's principal challenge for theory and policy is to find a new consensus that will include the lessons of the past and an understanding of the new reality. Globalization has narrowed the degree of freedom of national economic policy making. Global finance has played a particularly important role in this respect. Yet national governments are still considered accountable for economic prosperity and stability both by their electorate and the business community and by their international partners. The Western model of a democratic political system and socially conscious market economy developed during the decades following the end of the Second World War has led to unprecedented material prosperity and remarkable social progress. It has also shown great resilience, e.g., during and after the crises of the 1970s and the ones in the wake of the near meltdown of the international financial system in the autumn of 2008. Without freedom and without responsibility and solidarity, neither the system as a whole, nor its main components could have functioned properly or survived in the long run. Thus, freedom and responsibility and solidarity were and will remain key elements of the financial and monetary order also in the future.

References

Burret HT, Schnellenbach J (2013) Implementation of the fiscal compact in the Euro area member states. German Council of Economic Experts. Working paper no. 08

Dyson K, Featherstone K (1999) The road to Maastricht: negotiating economic and monetary union. Oxford University Press, Oxford

Erhard L (1957) Wohlstand für Alle. Econ, Düsseldorf

Erhard L (2009) Wohlstand für Alle. Anaconda, Köln

European Central Bank (2015a) Press conference of Mario Draghi, President of the ECB. Frankfurt am Main, 22 Jan

European Central Bank (2015b) Press release: ECB announces expanded asset purchase programme. Frankfurt am Main, 22 Jan

Fischer J (2014) Scheitert Europa? Kiepenhauer & Witsch, Köln

Fratzscher M (2014) Die Deutschland-Illusion. Carl Hanser, München

German Council of Economic Experts (Sachverständigenrat). Monetary policy and fiscal consolidation in the Euro-area. Annual economic report 2013/14, third chapter

Hieronymi O (ed) (1980) The new economic nationalism. Macmillan, London

Hieronymi O (1998) Agenda for a new monetary reform. Futures 30(8):769–781

Hieronymi O (2002) Wilhelm Röpke: The social market economy and today's domestic and international order. HEI-Webster University, Cahiers HEI No. 6

Hieronymi O (2005) The "social market economy" and globalisation: the lessons from the European model for Latin America. In: Fontela Montes E, Guzmàn Cueva J (eds) Brasil y la Economia Social de Mercado. Cuadernos del Grupo de Alcantara, Càceres, pp 247–300

Hieronymi O (2009a) Rebuilding the international monetary order: the responsibility of Europe, Japan and the United States. Revista de Economia Mundial 29:197–226

Hieronymi O (2009b) Globalization and the reform of the international banking and monetary system. Palgrave Macmillan, London

Hieronymi O, Stephanou C (2013) International debt. Economic, financial, monetary, political, and regulatory aspects. Palgrave Macmillan, London

International Monetary Fund (2014) World economic outlook: legacies, clouds, uncertainties. IMF, Washington, DC

Keeley B, Patrick L (2010) From crisis to recovery: the causes, course and consequences of the great recession. OECD Insights, Paris

Koo RC (2009) The Holy Grail of macroeconomics: lessons from Japan's great recession. Revised and updated. Wiley, Singapore

Koo RC (2011) The world in balance sheet recession: causes, cure, and politics. Nomura Research Institute, Tokyo

Koo RC (2015) The escape from balance sheet recession and the QE trap. Wiley, Singapore

Krugman PR (1998) It's baaack: Japan's slump and the return of the liquidity trap. Brookings Paper Econ Activ 2:137–205

Krugman PR (2010) How much of the world is in a liquidity trap? The New York Times, 17 Mar 2010

Lamfalussy A (1987) Current-account imbalances in the industrial world: why they matter. In: Essays in international finance, no. 169, Dec 1987. International Finance Section, Princeton University, Princeton, NJ, pp 31–37

OECD (2014) Going for growth: economic policy reforms, 2014 interim report

Paulson HM (2010) On the brink: inside the race to stop the collapse of the global financial system. Hachette, New York

Piketty T (2013) Le Capital au XXIe Siècle. Editions du Seuil, Paris

Röpke W (1951) Austerity. Reprinted in: Röpke W (1962) Wirrnis und Wahrheit. Eugen Rentsch, Zürich

Sinn HW (2014) The Euro trap. Oxford University Press, Oxford

Swiss National Bank (2015) Press release: Swiss National Bank discontinues minimum exchange rate and lowers interest rate to −0.75 %, 15 Jan 2015

Wolf M (2004) Why globalization works. The case for the global market economy. Yale University Press, New Haven, CT

Wolf M (2014) The shifts and the shocks: what we have learned and still have to learn from the financial crisis. Allen Lane, London

The European Twin Sovereign Debt and Banking Crises

Beniamino Moro

Abstract Europe currently faces a severe economic and financial Great Crisis. It is often described as a sovereign debt crisis, but in fact, it is really a sequence of interactions between sovereign problems and banking problems that caused a severe economic slowdown. It also caused a fragmentation of euro-area financial markets. The genesis of the crisis focuses on the imbalances in European Monetary Union (EMU) countries balance-of-payments, where the TARGET2 payment system became crucial, reflecting stress in the funding of banking systems in crisis-hit countries. The decisions by European leaders to set up a banking union and the announcement, as well as adoption, of non-standard measures by the European Central Bank (ECB) greatly contributed to restoring confidence in the euro-area financial markets, improving market sentiment and reversing the earlier trend towards market fragmentation. Ultimately, an expansion of the European aggregate demand is necessary to promote growth, and to this aim, the role of Germany is crucial.

1 The Origin and Development of the European Great Crisis

Eurozone countries are currently emerging from a severe economic and financial Great Crisis. The prospect of a slow recovery, the current account imbalances and the levels of debt accumulated by public and private sectors make the situation troublesome. Macroeconomic imbalances, which accumulated over a long time, are now being partially corrected, and some of the crisis-hit European countries are regaining competitiveness. Some progress is being made in consolidating public finances, and some important steps have been taken to reduce tensions in the financial markets. Nevertheless, the fragmentation of euro-area financial markets still remains.

B. Moro (✉)
Department of Economics and Business, University of Cagliari, Cagliari, Italy
e-mail: moro@unica.it

© Springer International Publishing Switzerland 2016
S.P.S. Rossi, R. Malavasi (eds.), *Financial Crisis, Bank Behaviour and Credit Crunch*, Contributions to Economics, DOI 10.1007/978-3-319-17413-6_2

Around mid-2012, the decisions by European leaders to set up a banking union and the announcement, as well as the adoption, of non-standard measures by the European Central Bank (ECB) greatly contributed to restoring confidence in the euro-area financial markets, improving market sentiment and reversing the earlier trend towards market fragmentation. Nonetheless, the crisis still remains significant and is unlikely to be overcome in the short run.[1]

How was it that Europe came to the recent Great Crisis? To answer this question, some stylized facts are presented in this chapter and extensively discussed. The origin of the current European crisis can be traced directly back to the global financial crisis of 2007–2009, which spilled over into a sovereign debt crisis in several euro-area countries in early 2010.

Although it is usually described as a sovereign debt crisis, it is really a sequence of interactions between sovereign problems and banking problems. With deteriorating public finances, sovereign risk has increased and worsened bank's balance sheets. In fact, as public debt approached sustainability limits in PIIGS countries (Portugal, Ireland, Italy, Greece, and Spain), a high bank exposure to sovereign risk gave rise to a fragile interdependence between fiscal and bank solvency and thus to the possibility of a self-fulfilling crisis.

The interdependence between sovereign credit and banking systems has been a running theme of this sequence of events. Eurozone sovereign debt is held in large amounts by Eurozone banks, with a significant bias towards the bonds of the country in which the bank is headquartered. This is partly due to policy choices made prior to the crisis, which in retrospect appear questionable. In particular, those choices include the risk-weighting at zero of Eurozone sovereign bonds in regulatory capital calculations, the longstanding acceptance of such bonds with no haircut by the ECB as collateral in its liquidity policies, and the possible instances of moral suasion by home-country public authorities that resulted in large holdings of the home country's sovereign debt (Véron 2011).

An important element that contributed to the European financial crisis was a mispricing of risk by capital markets and an ensuing misallocation of capital in the decade before the outbreak of the crisis. European monetary unification brought about a convergence of interest rates among euro-area members, as shown in Fig. 1.

Countries with weaker positions that had joined the Euro could refinance themselves at roughly the same cost as the most solvent states. Spreads of sovereign bonds of the PIIGS countries over Germany narrowed rapidly in the run-up to EMU membership and almost disappeared once they had become members of the euro area. By January 2001, the time of Greece's entry into the EMU, the yields on 10-year Greek bonds had fallen to 5 % from 25 % in 1992.

The sovereign risk of virtually all euro-area countries, including the PIIGS, was priced more or less the same as German sovereign debt. Financial markets were too optimistic, depending on the fact that the risk of euro-area central government

---

[1] A more extensive exposition of the arguments contained in this chapter can be found in Moro (2014). Further arguments appear in Moro (2012, 2013).

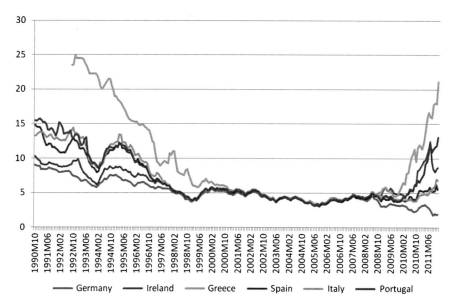

Fig. 1 10-Year government bond yields (% per annum), October 1990–December 2011. Source: Eurostat

bonds was weighted at zero in regulatory capital calculations and because the ECB treated such debt with no haircut—basically as risk-free—when these bonds were offered as collateral for repos and other collateral financing trades (Véron 2011). On the contrary, soon after the explosion of the European financial crisis in 2010, as also shown in Fig. 1, spreads of sovereign bonds of the PIIGS countries over Germany began to differentiate again.

The systematic mispricing of sovereign debt observed in the Eurozone also had the effect of giving wrong incentives to policymakers. During the boom years, when financial markets were blind to the sovereign risks, no incentives were given to policy makers to reduce their debts, as the latter were priced so favourably. Since the start of the financial crisis, financial markets driven by panic overpriced risks and gave incentives to policymakers to introduce excessive austerity programmes.

This implies measures aimed at reducing the debt burden. If, however, there is a disconnection between the spreads and the fundamentals, a policy geared exclusively towards affecting the fundamentals (i.e., reducing the debt burden) will not be sufficient. In that case, policy makers should also try to stop countries from being driven into a bad equilibrium. This can be achieved by more active liquidity policies by the ECB that aim to prevent a liquidity crisis from leading to a self-fulfilling solvency crisis (Wyplosz 2011; De Grauwe 2011).

To this aim, between December 2011 and February 2012, the ECB first provided two unconventional long-term refinancing operations (LTRO) for a total of more than 1.000 bn € at a fixed rate of 1 %, maturing 3 years later. Then, on September 6, 2012, the ECB approved the Outright Monetary Transactions (OMT) programme, under which the Bank announced to be ready to purchase in secondary markets unlimited sovereign bonds of troubled countries having a maturity of between 1 and 3 years.

The purpose of this programme was to reduce spreads in public bonds interest rates for the component not dependent on fundamentals, by contrasting fear and panic to take over. In fact, even if the OMT programme had not been activated until now, both of these unconventional monetary policy decisions have greatly contributed to the maintenance of calm in the financial markets during these last years.

2   The Misalignment of Internal Real Exchange Rates, TARGET2 Positions and EMU Countries' Balances of Payments

Hindsight has made it clear that the availability of cheap credit in the decade before the outbreak of the financial crisis led to an unsustainable accumulation of private and public debt in crisis-hit countries. The drop in real interest rates in these countries after their entry into the euro area and the inflowing capital fuelled unsustainable developments, including excessive credit dynamics and real estate bubbles. It also reduced the pressure for economic reform to improve competitiveness within the monetary union, as countries could easily finance their current account deficits through abundant inflowing capital.

The resulting appreciation of the real exchange rate decreased the competitiveness in these countries, which then caused rising current account imbalances (Fig. 2). These imbalances then sharply increased budget deficits and worsened debt indicators, triggering the sovereign debt crisis.

In fact, a high level of public debt is not a problem *per se*, as long as the government is able to refinance itself and roll over its debt. This requires public debt and the interest burden to grow more slowly than the economy and the tax base. Unfortunately, this is not the case in the PIIGS countries. The economic crisis in these countries is therefore not merely a debt crisis; it is first and foremost a competitiveness and growth crisis that has led to structural imbalances within the euro area (Holinski et al. 2012; Lane and Pels 2012; Bergsten and Kirkegaard 2012; Mayer 2011).

According to this field of research, below the surface of the sovereign public debt and banking crises lies a balance-of-payments crisis, caused by a misalignment of internal real exchange rates (Sinn 2012a; Sinn and Wollmershäeuser 2011; Neumann 2012; Lin and Treichel 2012).

In a fixed nominal exchange rate system, balance-of-payment imbalances can emerge when the real exchange rate is above or below its equilibrium value. In the first case, when the real exchange rate is over-valued, a country imports more than it exports so that the current account moves into deficit. At the same time, domestic asset prices in foreign currency are higher than foreign asset prices so that investors

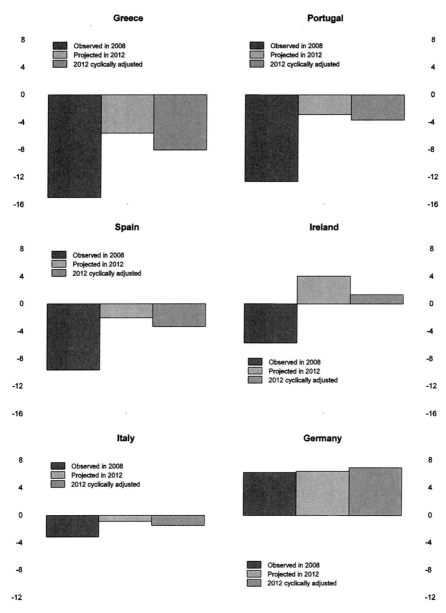

Fig. 2 Current account balances in Euro area countries in per cent of GDP. Source: OECD Economic Outlook 92 database and OECD calculations

sell the first and buy the latter. This leads to net capital outflows and, hence, a deficit in the capital account. The combined deficits of the current and capital accounts then lead to a deficit of the balance of payments.

In the second case, when the real exchange rate is under-valued, the current and capital accounts, and hence the balance of payments, are in surplus, and the central bank accumulates international reserves. This process comes to an end only when reserve accumulation has increased the money supply to an extent that inflation grows to intolerable levels and the authorities up-value the nominal exchange rate in an effort to regain price stability.

Because the EMU has been built as a union of sovereign states, each state has retained its own National Central Bank (NCB), which has become a member of the so-called Eurosystem with the ECB at the top. National inter-bank payment systems have been merged into a euro-area interbank payment system (TARGET2), where NCBs have assumed the role of the links between countries. So, TARGET2 plays a key role in ensuring the smooth conduct of monetary policy, the correct functioning of financial markets, and banking and financial stability in the euro area, by substantially reducing systemic risk.[2]

The settlement of cross-border payments between participants in TARGET2 results in intra-Eurosystem balances, that is, positions on the balance sheets of the respective NCBs that reflect claims/liabilities on/to the Eurosystem. They are reported, as in Fig. 3, on the NCBs' balance sheets as TARGET2 claims (if positive) or TARGET2 liabilities (if negative), vis-à-vis the ECB as the central counterpart.

According to Mayer (2011), a key consequence of this system is that each euro area country has a national balance of payments in the form of the net position of its central bank within TARGET2. This net position can result in a claim (balance of payment surplus) or liability (balance of payment deficit) against the ECB, which sits in the centre of the payment system. The consequence of this system is that a country with a balance of payments deficit automatically receives unlimited funding. Hence, Mayer's conclusion is that the ECB's funding operations become tilted towards the countries with overvalued real exchange rates.

Anyway, Mayer's idea that TARGET2 provides unlimited funding to the balance of payments deficits of peripheral EMU countries is questionable. TARGET2 flows reflect a kind of lender of last resort intervention by the ECB through the free allotment program. They just reflect the funding necessity of banks in different regions, periphery banks being the most in need.

In fact, as you can see in Fig. 4 before the beginning of the financial crisis, until July 2007, TARGET2 positions were balanced overall. Cross-border payments were flowing in both directions and were netted out to zero at close of business each day. The beginning of the financial crisis in August 2007 led to one-direction flows from "peripheral" countries (Greece, Ireland and Portugal) to "core" countries (Germany and the Netherlands). The divergences widened with the outbreak of the sovereign debt crisis in May 2010. Since the summer of 2011, as the crisis has

---

[2] TARGET is the "Trans-European Automated Real-time Gross Settlement Express Transfer" system. It was replaced by TARGET2 in November 2007, with a transition period lasting until May 2008, by which time all national platforms were replaced by a single platform. The processing and settlement of euro-denominated payments take place on an individual basis on the participants' accounts at NCBs connected to TARGET2. The transactions are settled in real time with immediate finality, thus enabling the beneficiary bank to reuse the liquidity to make other payments on that day.

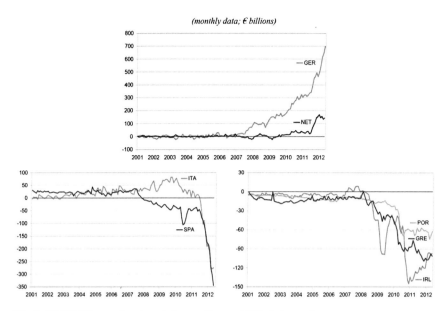

Fig. 3 TARGET2 cumulated net balances. Source: NCBs balance sheets

intensified and also affected Italy and Spain, divergences of TARGET2 positions have become even wider.

In mid-2012, the total value of TARGET2 claims (or equivalent liabilities) on the balance sheet of the euro NCBs reached 1 trillion €. In particular, German and Dutch net claims in TARGET2 increased from close to zero in the first half of 2007 to about 700 and 140 bn €, respectively, by the end of May 2012. Conversely, in Greece, Ireland and Portugal, net liabilities in TARGET2 increased from close to zero to 102, 97, and 63 bn €, respectively. Finally, the NCBs of Italy and Spain, which had slightly positive TARGET2 net claims before the start of the crisis, registered net liabilities of 275 and 345 bn € by the end of May 2012.

The domestic booms resulting from low real interest rates and capital inflows after accession to EMU led to large wage increases in excess of productivity growth and, hence, rising unit labour costs, as observed in Fig. 5, and higher price inflation than in Germany and other "core countries" of the euro area. The result was an erosion of competitiveness among the peripheral members of the euro area vis-à-vis the core countries, particularly Germany, which has been able to improve its price competitiveness significantly since the launch of the euro through wage constraints and structural reforms.

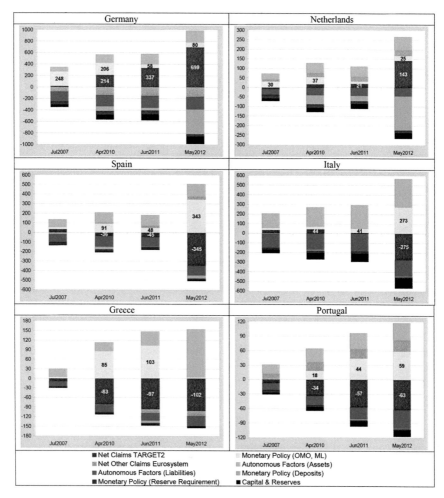

Fig. 4 NCBs balance sheets (bn €; outstanding amount at the end of the month). Source: Cecioni and Ferrero (2012)

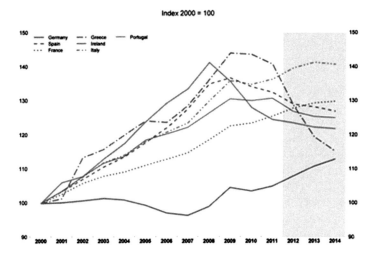

Fig. 5 Unit labour costs. Source: OECD Economic Outlook 92 database

3 The Accumulation of TARGET2 Imbalances

The identification of the balance-of-payment imbalances with TARGET2 positions is questionable. In fact, Cecioni and Ferrero (2012) showed that movements in the current account's deficits were significantly related to TARGET2 balances only for Greece whereas intra-area trade balances were not related to TARGET2 in any other country. For all countries, the large increase in TARGET2 liabilities appears to mostly have been related to capital flight, concerning both portfolio investments and cross-border interbank activity. At any rate, TARGET2 balances reflect funding stress in the banking systems of certain countries. Therefore, such imbalances must be interpreted with caution because they also reflect transactions among multi-country banking groups.

On the accumulation of TARGET2 imbalances, Sinn (2011, 2012b, c) and Sinn and Wollmershäeuser (2011, 2012) triggered the debate. The monetary expansion in the southern countries enabled a net outflow of central bank money to other Eurozone countries by way of international payment orders for the purpose of buying goods and assets. Sinn and Wollmershäeuser (2012) claimed that this outflow represents a classical imbalance of payments and that its accumulated value is measured by the TARGET2 balances. They also argued that the TARGET2 debts impose risks on the rest of the Eurozone countries in proportion to their share of the ECB capital, should the deficit countries default and leave the Eurozone.

The policy implication is that when exchange rate adjustments are impossible, the accumulation of credit and debit positions in TARGET2 must be limited, and imbalances in cross-border payment flows must be accommodated officially on an annual basis.

Many authors have rebutted these arguments, particularly Whelan (2011, 2012), Buiter et al. (2011b), Buiter and Rahbari (2012), Bindseil and König (2011), Deutsche Bundesbank (2011), ECB (2011), and Banca d'Italia (2012). These papers primarily concluded that what is important for the transmission of monetary policy is the net liquidity provided to euro-area banks, not the manner in which that liquidity is distributed. More generally, the increase in TARGET2 imbalances does not interfere with the conduct of monetary policy or the objective of price stability within the area.

Nevertheless, the increase in TARGET2 balances has been closely linked to balance-of-payments (BoP) imbalances. Before the crisis, both the BoP current account and the trade balance of the countries under stress were in deficit, with the exception of Italy where they were approximately balanced. These deficits were funded mostly from foreign investments in domestic securities and in the interbank market. The capital flowing in and out of the countries was almost completely netted out, leaving small average net balances for the individual items of the BoP financial account.

During the crisis, the absolute size of individual items in the BoP increased and its composition changed significantly. The main changes were in the financial accounts. The reversals of foreign investments in domestic securities and of liabilities issued by domestic Monetary and Financial Institutions (MFIs) were not matched by a similar increase in disinvestments of domestic capital previously invested abroad. Net outflows in the financial accounts of the BoP were compensated by a considerable increase in the respective NCB's TARGET2 liabilities with the ECB.

The timing of these changes was uneven across countries (Cecioni and Ferrero 2012). Referring to Fig. 4, during the global financial crisis (August 2007–April 2010) and in the first phase of the sovereign debt crisis (May 2010–June 2011), Italy's and Spain's financial accounts remained almost unchanged while those of Greece and Portugal showed the largest adjustments. In the latter countries, foreigners disinvested from the interbank and the securities markets, and some signs of deposit flight from domestic banks by residents appeared.

In the second phase of the sovereign debt crisis (July 2011–May 2012), access to international financial markets by the Italian and Spanish governments and MFIs was also impaired. During this period, Italy and Spain recorded net outflows from the MFIs, respectively, of 118 and 182 bn € and net outflows of portfolio investments of about 90 bn €. In Italy, in particular, net outflows of portfolio investments largely corresponded to a willingness in non-residents not to roll over maturing sovereign debt securities and, to a lesser extent, to sales by non-residents of sovereign debt securities on the secondary market. In the same period, TARGET2 liabilities increased for Italy and Spain to approximately 280 and 300 bn €, respectively.

Cecioni and Ferrero's main conclusion is that the ECB's unconventional monetary policies contrast the risks of segmentation in the money markets along national lines with the aim of preserving the transmission of the unique monetary policy. Any institutional change that would limit the flow of payments through

TARGET2 would have a pro-cyclical effect by tightening further liquidity conditions in troubled countries. Furthermore, it would increase asymmetries within the euro area, undermining the existence of the unique monetary policy.

Nevertheless, the banking system cannot permanently rely on central bank funds for its main source of funding. In the medium term, peripheral countries cannot continue to substitute inflows of foreign private sector liquidity with TARGET2 liabilities. Stressed countries must return to private markets and attract funds from the rest of the area. This requires the restoration of confidence in both the banking sector and in the sustainability of public finance.

To conclude on this point, according to Cecchetti et al. (2012), interpretations of TARGET2 balances fall into two camps. The first is that these balances correspond to current account financing, which can be labelled as the *flow* interpretation. Proponents of this view include most prominently Sinn and Wollmershäuser (2011, 2012). The second camp, including Buiter et al. (2011a), Mody and Bornhorst (2012), Bindseil and König (2012), and Cecioni and Ferrero (2012), interprets TARGET2 balances as a "capital account reversal". That is, they see this as one symptom of a balance-of-payments crisis. This is the *stock* interpretation of TARGET2 balances.

4 The ECB's Loss of Control Over Interest Rates in the Crisis-Hit Countries

The crisis has not only had a strong impact on the financial situation of many European countries but has also affected investors' and lenders' confidence and the effectiveness of the financial sector. The tensions in sovereign debt markets and within the banking sector have fed each other, creating severe funding problems for many borrowers. These developments have also led to the fragmentation of the financial system along national borders, with a retrenchment of financial activities to national domestic markets.

The resulting limited or costly access to funding for many businesses and households wishing to invest has been a major obstacle to recovery across Europe to date. At the same time, high levels of indebtedness mean that many economic actors must reduce their financial exposure or increase their savings. Such "deleveraging" can also hamper recovery in the short term. The problems are particularly acute in the vulnerable euro-area member States.

To overcome these problems and tensions, President Mario Draghi announced in July 2012 that the ECB would do "whatever it takes" to preserve the euro and fight against the crisis. Then, on September 6, 2012, the ECB approved the Outright Monetary Transactions (OMT) programme.

Under this programme, the Bank decided to buy unlimited sovereign bonds of troubled countries in secondary markets with a maturity of between 1 and 3 years. The purpose of this programme, first, was to reduce the spreads in the interest rates for public bonds of troubled countries with respect to German public bonds, and second, to safeguard the monetary policy transmission mechanism in all countries of the euro area, preserving the uniqueness of Eurozone monetary policy and ensuring the proper transmission of the policy stance to the real economy throughout the area.

As shown in Fig. 6, soon after Draghi's announcement, TARGET2 net positions began to converge again towards lower levels, and eventually towards zero. This is clearly the evidence of the strong power that the ECB has in influencing the expectations of financial flows among euro-area countries. In fact, the spreads in public bonds interest rates have considerably fallen, which is in line with interest rate reductions among European crisis-hit countries.

Since then, Spanish and Italian bond yields have also greatly decreased, and now, they only incorporate the country-risk due to fundamentals, without any risk premium due to the possible break-up of the European monetary union. The ECB has bought time for governments to overhaul their economies and banks, but politicians have taken advantage of the financial-market calm to slow their recovery efforts.

Eurozone leaders agreed during the 29 June 2012 summit to build a banking union that would include a single banking supervisor housed within the ECB, a common deposit insurance for households and a common bank resolution rule. However, the lack of progress on the banking union and doubts about the financial strength of the banks in crisis-hit countries are hindering cross-border lending. So, the fragmentation of the financial system along national borders and the retrenchment of financial activities to national domestic markets persist.

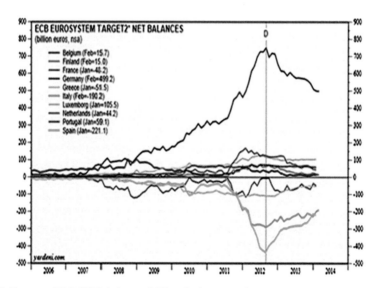

Fig. 6 European TARGET2 balances (billion €). Source: Il Sole-24Ore

In fact, the precise transmission mechanism of the ECB monetary policy is not so clear. The problem of troubled EMU countries, especially in Italy and Spain but also the UK, is that the interest rates that small and medium-sized enterprises (SMEs) must pay to borrow money are far above those set by the ECB and those paid to depositors. Therefore, the link between the ECB's policy rate and borrowing in the real economy is broken (Van Rixtel and Gasperini 2013; Neri 2013).

One explanation for this situation is found in Bernanke and Gertler's (1995) "black box" analysis, which notes that when interest rates rise, credit supply might fall. This is known as the "credit channel paradox", which works as follows. Because of the capital rules of lending, banks can loan to small and medium enterprises (SMEs) only if they have a corresponding amount of capital or deposits on hand while the rule does not apply when banks buy public bonds.

High interest rates on public bonds therefore crowd out the bank-lending channel to SMEs. Furthermore, banks lose deposits as customers decide instead to use them to buy public bonds with higher rates of return. To plug the gap, banks offer long-term deposits that also pay higher interest rates. So, the entire cost of funding for the banks increases. As their own costs rise, banks' loans become scarcer and dearer. This then slows the economy by increasing costs for bank-dependent borrowers, which is the case for SMEs.

For the bank-lending channel to hold, banks' costs must first rise, which depends on the shortfall of customers' deposits plus the deterioration of insolvencies by firms and households. This circumstance will be important only in countries where firms are dependent on bank borrowing. This is the case where SMEs prevail, as in Italy, Spain and the UK, where the loans that banks make exceed the cash they collect as deposits.

In 2008, as the Eurozone started to contract, the ECB slashed its main rate from 4.25 to 1 %, but because investors were worried about the state of the banks, the returns that banks had to offer on their own bonds rose. This offset the ECB's easing, so that firms' borrowing rates fell by less than normal. When the euro crisis intensified in 2010, the ECB's influence on interest rates in Spain and Italy waned even further. Banks' bond yields rose in line with their governments' cost of borrowing. The supply of loans contracted as predicted by the bank-lending channel; however, the contraction now is a result of a change that the ECB did not control.

The amount of borrowing in Italy and Spain has now started to fall again. Some of this may be due to weak demand, but Cappiello et al. (2010) provided empirical evidence for the existence of a bank-lending channel of monetary policy transmission in the euro area. Furthermore, they found that changes in the supply of credit, both in terms of volume and credit standards applied on loans to enterprises, had significant effects on real economic activity.

To support the smooth transmission of its interest rate decisions to the wider economy, the ECB decided to accommodate the liquidity needs of banks that could not be satisfied in the financial market. Thus, since October 2008, the Eurosystem has been conducting most of its liquidity-providing tenders with a fixed-rate, full allotment procedure. This means that all bids received from counterparties are fully satisfied against adequate collateral. In the context of a dysfunctional interbank market, banks could thus turn to the Eurosystem for liquidity. This enabled them to build up buffers to meet future liquidity needs while access to interbank funding was uncertain. Consequently, the Eurosystem provided more liquidity than needed by the banking sector on average while at the same time taking on an intermediation function. This prevented a disorderly deleveraging process and the ensuing adverse consequences for the euro-area economy and price stability.

As the sovereign debt crisis emerged in some euro-area countries starting in spring 2010, the segmentation in funding markets for banks became more delineated along national borders. The central bank intermediation allowed the banking systems in those countries to withstand the withdrawal of private capital and the reversal of cross-border capital flows. The recourse to central bank funding is therefore closely linked to the emergence of significant TARGET2 liabilities for countries most affected by the crisis, and on aggregate, at the euro-area level.

The sovereign debt crisis and resulting bank funding market segmentation also led to a flow of capital into the more resilient countries. This resulted in significant amounts being directed towards the central banks' liquidity absorbing facilities, for example, via use of the deposit facility or via counterparties accruing amounts in excess of their reserve requirements in their current accounts at the central bank. In particular, the repatriation of previous investments and the lack of renewed lending to banks in crisis-hit countries led to significant net payment inflows, a concurrent increase in the TARGET2 claims of the NCBs in the more resilient countries and an increase in liquidity in the banking systems of those countries.

In the second half of 2011 and the first half of 2012, the sharp increase in TARGET2 liabilities and claims was also due to concerns about the integrity of the monetary union. A number of banks from resilient countries had decided to replace head office funding for subsidiaries in financially stressed jurisdictions with local funding. This meant that borrowing from the Eurosystem replaced inter-group funding from resilient countries. This behaviour was in some cases encouraged by national banking regulators aiming to safeguard their domestic banking system (ECB 2013).

5   Final Remarks: The Role of Germany in Promoting European Recovery

The present European economic and financial Great Crisis has demonstrated once more that any fixed exchange rate arrangement (including the monetary union) is prone to crisis if countries do not adjust their economies internally and if imbalances are allowed to grow too large. If economic policies cannot keep the domestic price level competitive vis-à-vis the rest of the integrating area, and if external adjustments via the nominal exchange rate are precluded, real exchange rate appreciation will erode the countries' competitiveness. In most cases, this will lead to current account deficits that at some point will trigger a balance-of-payments crisis.

Therefore, structural reforms are unavoidable in indebted countries to improve productivity and increase competitiveness. Unfortunately, they will produce positive results only in the long run. In the medium term, there is widespread consensus that a successful crisis resolution must include at least a fiscal union or fiscal pact, along with a banking union. A Fiscal Compact entered into force on 1 January 2013, and in March 2014, Eurozone leaders agreed to build a banking union that would include a single banking supervisor housed within the ECB, a common deposit insurance for households and a common bank resolution rule. These decisions have enforced the new convergence-to-zero process of TARGET2 balances.

However, fiscal consolidation will be difficult to achieve without a strong recovery of the European economy. There is no national way out of the crisis. Expansionary measures are impossible at the level of member states, which are obliged to choose fiscal consolidation as a priority. Therefore, in the short run, one possible way to overcome the crisis is to launch a new phase of growth at the European level and promote a substantial increase in European employment.

In this regard, there is now a deep division between the economies of the prosperous North (Germany, Austria, the Netherlands and Finland) and those of the austerity-hit South (France, Italy, Spain, Greece and Portugal). A long-simmering growth-versus-austerity debate has boiled over with increasing calls from outside Germany to rethink crisis-fighting measures. Up to now, Germany has been a staunch advocate of austerity, outlining plans to balance its own budget in 2014, a year ahead of schedule, while France, Italy and Spain as well as the European Commission have all indicated their strong concerns to promote growth without delaying fiscal consolidation.

Additionally, there is only one way to promote growth in the European Union without interfering in the fiscal consolidation needs of the austerity-hit southern countries. This is possible if Germany does not maintain a balanced public budget for the next few years and commits itself to promoting an expansionary fiscal policy with deficits ranging from 1 to 3 % of GDP. In fact, Germany is the only country in the EU that can expand its aggregate demand without paying a substantial increase in domestic inflation.

To expand European aggregate demand to the extent necessary to promote growth, Germany could also let domestic wages increase. In fact, according to 2013 national agreements, three million German metalworkers increased their wages by 3.4 % in 2013, and a further increase of 2.2 % was added in 2014.

The combined effects of the two policies (budget deficit plus wage increases) and the ensuing moderate increase in domestic inflation could be sufficient to appreciate the real exchange rate in Germany, permitting the austerity-hit Southern EMU countries to regain their external competitiveness. In this way, German surplus of the current account (7 % of GDP in 2014) will decrease, while exports of deficit EMU countries will increase, fuelling again the economic growth of the entire Union.

The final effect of this policy will be a further reduction of net claims and liabilities in the TARGET2 payment system.

References

Banca d'Italia (2012) Recent evolution of the balances of the TARGET2 payment system. Economic Bulletin, 63, January

Bergsten F, Kirkegaard JF (2012) The coming resolution of the European crisis. In Peterson Institute for International Economics, policy brief, January. Available via http://www.iie.com/publications/pb/pb12-1.pdf

Bernanke B, Gertler M (1995) Inside the black box: the credit channel of monetary policy transmission. J Econ Perspect 9(4):27–48

Bindseil U, König P (2011) The economics of target2 balance. SFB 649 working paper no. 35. Available via http://sfb649.wiwi.hu-berlin.de/papers/pdf/SFB649DP2011-035.pdf

Bindseil U, König P (2012) TARGET2 and the European sovereign debt crisis. Kredit und Kapital 45(2):135–174

Buiter WH, Rahbari E (2012) Target2 redux: the simple accountancy and slightly more complex economics of Bundesbank loss exposure through the Eurosystem. CEPR discussion paper no. 9211. Available via http://www.willembuiter.com/target2redux.pdf

Buiter WH, Rahbari E, Michels J (2011a) TARGETing the wrong villain: Intra-Eurosystem imbalances in credit flows. Citi global economics view, June

Buiter WH, Rahbari E, Michels J (2011b) The implications of intra-Euro area imbalances in credit flows. CEPR policy insight 57, August

Cappiello L et al (2010) Do bank loans and credit standards have an effect on output? A panel approach for the Euro area. ECB working paper no. 1150, January

Cecchetti SG, McCauley RN, McGuire P (2012) Interpreting TARGET2 balances. BIS working paper no. 393, December

Cecioni M, Ferrero G (2012) Determinants of TARGET2 imbalances. Banca d'Italia, Questioni di Economia e Finanza (Occasional papers) no. 136, September

De Grauwe P (2011) The European Central Bank: lender of last resort in the government bond markets? CESifo working paper no. 3569

Deutsche Bundesbank (2011) The dynamics of the Bundesbank's TARGET2 balances. Monthly report, March

ECB (2011) TARGET2 balances of national central banks in the Euro area. Monthly Bulletin, October

ECB (2013) TARGET balances and monetary policy operations. Monthly Bulletin, May

Holinski N, Kool C, Muysken J (2012) Persistent macroeconomic imbalances in the Euro area: causes and consequences. FRB St Louis Rev 94(1):1–20

Lane PR, Pels B (2012) Current account imbalances in Europe. CEPR discussion paper no. 8958

Lin JY, Treichel V (2012) The crisis in the Euro zone: did the Euro contribute to the evolution of the crisis? World Bank policy research working paper no. 6127

Mayer T (2011) Euroland's hidden balance-of-payments crisis. EU monitor 88, Oct 26. Available via http://www.dbresearch.com/PROD/DBR_INTERNET_EN-PROD/PROD0000000000279906/Euroland%E2%80%99s+hidden+balance-of-payments+crisis.pdf

Mody A, Bornhorst F (2012) TARGET imbalances: financing the capital-account reversal in Europe. VoxEU, Mar 7

Moro B (2012) The theoretical debate on the recent great crisis. J Ital Econ Assoc XVII(1):3–42

Moro B (2013) The run on repo and the liquidity shortage problems of the current global financial crisis: Europe vs US. Ekonomi-tek 2:41–77

Moro B (2014) Lessons from the European economic and financial great crisis: a survey. Eur J Polit Econ 34(S):9–24

Neri S (2013) The impact of the sovereign debt crisis on bank lending rates in the Euro area. Bank of Italy occasional paper no. 170, June

Neumann MJM (2012) The refinancing of banks drives target debt. CESifo forum 13, special issue, January

Sinn HW (2011) The ECB stealth bailout. VoxEu, June 1

Sinn HW (2012a) The European balance of payments crisis: an introduction. CESifo forum 13, special issue, January

Sinn HW (2012b) Fed versus ECB: how target debt can be repaid. Vox, Mar 10. Available via http://www.voxeu.org/article/fed-versus-ecb-how-target-debts-can-be-repaid

Sinn HW (2012c) TARGET losses in case of a Euro breakup. Vox, Oct 22

Sinn HW, Wollmershäeuser T (2011) Target loans, current account balances and capital flows: the ECB's rescue facility. NBER working paper no. 17626, November

Sinn HW, Wollmershäeuser T (2012) Target balances and the German financial account in light of the European balance-of-payments crisis. CESifo working paper no. 4051. Available via http://www.cesifo-group.de/portal/pls/portal/docs/1/1218218.PDF

Van Rixtel A, Gasperini G (2013) Financial crisis and bank funding: recent experience in the Euro. BIS working paper no. 405, March

Véron N (2011) The European debt and financial crisis: origins, options and implications for the US and Global Economy. Working paper, Sept 22. Available via http://banking.senate.gov/public/index.cfm?FuseAction=Files.View&FileStore_id=9bec6123-d58d-423d-bf17-4fdcb9b113c3

Whelan K (2011) Professor Sinn misses the target. VoxEu, June 9

Whelan K (2012) TARGET2 and Central Bank balance sheets. University College Dublin, School of Economics working paper no. 12/29, November. Available via http://www.ucd.ie/t4cms/WP12_29.pdf

Wyplosz C (2011) A failsafe way to end the Euro area crisis. VoxEu, Sept 26. Available via http://voxeu.org/index.php?q=node/70

Part II
Bank Opportunistic Behaviour and Structural Reforms

Moral-Hazard Conduct in the European Banks During the First Wave of the Global Financial Crisis

Paolo Mattana and Stefania P.S. Rossi

Abstract This paper investigates the extent to which public interventions, largely implemented to countervail the effects of the 2007–2009 financial crisis, have generated moral hazard behaviour in large European banks, twisting their risk-taking and profitability profiles according to the so-called "too-big-to-fail" hypothesis. To this end, we devise an empirical framework linking credit risk and profitability changes to bank dimension. By applying a Quantile Regression Approach to a sample of 1476 European financial institutions, and considering the combination of risk and profit size sensitivities at quantile level, we observe that the theoretical hypothesis behind the *too big to fail* is confirmed when the change in ROA proxies for the risk undertaking. We obtain a different picture—much less consistent with our moral hazard hypothesis—when the change in ROE is employed instead. We also provide a possible explanation for this contradictory pattern by discussing the role of managers versus shareholders in the bank strategic design.

1 Introduction

During the first wave of the present financial crisis, substantial policy interventions were implemented to countervail bank defaults and protect the global economy from disastrous financial instability. A large swath of the literature (cfr. *inter al.*, Hetzel 2009; De Nicolò et al. 2010; Hakenes and Schnabel 2010; Ioannidou and Penas 2010; Dam and Koetter 2012; Bertay et al. 2013; Gropp et al. 2011, 2014) has linked these policy interventions (in the form of direct capital injections and/or implicit/explicit bailout guarantees) to a number of adverse effects, not the least of

P. Mattana • S.P.S. Rossi (✉)

Department of Economics and Business, University of Cagliari, Cagliari, Italy

e-mail: mattana@unica.it; stefania.rossi@unica.it

© Springer International Publishing Switzerland 2016

S.P.S. Rossi, R. Malavasi (eds.), *Financial Crisis, Bank Behaviour and Credit Crunch*, Contributions to Economics, DOI 10.1007/978-3-319-17413-6_3

which have been a reduction in market discipline and the temptation to engage in moral hazard.

According to the so-called "too big to fail" hypothesis (TBTF), large banks are deemed to be particularly involved in the phenomenon. In this regard, contributions to the literature have mainly focused on the effects and distortions that government bailout guarantees may have on the risk appetite of banks (Mishikin 2006; Stern 2009; Barrell et al. 2011; Hakenes and Schnabel 2011; Molyneux et al. 2011; Völz and Wedow 2011; Beltratti and Stulz 2012; Brewer and Jagtiani 2013). Conversely, other studies (cfr., *inter al.*, Freixas 1999; Chang 2010; Mattana et al. 2015) have analysed the implications that distorted incentives may have on banks' strategic choices regarding *both* risk appetite and profitability.

The present paper contributes to the TBTF literature by studying the role of size in the combination of risk and profitability chosen by a large sample of European banks (1476) observed across the time period from 2007 to 2009. To approach the problem, we first set up an empirical model and then apply a Quantile Regression Methodology to estimate the effect of bank size on specific parts of the conditional distribution of our risk-taking and profit variables. What we expect is that, if banks have engaged in moral hazard behaviour, size should become positive and significant at the right of a given (endogenous) threshold in the conditional distribution of the risk and profit variables.

The paper is structured as follows. Section 2 will discuss the model specifications. In Sect. 3 a description of the data will be provided. The empirical methodology and results will be presented in Sect. 4. Section 5 provides conclusions based on the analyses.

2   Size-Induced Strategic Choices

2.1   *The Empirical Framework*

Consider the following empirical model:

$$Credit\_Risk_i = \alpha_0 + \alpha_1 Size_i + \sum \varphi_{1j} Z_j + e_1 \tag{1}$$

$$Prof\_Index_i = \beta_0 + \beta_1 Size_i + \sum \varphi_{2j} Z_j + e_2 \tag{2}$$

where $Credit\_Risk_i$ and $Prof\_Index_i$ are i-*th* bank measures of credit risk appetite and profitability measures, $Size_i$ proxies for the dimension of bank i-*th*, and Z_j is the vector of control variables. In Eq. (1), α_0 measures the "autonomous" fraction of the variation in credit risk undertakings over the financial crisis. α_1 is the parameter of interest, measuring the effect of size on the credit risk variable. φ_{1j} is the vector of parameters associated with the control variables while e_1 is the error term. In

Eq. (2), β_0 measures the "autonomous" part in the profit retention rate over the financial crisis. β_1 is the parameter of interest, measuring the effect of size on the profitability retention rate. φ_{2j} is the vector of parameters associated with the control variables. e_2 is the error term.

According to this setting, the strategic behaviour of banks—at least from the perspective of the TBTF hypothesis—requires that risk appetite increases, under distorted incentives, in the expectation of higher profits (cf. Mattana et al. 2015, for a formal model).

To capture the existence of size-induced distorted strategic choices dependent upon the expectation of policy intervention (either in the form of direct capital injections and/or implicit/explicit bailout guarantees), we propose a Quantile Regression Estimation[1] of Eqs. (1) and (2). The quantile approach permits the estimation of various quantile functions of a conditional distribution. Each quantile regression characterizes a particular point (centre or tail) on the conditional distribution. Taken together, the ensemble of estimated conditional quantile functions offers complete information about the effect of covariates on the entire distribution of the response variable. The method is very interesting because we can become aware of any heterogeneity in the estimation of the sensitivity coefficients in different points of the quantile distribution of the dependent variable. Notice also that the Quantile Regression Approach overcomes various problems that confront OLS (heteroscedasticity being one example). Additionally, quantile regressions will be more robust in response to large outliers.

Given the capacity of quantile regression to provide evidence that the banking industry has actually engaged in moral hazards in the form of TBTF during the present financial crisis, we should therefore observe significant point estimates of the alpha and beta sensitivities only at the right of some point of the conditional distributions of risk and profit variables. More specifically, provided that the conditioning set Z_j is effective in eliminating all residual heterogeneity, size should become a relevant covariate only for the group of banks that have increased their risk appetite the most across the first wave of the present financial crisis. Conversely, if moral hazard behaviour is not present, again provided the conditioning set Z_j is effective in eliminating heterogeneity across units, size should not bear explanatory power at any point of the conditional distributions for risk and profit.

2.2   Variables

A crucial point of our analysis concerns the identification of appropriate measures for credit risk and profitability. Credit risk, in the empirical literature regarding moral hazard in the banking industry, is typically estimated by a normalised measure of impaired loans (IL). The idea is that a higher value of IL, *ceteris paribus*, is meant to imply higher default risk (cf. Sironi 2003; Gropp and Vesala

---

[1] The approach has been first suggested by Koenker and Bassett (1978).

2004). However, banks are also likely to consider loan loss provisions (LLP) in their accounting statements. Therefore, as a proxy for credit risk, the value of LLP, again in normalised terms, is alternatively designated in the literature to indicate credit risk profile (cf. Berger and DeYoung 1997; Bushman and Williams 2012). The two variables ordinarily show comparable developments: the latter being more a proxy for the expected (ex-ante) risk while the former is more of an ex-post risk indicator.

The normalisation variable is usually taken from the assets side of banks' balance sheets, as either Total Gross Loans or Total Assets. In this regard, in our empirical investigation, we face two substantial obstacles to the use of either one of these quantities. On the one hand, given the period under investigation, the variable Total Gross Loans has undergone wild variations in our sample.[2] Therefore, using this variable as a divisor for the calculation of a proxy of credit risk might significantly alter the actual capability of the normalised variable to capture banks' strategic choices. On the other hand, Total Assets is also our independent variable, and therefore, it seems inappropriate to use it for normalisation purposes in the left hand side of our empirical relationships. Thus, we prefer using Total capital (TC) to normalise our credit risk variables. This variable has the advantage that, in addition to considering the value of ownership interests in a company (Equity), TC also encompasses the total value of debts owed by the company in the form of loans and bonds. The variable TC appears, moreover, far more stable across banks in our sample, with an average recorded value for the 2009–2007 time period of 11.03 % and a SD of just 29.32 %.

For profitability proxies we employ ROA and ROE ratios. ROA tells how effectively a bank is taking earnings advantage of its base of assets. It is a typical performance indicator which mainly reflects managerial strategic moves. ROE on the other hand looks at how effectively a bank is using equity capital and mainly reflects the owners' interest in the business.

Furthermore, and consistent with our information needs, because we aim to evaluate the impact of public policy on the *change* in risk appetite and profitability since the outbreak of the economic crisis, both our credit risk and profitability variables are calculated in difference terms between the recorded values at the end of 2009 and the balance-sheet values at the beginning of the global financial crises in 2007.[3] This is an important point because our choice prevents many spurious elements from interfering in our investigation that come from the dangerous build-

[2] The average recorded value of Total Gross Loans in our sample is 24.19 %, with a SD of 461.63 %.

[3] Notice that, from a more technical point of view, the use of the difference operator can be considered as having a number of positive effects. First, it reduces the risk that endogeneity impacts the results of the estimation. Perhaps more importantly, the use of the difference operator is also an effective method of casting away heterogeneity at the single unit level: particularly for the profitability indicator, the use of the difference operator precludes many spurious elements, one for all economies of scale, from interfering with the task of estimating the interplay between credit risk and profitability in relation to bank size.

up of public budget deficits and debt. Therefore, the variables $\Delta ILTC_i$ and $\Delta LLPTC_i$ represent bank i-th change (2009 minus 2007) in the normalised values of IL and LLP. In parallel terms, ΔROE_i and ΔROA_i measure variations (2009 minus 2007) in bank i-th ROE and ROA profitability indices. Descriptive statistics for these variables are reported in Table 2.

To proxy bank dimension (Size), we compute the log of the total assets of each bank, at the initial period 2007, scaled for the average bank size in the country of origin, so that any country dimension bias will be avoided.

Regarding the set of control variables, we use only strictly exogenous variables, such as country and bank specialisation dummies, as well as a dummy variable separating listed from non-listed banks.

3 Data and Descriptive Statistics

Our dataset is composed of single-bank records for European countries, consisting of annual accounting data derived from the financial statements of banks made available through the BankScope database of Bureau van Dijk and Fitch/Ibca. We selected data for 16 European countries (cf. Table 1). Regarding bank specialisation, we include in the sample only institutions for which credit risk is an appropriate indicator of risk-taking, such as commercial banks, cooperative banks, savings banks, real estate and mortgage banks, as well as specialised governmental credit institutions. In the sample selection, we have also concentrated on choosing the most appropriate accounting standards. In this regard, we prefer financial statements using IAS over those using national standards. We also use consolidated balance sheets whenever available, to avoid double-counting institutions and to convert all values into a single currency (US$).

The sample contains 1476 banks, observed from 2007 to 2009. Table 1 reports the stratification in the resulting sample by bank nationality.

The balance sheet variables employed in the empirical analysis cover the following quantities: Total Assets (used to calculate our proxy for bank size, computed as the log of total assets at the initial period of 2007, scaled for each bank, for the average bank size in the country of origin), IL, LLP, TC, ROA and ROE. As discussed above, we first construct the ratios, ILTC, LLPTC and then calculate the 2009/2007 difference in the ratios. The same 2009/2007 difference is computed for ROA and ROE.

Given our estimation strategy, we present in Figs. 1 and 2 some distribution graphs of our dependent variables. In all cases, for a clearer representation, extreme values are dropped; the minimum and maximum values, however, are reported in Table 2.

Table 1 Stratification of the sample by country of origin

Country	Banks	% of the sample
Austria	54	3.66
Belgium	12	0.81
Denmark	58	3.93
Finland	9	0.61
France	109	7.38
Germany	513	34.76
Greece	14	0.95
Ireland	13	0.88
Italy	197	13.35
Netherlands	21	1.42
Norway	85	5.76
Portugal	14	0.95
Spain	61	4.13
Sweden	18	1.22
Switzerland	229	15.51
UK	69	4.67
Total	**1,476**	**100.00**

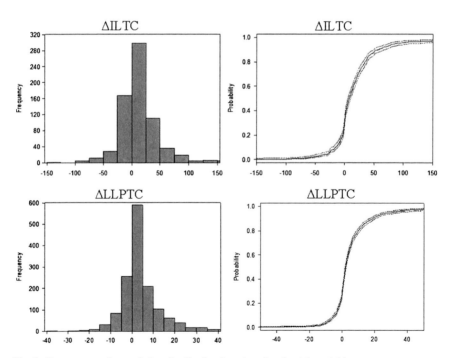

Fig. 1 Frequency and cumulative distribution functions for the risk variables

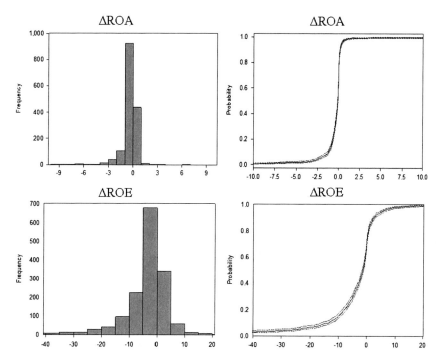

Fig. 2 Frequency and cumulative distribution functions for the profitability variables

Table 2 Descriptive statistics

Variable	Year	N	Mean	Std. dev.	Min	Max
Size	2007	1,476	1.06	5.71	0.01	62.82
ΔILTC	2009–07	693	18.28	53.65	−417.85	569.64
ΔLLPTC	2009–07	1,476	5.01	25.50	−338.20	111.68
ΔROA	2009–07	1,476	−0.38	1.26	−26.71	6.98
ΔROE	2009–07	1,476	−4.85	15.43	−205.34	78.04

Size is the total assets of each bank, in 2007, scaled for the average bank size in the country of origin. The other variables are 2009/2007 differences in the ratios, in percentage

Descriptive statistics for the variables employed in the empirical analysis are presented in Table 2. As it emerges, we do not have a balanced dataset, and the full dimension of the sample is retained only in the cases of ΔLLPTC, ΔROA, and ΔROE. Conversely, the number of observations decreases to 693 for the cases of ΔILTC. This is because data on impaired loans at the bank level are not always available in the BankScope dataset.

4   Results

Table 3 contains results of the Quantile Regression estimation of Eqs. (1) and (2). For the purpose of our analysis, we divide the distribution of our dependent variables (ΔILTC, ΔLLPTC, ΔROA, ΔROE) into 20 quantiles, represented in ascending order from "low" classes of risk and profitability to "high" classes of risk and profitability.[4] As discussed in Sect. 2.1, for our hypothesis of TBTF to be verified, we expect coefficients to become positive and significant at the right of the conditional distribution of our risk and profit variables (namely only for "high" quantiles). Regarding the estimation method, we propose the Simultaneous Quantile Regression Estimation (SQRE) variant of the quantile regression method. The SQRE generates a bootstrapped variance-covariance matrix of the estimators that includes between-quantiles blocks. Thus, very crucially, one can test and construct confidence intervals comparing coefficients describing different quantiles. For convenience, we omit α_0 and β_0 estimates and the coefficients of the control variables.[5]

We first comment on the quantile point estimates of the α_1 sensitivity. The evidence obtained by the SQRE estimator (first and second columns in Table 3) presents some interesting features. Surprisingly, coefficients are positive *across* all quantiles for both the ΔILTC and ΔLLPTC variables. The statistical fit is quite robust, particularly for the ΔLLPTC. These results imply that, *within* quantiles, size always plays a role in increasing the risk exposure of banks. In our opinion, these findings reflect indications that the conditioning set (Z_j vector) is unable to eliminate all size-induced heterogeneity unrelated to moral hazards. Several elements may explain this result. First of all, our conditioning set does not provide an indicator of size-dependent diversification policy pursued at single unit (bank) level.[6] Moreover, during the global financial turmoil, larger banks might have undergone higher risk exposure, *vis à vis* smaller banks, because small banks have a superior capability of monitoring the loan granting process, minimizing the non-performing loans and loss provisioning.

However, if we confront the magnitude of the α_1 coefficients *across* quantiles, we observe a sharp tendency of the coefficient to increase for banks that have increased their risk exposure the most. As reported in the last line of Table 3, F-testing the null of parameters invariant *across* quantiles confirms that coefficients significantly differ at the quantile level. Furthermore, when we instruct the software to test sequentially the null of parameters invariant *across* quantiles, we observe

---

[4] The chosen number of intervals in the conditional distribution of the dependent variables is an important issue. Of course, the higher the number of intervals, the more details can be obtained on the parameter estimations at various points along the conditional distributions. There is a trade-off, however, with the number of observation points in the various quantiles. We have solved this trade-off by dividing the distribution of the dependent variables into 20 quantiles.

[5] The full estimates are available upon request.

[6] Unfortunately, BankScope does not allow proxy construction of the bank's diversification policy.

Table 3 SQRE estimation; α_1 and β_1 size sensitivities

Quantiles	ΔILTC	ΔLLPTC	ΔROA	ΔROE
05	1.34	0.17**	−0.02*	−0.27
10	2.02**	0.17***	−0.02**	−0.17
15	1.70**	0.23***	−0.01*	−0.06
20	1.56**	0.29***	−0.01*	−0.15
25	1.58***	0.30***	−0.02**	−0.27*
30	1.36***	0.33***	−0.02***	−0.29**
35	1.41***	0.36***	−0.01**	−0.31***
40	1.43***	0.46***	−0.01**	−0.32***
45	1.35***	0.51***	−0.01**	−0.36***
50	1.30***	0.47***	−0.01**	−0.37***
55	1.30***	0.51***	−0.01	−0.39***
60	1.24**	0.49***	−0.01**	−0.42***
65	1.23**	0.46***	−0.01*	−0.36***
70	1.39***	0.46***	−0.01	−0.38***
75	1.42***	0.51***	−0.00	−0.53***
80	1.85***	0.59***	−0.00	−0.56***
85	2.86**	0.56**	0.00*	−0.65***
90	2.80*	0.67**	0.01*	−0.75***
95	3.72*	1.09***	0.02*	−1.56***
H_0	$F(17, 666) = 96.53$ Prob > F = 0.00	$F(18, 1448) = 5.42$ Prob > F = 0.00	$F(18, 1449) = 16.07$ Prob > F = 0.00	$F(18, 1449) = 1.63$ Prob > F = 0.04

***, **,* denote significance at the 1 %, 5 % and 10 % levels, respectively

that the null is rejected starting from the 80th percentile of the distribution for the case of ILTC and from the 90th percentile for the case of the delta LLPTC. These results yield evidence that if we look at the banks that had the most increased risk during the first wave of the present financial turmoil, we find evidence of an amplified role of bank size relative to that of banks showing a less pronounced risk disclosure over the crisis.

The SQRE estimation of Eq. (2) also provides surprising details on the relationship between bank size and profit retention during the crisis. In the case of ΔROE, we observe that point estimates are negative at all points along the conditional distribution. They are also statistically significant starting from the 25th percentile. Again, probably because of the inability of our conditioning set to remove all size heterogeneity unrelated to moral hazards at the single unit level, we observe a role for size in reducing the profit dip at all classes of the conditional distribution. However, when we consider the behaviour of the β_1 sensitivity as we move rightwards in the conditional distribution of ΔROE, we observe a downward behavioural trend which becomes suddenly steeper at the 70th percentile. The null of parameters invariant *across* quantiles is strongly rejected by the F-test. Furthermore, when we instruct the software to test sequentially the null of parameters invariant *across* quantiles, we observe that the null is rejected at the 85th percentile of the distribution.

Interestingly, when the size sensitivity of profit retention is estimated using ΔROA, a different pattern emerges; specifically, the β_1 coefficient, despite remaining negative for a great part of the left distribution of the profit variable (the lowest sensitivity being measured for the first quantile at a value around -0.02), shows an almost monotone upward trend, and becomes positive at the very right of the conditional distribution of the profit retention rate variable. F-testing confirms the appropriateness of our quantile approach in this case, as well. Implications, from our perspective, are crucial. In particular, for the group of least performing banks (including the left distribution up to the 80th percentile), larger size implies, on average, a deterioration in the bank's capability to retain profits across the crisis. Conversely, for the group of the best performing banks (from the 85th percentile included) a positive correlation emerges between size and profit retention. F-testing strongly rejects the null of parameter invariant *across* quantiles.

4.1 An Interpretation of the Results in Terms of TBTF

What can we infer from the aforementioned results with regard to engagement in moral hazards in the form of TBTF in the European banking industry during the first wave of the present financial crisis?

Mattana et al. (2015), to derive information regarding banks' strategic choices during the financial crisis, combined information about risk/profit size sensitivities. In our case, there is a critical obstacle with regard to the possibility of jointly looking at the risk/profit coefficients: simply put, our method does not allow us to obtain combinations of the coefficients at the bank level. Admittedly, then, we do not know yet whether the sample intersection of the quantiles is populated by the same banks. However, by assigning each bank its quantile risk and profit size sensitivity and computing correlations, we can discover some important additional information. Specifically, we discover a high positive correlation between bank-level alphas (both in the case of ΔILTC and ΔLLPTC) and beta coefficients when ΔROA proxies for profit retention. In this instance, the correlation is high and negative when the alphas are linked with the beta sensitivities where profit retention is proxied by ΔROE. Thus, the quantile alpha/beta combinations can be used as an approximation of bank-level combinations of the coefficients.

Consider, in Fig. 3, the scatterplots for risk and profit size sensitivities. For an easier appraisal, coefficients are standardised. To unveil tendencies, points are joined by means of the nearest neighbour fit method.

Consider first the combination of the α_1 sensitivities with the β_1 coefficients obtained when ΔROA is used to proxy for profitability retention during the crisis. Consistent with the theoretical hypothesis behind the TBTF form of moral hazard, both size sensitivities show a sudden escalation at the very right of the conditional distributions.

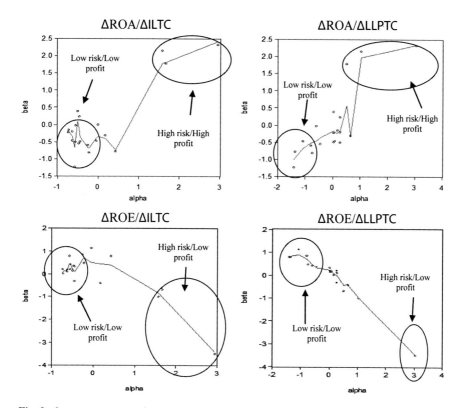

Fig. 3 β_1 *versus* α_1 scatterplots

In contrast, when we consider the combination of the α_1 sensitivities with the β_1 coefficients obtained when ΔROE proxies for profitability retention during the crisis, we obtain a different picture, much less consistent with our hypothesis regarding TBTF. In this case, scatterplots and tendency curves show that high risk-size sensitivities go hand in hand with low profit-size sensitivities.

What may be the reasons behind this ΔROA/ΔROE contradictory pattern? We believe that in the discussion of moral hazard in the form of the TBTF, there is one more subtle issue to be considered. Here, we specifically refer to the actors (managers and/or owners) behind the moral hazard behaviour. Admittedly, bank managers and owners are described as generally responding to different sets of incentives (cf. Haq et al. 2011). Unless their interest is closely aligned with that of the value-maximising owner, bank managers tend to be more risk averse because their wealth (both tangible and human capital) depends on the bank they manage sustaining operations. Conversely, limited liability gives bank owners an incentive to expropriate wealth from bondholders/depositors by increasing risk. In the presence of a bailout policy, the government protects bondholders (particularly depositors) from the consequences of bank risk-taking behaviour; therefore, the owners' incentive to monitor and constrain risk-taking is weak.

In this regard, as also discussed above in Sect. 2.2., ROA is a typical performance indicator which mainly reflects managerial strategic moves, whereas ROE looks more at how effectively a bank is using equity capital and mainly reflects the owners' interest in the business. If we take these considerations for granted, our results imply that moral hazard in the form of TBTF emerges in the European banking industry only as a result of strategic choices taken from the managers' side. Conversely, there are no signs of owners' having driven moral hazard behaviour. On that point, however, we are aware that further research is warranted.

5 Conclusions

We devised an empirical model to investigate the extent to which bank size has played a role in the strategic combination of risk and profitability chosen by a vast sample of European banks (1476) during the first wave of the present global financial crisis (2007–2009). The idea is that because of the dramatic policy interventions, to counter the bank defaults and avoid disastrous financial instability, large banks might have been influenced toward expansion, taking advantage of moral hazard behaviour in the form of the TBTF phenomenon.

Two equations were separately estimated using a Robust Quantile Approach. In the first equation, the dependent variable was the change in risk profile (alternatively proxied by the 2009/2007 variation of the ratio of impaired loans over total capital and the ratio of loan loss provisioning over total capital). In the second equation, the dependent variable was the change 2009/2007 in bank profitability (alternatively proxied by ROA and ROE). In both specifications *Size*, (measured as the log of the ratio of bank assets in 2007 to country-of-origin average bank size) was the independent variable. A set of strictly exogenous control variables was also taken into consideration in the model. Finally, information obtained separately at quantile level for the two strategic variables were then conveyed at single bank level. As a result, evidence that the banking industry has actually indulged in our moral hazard hypothesis simply derives from the contemporaneous presence at a quantile level of positive and significant estimates of risk and profit size sensitivities.

Overall, our results can be summarised as follows. First of all, we found that, *within* quantiles, size always played a role in increasing the risk exposure of banks. However, more consistently with our idea of TBTF, when we confronted the magnitude of the size sensitivities of risk exposure *across* quantiles, we observed a sharp tendency of the coefficient to increase for banks that have increased their risk exposure the most (the very right of the conditional distribution of the dependent variable).

Secondly, we observed that the size sensitivity of the profit retention rate, proxied by ΔROA, although remaining negative for a great part of the left distribution, displayed an almost monotone upward trend, becoming positive—at the very right of the conditional distribution—for those banks that have increased the profit retention rate the most. Therefore, consistently with the theoretical hypothesis of TBTF, these findings suggested the existence of a form of moral hazard conduct in the

European banks considered in our analysis. However, this evidence could not be confirmed when the change in profitability was estimated using ΔROE. We provided a possible explanation for this contradictory pattern (ΔROA *versus* ΔROE) by discussing the role of managers/shareholders in the bank strategic choices.

At the end of the paper, the implications of the findings in terms of moral hazard conduct in the European banking industry were presented.

Acknowledgements A version of this paper has been presented at the Conference on "Financial crisis and credit crunch: Micro and macroeconomic implications" held at the Department of Economics and Business, University of Cagliari, Italy. Results have also been discussed in the Seminars at the University of Malaga, Spain, and at the Department of Economics, Business, Mathematics and Statistics (DEAMS), University of Trieste, Italy. We would like to thank participants for useful comments. The usual disclaimer applies. Research grant from the Autonomous Region of Sardinia, *Legge Regionale 2007, N. 7* [Grant Number CRP-59890, year 2012] is gratefully acknowledged.

References

Barrell R, Davis EP, Fic T et al (2011) Is there a link from bank size to risk taking? NIESR discussion paper no. 367. Available via http://niesr.ac.uk/sites/default/files/publications/dp367.pdf

Beltratti A, Stulz R (2012) Why did some banks perform better during the credit crisis? A cross-country study of the impact of governance and regulation. J Financ Econ 105:1–17

Berger AN, DeYoung R (1997) Problem loans and cost efficiency in commercial banks. J Bank Finance 21:849–870

Bertay AC, Demirgüc-Kunt A, Huizinga HP (2013) Do we need big banks? Evidence on performance, strategy and market discipline. J Financ Intermed 22:532–558

Brewer E III, Jagtiani J (2013) How much did banks pay to become too-big-to-fail and to become systemically important? J Financ Serv Res 43:1–35

Bushman RM, Williams CD (2012) Accounting discretion, loan loss provisioning, and discipline of banks' risk-taking. J Account Econ 54:1–18

Chang J (2010) The too big to fail policy and its implications. Korean Capital Market Institute, KCMI capital market perspective no. 2, vol 2

Dam L, Koetter M (2012) Bank bailouts and moral hazard: evidence from Germany. Rev Financ Stud 25:2343–2380

De Nicolò G, Dell'Ariccia G, Laeven L et al (2010) Monetary policy and bank risk taking. IMF staff position note, SPN/10/09

Freixas X (1999) Optimal bailout policy, conditionality and constructive ambiguity. Economics working papers 400. Available via SSRN. http://ssrn.com/abstract=199054 or http://dx.doi.org/10.2139/ssrn.199054

Gropp R, Vesala J (2004) Deposit insurance, moral hazard and market monitoring. Rev Finance 8:571–602

Gropp R, Hakenes H, Schnabel I (2011) Competition, risk-shifting, and public bail-out policies. Rev Financ Stud 24:2084–2120

Gropp R, Grundl C, Guttler A (2014) The impact of public guarantees on bank risk taking: evidence from a natural experiment. Rev Finance 18:457–488

Hakenes H, Schnabel I (2010) Bank without parachutes: competitive effects of government bailout policies. J Financ Stabil 6:156–168

Hakenes H, Schnabel I (2011) Bank size and risk taking under Basel II. J Bank Finance 35: 1436–1449

Haq M, Pathan S, Williams B (2011) Managerial incentives, market power and bank risk taking. SSRN working paper series, July 29. Available via SSRN. http://ssrn.com/abstract=1898933 or http://dx.doi.org/10.2139/ssrn.1898933

Hetzel RL (2009) Should increased regulation of bank risk taking come from regulators or from the market? Econ Q 95:161–200

Ioannidou VP, Penas MF (2010) Deposit insurance and bank-risk taking: evidence from internal loan ratings. J Financ Intermed 19:95–115

Koenker R, Bassett G (1978) Regression quantile. Econometrica 46:33–50

Mattana P, Petroni F, Rossi SPS (2015) A test for the too-big-to-fail hypothesis for the European banks during the financial crisis. Appl Econ 47(4):319–332

Mishikin FS (2006) How big a problem is too big to fail? A review of Gary Stern and Ron Feldman's too big to fail: the hazards of bank bailouts. J Econ Lit 54:988–1004

Molyneux P, Schaeck K, Zhou TM (2011) Too systemically important to fail, in banking. Bangor Business School working paper no. 11/011. Available via SSRN. http://ssrn.com/abstract=1986013 or http://dx.doi.org/10.2139/ssrn.1986013

Sironi A (2003) Testing for market discipline in the European banking industry: evidence form subordinated debt issues. J Money Credit Bank 35:443–572

Stern GH (2009) Better late than never: addressing too-big-to-fail. Brookings Institution, Washington, DC, Mar 31

Völz M, Wedow M (2011) Market discipline and too-big-to-fail in the CDS market: does banks' size reduce market discipline? J Empir Finance 18:195–210

Agency Problems in Banking: Types of and Incentives for Risk Shifting

Miguel A. Duran and Ana Lozano-Vivas

Abstract The banking literature has extensively examined risk shifting, especially in theoretical terms and in relation to the safety net and regulation. To set a framework of analysis for this moral hazard problem, we provide a brief synthesis of the incentive scheme underlying risk shifting. Then, we propose an empirical method to determine whether banks engage in risk shifting. This method also allows us, first, to classify risk shifting practices depending on the group of creditors to which shareholders transfer risk (that is, our method implies a taxonomy of risk shifting), and second, to identify positive and negative incentives for risk shifting. We apply our method to the banking systems of the United States and the European Union and discuss the resulting findings.

1 Introduction

Since Jensen and Meckling (1976) stressed the view of risk shifting as an agency problem, this view has been a pillar of the standard understanding of the conflicts between firm shareholders and creditors. In the banking sector, such conflict may be particularly severe, due to the relatively high level of leverage in this industry and as a result of the incentives created by the safety net. Indeed, the banking literature has paid a great deal of attention to risk shifting, but with a particular focus on how it is affected by regulation and the safety net (Berger et al. 1995; VanHoose 2007; Freixas and Rochet 2008).

The incentive structure behind risk shifting can be illustrated in a simple setting. Let a limited liability firm with no initial debt have the chance to invest in two mutually exclusive, equal-cost projects, projects 1 and 2, which will be financed via non-coupon bearing debt with a face value of X^* and maturing at T. As a result of these investments, the value of the assets of the firm at T is a random amount, $\widetilde{X}_j$, with $j = 1, 2$. Under some simplifying assumptions, the value of debt at T, D_j, is X^*

M.A. Duran (✉) • A. Lozano-Vivas
University of Malaga, Malaga, Spain
e-mail: maduran@uma.es; avivas@uma.es

© Springer International Publishing Switzerland 2016   53
S.P.S. Rossi, R. Malavasi (eds.), *Financial Crisis, Bank Behaviour and Credit Crunch*, Contributions to Economics, DOI 10.1007/978-3-319-17413-6_4

if the firm is solvent, that is, if $X^* < \widetilde{X}_j$, and the value of debt is just $\widetilde{X}_j$ under insolvency, because limited liability protects shareholders; that is, $D_j = min\left[X^*, \widetilde{X}_j\right]$. By contrast, the value of equity at T, S_j, is the residual value $\widetilde{X}_j - X^*$ if the firm is solvent, and 0 otherwise; that is, $S_j = max\left[0, \widetilde{X}_j - X^*\right]$. Therefore, shareholders' stake in a firm is similar to a European call option on the value of the firm, with exercise price equal to the face value of debt. This implies that funding through debt is equivalent to shareholders selling the firm to creditors, with the right to buy it back at T for price X^*. Let us assume that the distributions of $\widetilde{X}_1$ and $\widetilde{X}_2$ are identical except for the fact that positive and negative extreme values are more frequent under the distribution of $\widetilde{X}_2$. This implies that the expected values of firm assets at T are the same under projects 1 and 2, but the latter project is riskier. Given the structure of payoffs of equity and debt, shareholders have a strong incentive to issue debt and then to choose project 2 at the expense of creditors. That is, shareholders prefer high-risk investments, "which promise (them) very high payoffs if successful even if they have a very low probability of success." When these investments "turn out well," shareholders capture "most of the gains" (in our example, $\widetilde{X}_2 - X^*$) and when "they turn out badly, the creditors bear most of the costs" (in our example, $X^* - \widetilde{X}_2$) (Jensen and Meckling 1976: 334).

If these incentives lead shareholders to actually choose high-risk projects, we should observe that leverage-increasing firms become riskier; that is, observing this relation between leverage and risk implies that shareholders shift risk to creditors. Analysis of this empirical implication in the banking sector is one of the aims of this paper; specifically, we analyse the presence of risk shifting by testing whether there is a positive relation between risk and leverage. It is worth noting that our analysis, therefore, is based on a sufficient condition, not a necessary one: risk shifting practices may be present although a positive relation between leverage and risk is not observed. In addition, the empirical method that we propose to determine whether banks engage in risk shifting allows us to classify these practices in terms of the group of creditors to whom risk is shifted; that is, by differentiating between depositors and non-depository creditors, we can determine the type of risk shifting observed, if any. Additionally, our method enables us to identify which variables incentivise or disincentivise risk shifting.

We study risk shifting in the banking sectors of the United States (US) and in the first 15 members of the European Union (EU15) (Duran and Lozano-Vivas 2014, 2015). In both banking sectors, we focus on risk-increasing banks, because increases in risk are a key feature of risk shifting, and to exclude ambiguous situations in interpreting our results. The main common conclusions for both banking systems are that: (1) banks seem to have engaged in risk shifting practices; (2) the type of observed risk shifting implies that shareholders shift risk to non-depository creditors; and (3) capital buffers appear to disincentivise risk shifting. The latter result suggests that the incentives that lead banks to maintain a relatively high capital ratio and to avoid risk shifting practices are aligned; hence, this finding provides support to the regulation of conservation capital buffers introduced in Basel III.

The main difference between the US and the EU15 is that the return rate appears to have opposite effects in each sample: It disincentivises (incentivises) risk shifting in the US (EU15). The EU15 sample allows examination of the effect of banking regulation. The main conclusion in this regard is that hardening the three pillars of Basel II does not seem to disincentivise risk shifting.

2   Method of Analysis

To analyse risk shifting in the banking industry, we extend to other funding sources the way in which Shrieves and Dahl (1992) model the relation between changes in risk and equity. In particular, we differentiate among three funding sources for banks, and hence, three funding groups of agents: capital, deposits, and non-depository debt claims. In Eq. (1) below, *fsta* denotes the ratios of any of these sources to assets; that is, *fsta* represents the capital-to-assets ratio, *CR*, the deposits-to-assets ratio, *DR*, or the ratio of non-depository debt to assets, *NDR*. We also divide observed changes in *fsta* or risk into two components; one is endogenous or discretionary and depends on the decisions of banks, the other is an exogenous component that reflects unanticipated and randomly distributed shocks. We suppose that the former follows a partial adjustment process, which means that the discretionary changes in risk (*fsta*) are proportional to the difference between the target value of risk (*fsta*) and the level of risk (*fsta*) in the preceding period. Therefore, the changes in risk and *fsta* of bank k in period t are defined as follows:

$$
\begin{aligned}
\Delta RISK_{k,t} &= \Delta RISK_{k,t}^{M} + u_{k,t} = \alpha \cdot \left(RISK_{k,t}^{*} - RISK_{k,t-1} \right) + u_{k,t}, \\
\Delta fsta_{k,t} &= \Delta fsta_{k,t}^{M} + e_{k,t} = \beta \cdot \left(fsta_{k,t}^{*} - fsta_{k,t-1} \right) + e_{k,t},
\end{aligned}
\tag{1}
$$

where, for bank k, $\Delta RISK_{k,t}$ ($\Delta fsta_{k,t}$) is the change in risk (*fsta*) from period $t-1$ to period t; $\Delta RISK_{k,t}^{M}$ ($\Delta fsta_{k,t}^{M}$) is the discretionary change in risk (*fsta*) from $t-1$ to t; $RISK_{k,t}^{*}$ ($fsta_{k,t}^{*}$) is the target value of risk (*fsta*) in t; and $RISK_{k,t-1}$ ($fsta_{k,t-1}$) is the level of risk (*fsta*) in $t-1$. The error term $u_{k,t}$ ($e_{k,t}$), which is assumed to be independent and identically distributed (i.i.d.) over time and across banks, represents the exogenous changes in risk (*fsta*). The coefficient α (β) captures the speed at which the observed value of risk (*fsta*) converges to its target value.

Given that target values are not observable, we assume that they depend linearly upon a set of explanatory variables and a stochastic error term. This set includes *Δfsta* for *RISK**, and *ΔRISK* for *fsta**. Thus, we note that risk and funding decisions are mutually related and must be analysed in a simultaneous setting. Following previous works that analyse the simultaneous relation between changes in risk and capital, other explanatory variables include size, *SIZ*, profitability, *PROF*, and the capital buffer, BUF.[1] We also consider an additional variable that captures the generosity of deposit insurance schemes, DI. In addition, for EU15, we include a control variable that proxies for restrictions on bank activities, $REST$, and three variables that reflect the pillars of Basel II: capital requirements, CAP, official supervisory power, $SUPERV$, and market discipline, $MKDISC$.[2]

The three funding sources into which we divide the financial structure of banks complement one another in the sense that, by definition, for bank k in period t, $CR_{k,t} + DR_{k,t} + NDR_{k,t} \equiv 1$. As a result, analysing risk shifting via a model containing these three ratios in the same equation would raise multicollinearity concerns. To avoid this, we estimate three equation systems based on Eq. (1), one for each of the funding sources. This estimation method is accurate and is, hence, not expected to have a substantial impact on our results if the speed at which risk values converge to target risk values (i.e., α in Eq. (1)) is approximately the same in all three equation systems.

Therefore, the model to be estimated is formed by three systems of two simultaneous equations. To simplify notation, for bank k at year t, let $X_{k,t}$ stand for the set of explanatory variables on which $RISK^*_{k,t}$, $CR^*_{k,t}$, $DR^*_{k,t}$, and $NDR^*_{k,t}$ depend.[3] The first equation system, which refers to changes in risk and capital, is then:

$$
\begin{aligned}
\Delta RISK_{k,t} &= \alpha_0^C + \alpha_1^C \cdot \Delta CR_{k,t} + \alpha_2^C \cdot X_{k,t} - \alpha_3^C \cdot RISK_{k,t-1} + u_{k,t}^C, \\
\Delta CR_{k,t} &= \beta_0^C + \beta_1^C \cdot \Delta RISK_{k,t} + \beta_2^C \cdot X_{k,t} - \beta_3^C \cdot CR_{k,t-1} + e_{k,t}^C,
\end{aligned}
\tag{2i}
$$

where $u_{k,t}^C$ and $e_{k,t}^C$ are i.i.d. error terms.

The second system relates risk and deposits:

$$
\begin{aligned}
\Delta RISK_{k,t} &= \alpha_0^D + \alpha_1^D \cdot \Delta DR_{k,t} + \alpha_2^D \cdot X_{k,t} - \alpha_3^D \cdot RISK_{k,t-1} + u_{k,t}^D, \\
\Delta DR_{k,t} &= \beta_0^D + \beta_1^D \cdot \Delta RISK_{k,t} + \beta_2^D \cdot X_{k,t} - \beta_3^D \cdot DR_{k,t-1} + e_{k,t}^D,
\end{aligned}
\tag{2ii}
$$

where $u_{k,t}^D$ and $e_{k,t}^D$ are i.i.d. error terms.

The third equation system focuses on the relation between risk and non-depository debt:

$$
\begin{aligned}
\Delta RISK_{k,t} &= \alpha_0^{ND} + \alpha_1^{ND} \cdot \Delta NDR_{k,t} + \alpha_2^{ND} \cdot X_{k,t} - \alpha_3^{ND} \cdot RISK_{k,t-1} + u_{k,t}^{ND}, \\
\Delta NDR_{k,t} &= \beta_0^{ND} + \beta_1^{ND} \cdot \Delta RISK_{k,t} + \beta_2^{ND} \cdot X_{k,t} - \beta_3^{ND} \cdot NDR_{k,t-1} + e_{k,t}^{ND},
\end{aligned}
\tag{2iii}
$$

where $u_{k,t}^{ND}$ and $e_{k,t}^{ND}$ are i.i.d. error terms. The requirement that the speed of adjustment of risk be similar in the three systems above implies that α_3^C, α_3^D, and α_3^{ND}, which are equivalent to α in Eq. (1), must have nearly identical values.

---

[1] In addition to Shrieves and Dahl (1992), see, e.g., Jacques and Nigro (1997), Aggarwal and Jacques (2001), Rime (2001), Bichsel and Blum (2004), Heid et al. (2004), Jokipii and Milne (2011).

[2] See the Appendix for definitions of the variables.

[3] Note that we do not include $\Delta CR_{k,t}$, $\Delta DR_{k,t}$, $\Delta NDR_{k,t}$, or $\Delta RISK_{k,t}$ in the set $X_{k,t}$.

2.1 Interpretations

The coefficients of equation systems (2i)–(2iii) allow us to determine not only when banks engage in risk shifting, but also its type and the variables that incentivise/disincentivise it. This section explains how to interpret these coefficients.

2.1.1 Types of Risk Shifting

Our analysis focuses on risk-increasing banks. There are two reasons for this. First, increases in risk are a key feature of the definition of risk shifting itself. Second, the sufficient condition for risk shifting that we analyse requires changes in risk and leverage to be positively related, i.e., $\Delta RISK$ and ΔCR must be negatively related. Thus, the basic condition for concluding that banks seem to engage in risk shifting is that α_1^C in Eq. (2i) is negative. However, this basic condition for risk shifting can be interpreted in a straightforward way only if we focus on risk-increasing banks. In this case, a negative α_1^C implies that the larger the decrease in the capital ratio, the larger the increase in risk.[4]

If the empirical analysis shows that $\Delta RISK$ and ΔCR are negatively related and, hence, that risk-increasing banks appear to engage in risk shifting, the next step is to analyse the type of risk shifting. In this sense, dividing the financial structure of banks into capital, deposits, and non-depository debt allows us to determine the group of creditors to which risk is shifted. In particular, risk could be transferred to depositors, other creditors, or to both, so four different types of risk shifting are differentiated. As Table 1 shows,[5] the type of risk shifting depends on the signs of

Table 1 Types of risk shifting

Type	Coefficients		
	System (2i) (ΔCR)	System (2ii) (ΔDR)	System (2iii) (ΔNDR)
Double-sided	$\alpha_1^C < 0$	$\alpha_1^D > 0$	$\alpha_1^{ND} > 0$
Deposit-based	$\alpha_1^C < 0$	$\alpha_1^D > 0$	$\alpha_1^{ND} < 0$ (or n.s.)
Other debt-based	$\alpha_1^C < 0$	$\alpha_1^D < 0$ (or n.s.)	$\alpha_1^{ND} > 0$
Unclassified	$\alpha_1^C < 0$	n.s.	n.s.
Not risk shifting	$\alpha_1^C > 0$	$\alpha_1^D < 0$ (or n.s.)	$\alpha_1^{ND} < 0$ (or n.s.)
Unclear	Other combinations		

This table shows how the type of risk shifting is defined by the signs of α_1^C, α_1^D, and α_1^{ND} in equation systems (2i)–(2iii)

---

[4] If we do not focus on risk-increasing banks, a negative relation between $\Delta RISK$ and ΔCR could also correspond to a situation in which banks that increase their capital ratio more also reduce their risk to a greater extent, which can hardly be considered a case of risk shifting.

[5] See Duran and Lozano-Vivas (2014, 2015).

the coefficients of ΔCR, ΔDR, and ΔNDR in the first equations of the systems (2i)–(2iii), that is, α_1^C, α_1^D, and α_1^{ND}.

The first type is double-sided risk shifting. Under this type, risk shifts to both depositors and non-depository creditors; that is, banks that reduce their equity-to-assets ratio over the preceding period, but that increase their deposits-to-assets ratio and the ratio of non-depository debt to assets, are expected to increase their overall risk. In terms of the coefficients in Eqs. (2i)–(2iii), this type requires α_1^C to be negative and significant, whereas α_1^D and α_1^{ND} are positive and significant.

The second type, deposit-based risk shifting, implies that shareholders transfer risk to depositors. This means that risk-increasing adjustments take place after reducing CR and increasing DR, whereas NDR decreases or is related to risk changes in a non-significant way; that is, α_1^C is negative and significant, α_1^D is positive and significant, and α_1^{ND} is either negative and significant or non-significant.

We refer to the third type as other-debt-based risk shifting. Banks engage in this type if shareholder risk-shift to non-depository creditors, so that changes that increase risk and reduce CR are observed together with changes that increase NDR. As regards changes in DR, they are either negative or have a non-significant relationship with risk changes. Therefore, α_1^C is negative and significant, α_1^{ND} is positive and significant, and α_1^D is either positive and significant or non-significant.

There are also situations where risk shifting is present, that is, α_1^C is negative and significant, but our method does not provide information about the group of agents to whom risk is shifted. This occurs if the adjustments in DR and NDR are not related to changes in risk in a statistically significant way, so that α_1^D and α_1^{ND} are not significant.

Risk shifting is not observed if two conditions hold. First, the basic requirement for risk shifting is not satisfied, that is, α_1^C is positive and significant, which means that risk increases after shareholders put more "skin in the game." Second, one of the following situations takes place: (1) DR and NDR do not change significantly (α_1^D and α_1^{ND} are not significant); (2) DR and NDR decrease (α_1^D and α_1^{ND} are negative and significant); or (3) DR (NDR) decreases and NDR (DR) does not change significantly [α_1^D is negative and significant (non-significant) and α_1^{ND} is not significant (negative and significant)]. For other situations in which the changes in both capital ratio and risk are, on average, positive, our method does not allow us to obtain clear conclusions about whether banks engage in risk shifting.

2.1.2   Variables That Incentivise/Disincentivise Risk Shifting

Our model also allows us to analyse whether incentives to shift risk are strengthened or weakened by any of the explanatory variables, Var, that help to define the target values of risk and $fsta$, that is, any of the variables included in the set X in equation systems (2i)–(2iii).

Table 2 Variables that incentivise/disincentivise risk shifting

Risk shifting type	Coefficients		
	System (2i) (Δ**CR**)	System (2ii) (Δ**DR**)	System (2iii) (Δ**NDR**)
Double-sided	$\beta_{Var}^{C} < 0$	$\beta_{Var}^{D} > 0$	$\beta_{Var}^{ND} > 0$
Deposit-based	$\beta_{Var}^{C} < 0$	$\beta_{Var}^{D} > 0$	$\beta_{Var}^{ND} < 0$ (or n.s.)
Other debt-based	$\beta_{Var}^{C} < 0$	$\beta_{Var}^{D} < 0$ (or n.s.)	$\beta_{Var}^{ND} > 0$
Unclassified	$\beta_{Var}^{C} < 0$	$\beta_{Var}^{D} < 0$ (or n.s.)	$\beta_{Var}^{ND} < 0$ (or n.s.)
Not risk shifting	$\beta_{Var}^{C} > 0$	$\beta_{Var}^{D} < 0$ (or n.s.)	$\beta_{Var}^{ND} < 0$ (or n.s.)
Unclear	Other combinations		

This table summarizes the type of risk shifting incentivised by the set of explanatory variables that define the target values of risk and fsta, where the latter stands for capital-to-assets ratio, deposit-to-assets ratio, or ratio of non-depository debt to assets. The table is based on the signs of the coefficients of the explanatory variables in the second equation of equation systems (2i)–(2iii). The subscript Var indicates the explanatory variable considered

Each type of risk shifting requires the ratios of the funding sources to change in a particular way. In this sense, double-sided risk shifting requires ΔCR to decrease and ΔDR and ΔNDR to increase. Thus, bearing in mind that we focus on risk-increasing banks, we conclude that *Var* seems to incentivise this type of risk shifting if it caused these effects. As Table 2 shows,[6] this is the case if the coefficient of *Var* in the second equation of Eq. (2i), β_{Var}^{C}, is negative and significant, and its coefficients in the second equations of Eqs. (2ii) and (2iii), β_{Var}^{D} and β_{Var}^{ND}, are both positive and significant.

Using similar reasoning, if *Var* causes ΔCR to decrease (i.e., β_{Var}^{C} is negative and significant), ΔDR to increase (i.e., β_{Var}^{D} is positive and significant), and has a negative or non-significant effect on ΔNDR (i.e., β_{Var}^{ND} is negative and significant or not significant), *Var* incentivises deposit-based risk shifting. This variable favours other debt-based risk shifting if it affects ΔCR negatively (i.e., β_{Var}^{C} is negative and significant), ΔDR positively (i.e., β_{Var}^{D} is positive and significant), and ΔNDR negatively or in a non-significant way (i.e., β_{Var}^{ND} is negative and significant or not significant). The unclassified type of risk shifting is incentivised by *Var* if its effect on ΔCR is negative (i.e., β_{Var}^{C} is negative and significant), whereas the effect on ΔDR and ΔNDR is negative or not significant (i.e., β_{Var}^{D} and β_{Var}^{ND} are both negative and significant or not significant, or one is negative and significant and the other is not significant).

Nevertheless, *Var* can also disincentivise risk shifting practices. This happens when β_{Var}^{C} is positive and significant and the conditions for β_{Var}^{D} and β_{Var}^{ND} under the unclassified risk shifting type hold. Finally, there are situations in which the effect of *Var* on risk shifting are unclear. This result arises in the case where β_{Var}^{C}, β_{Var}^{D},

---

[6] See Duran and Lozano-Vivas (2014, 2015).

and β_{Var}^{ND} are positive and significant, or if β_{Var}^{C} and β_{Var}^{D} (β_{Var}^{ND}) are positive and significant but β_{Var}^{ND} (β_{Var}^{D}) is negative and significant or not significant.

3   Results

We apply the method described in Sect. 2 to two different samples. The first comprises US commercial banks regulated by the Federal Reserve System, the Federal Deposit Insurance Corporation, and the Comptroller of the Currency in the period 1998–2011 (Duran and Lozano-Vivas 2014). The second sample consists of EU15 commercial, cooperative, and savings banks in the period 2002–2009. The countries included in the latter sample are Austria, Belgium, Denmark, Finland, France, Germany, Greece, Ireland, Italy, Luxembourg, Netherlands, Portugal, Spain, Sweden, and the United Kingdom, that is, the first 15 members of the European Union (Duran and Lozano-Vivas 2015).

For the US sample, bank accounting data were collected from the Reports of Condition and Income. For the periods 1998–2009 and 2010–2012, reports are provided, respectively, by the data distribution sites of the Federal Reserve Bank of Chicago and the Federal Financial Institutions Examination Council. As regards the EU15, bank-specific data were obtained from the annual financial statements provided by Fitch IBCA's Bankscope database by Bureau van Dijk.

Information on deposit insurance schemes is taken from the World Bank's "Deposit Insurance around the World Dataset," drawn up by Demirgüç-Kunt and Sobaci (2001) and Demirgüç-Kunt et al. (2005). Data concerning regulation and supervision are from the World Bank database developed by Barth et al. (2001) and updated by Barth et al. (2004, 2008).[7]

After excluding banks that have missing or unreliable values for the relevant variables and those whose data cover less than a 4-year period, the US sample of risk-increasing banks includes 34,842 observations, and the EU15 sample includes 7171 observations.[8]

To analyse risk shifting in the US banking system, the ratio of risk-weighted assets to total assets, *RWAR*, is used to proxy changes in risk. For the EU15 sample, and due to data availability, we use the additive inverse of the Z-Score, *ZS*, to capture changes in overall risk.[9] Changes in variables are measured as the

---

[7] For further details about how these datasets are used to generate the variables of our analysis, see the Appendix.

[8] Risk-increasing banks account for 46 % and 44 % of the total (cleaned-up) US and EU15 samples, respectively.

[9] We use the additive inverse of the Z-score instead of the Z-score itself because the latter is an inverse measure of risk, i.e., a larger Z-score indicates less risk. See the Appendix for the definition of *ZS*.

Table 3 Risk shifting in the US and EU15

	US sample			EU15 sample		
	System (2i) (ΔCR)	System (2ii) (ΔDR)	System (2iii) (ΔNDR)	System (2i) (ΔCR)	System (2ii) (ΔDR)	System (2iii) (ΔNDR)
Panel I. Dependent variable: $\Delta RISK$						
ΔCR	−0.0710* (0.0142)	–	–	−0.8966* (0.0085)	–	–
ΔDR	–	−0.0911* (0.0058)	–	–	−0.0538* (0.0094)	–
ΔNDR	–	–	0.0969* (0.0059)	–	–	0.0644* (0.0049)
Lagged RISK	−0.1079* (0.0023)	−0.1016* (0.0023)	−0.1023* (0.0023)	−0.0005* (0.0001)	−0.0008* (0.0001)	−0.0008* (0.0001)
Panel II. Dependent variables: ΔCR, ΔDR, *and* ΔNDR						
SIZ	0.0003* (0.00005)	−0.0036* (0.0002)	0.0032* (0.0002)	0.0004*** (0.0003)	0.0897* (0.0167)	0.0052** (0.0020)
PROF	0.3241* (0.0072)	−0.3135* (0.0196)	−0.0339*** (0.0193)	−2.1658* (0.0617)	−0.8801* (0.2183)	2.8907* (0.4136)
BUF	0.1372* (0.0014)	−0.0308* (0.0029)	−0.0595* (0.0029)	6.4032* (0.0669)	−0.0731 (0.0598)	−0.0316 (0.1114)
DI	0.0092* (0.0015)	0.0208* (0.0039)	−0.0321* (0.0039)	−0.0079** (0.0035)	0.0017 (0.0125)	−0.0286 (0.0237)
CAP	–	–	–	0.0012 (0.0008)	0.0005 (0.0029)	0.0003 (0.0057)
SUPERV	–	–	–	0.0045* (0.0006)	0.0058** (0.0023)	−0.0047 (0.0044)
MKDISC	–	–	–	−0.0192* (0.0016)	−0.0234* (0.0057)	0.0297* (0.0107)
REST	–	–	–	0.0143* (0.0045)	−0.0100 (0.0161)	0.0405 (0.0306)

This table reports the main results from the estimation of equation systems (2i)–(2iii) for the US and EU15 banking systems in the periods 1998–2011 and 2002–2009, respectively. In the US sample, $\Delta RISK$ is proxied by means of the change over the previous year in the ratio of risk-weighted assets to total assets; and in the EU15 sample, it is proxied by means of the change over the previous year in the additive inverse of the Z-Score. Panel I shows the results associated with the equations where $\Delta RISK$ is the dependent variable. Panel II refers to the equations where ΔCR, ΔDR, or ΔNDR is the dependent variable. For more details regarding definitions of the variables, see the Appendix. ***, **, and * represent significance at the 1 %, 5 %, and 10 % levels, respectively

difference between the values in the current and preceding years. The main results from this analysis are displayed in Table 3.[10]

---

[10] Table 3 does not display results that are not essential to determining whether there is risk shifting, its type, or which variables incentivise/disincentivise it. Similarly, we do not show or discuss robustness checks. Information on these matters is available upon request. In addition, for a more detailed discussion, see Duran and Lozano-Vivas (2014, 2015).

Panel I of Table 3 indicates that the speeds at which risk adjusts to its target value are very close across equation systems (2i)–(2iii); specifically, for ΔCR, ΔDR, and ΔNDR, these speeds are, respectively, in the US sample, 0.1079, 0.1016, and 0.1023, and in the EU15 sample, 0.0005, 0.0008, and 0.0008. Therefore, the condition that requires α_3^C, α_3^D, and α_3^{ND} to have similar values holds, which means that using a different equation system for each of the funding sources does not have a significant impact on our results.

In tune with our approach to risk shifting, a basic condition necessary to conclude that banks engage in this type of practice is to observe that changes in risk and leverage are positively related. The negative signs of the coefficients of ΔCR in Panel I of Table 3 for both the US and EU15 samples suggest that this condition is satisfied; that is, US and EU15 banks whose shareholders reduce their "skin in the game" more are also those that increase their risk to a greater extent.

Once risk shifting is present in a banking system, we can determine its type. According to Table 1, the specific type depends on the coefficients of ΔDR and ΔNDR. In our empirical analysis, for both the US and EU15 samples, the coefficient of ΔDR is negative and significant, whereas the coefficient of ΔNDR is positive and significant. These results suggest that US and European banks shift risk to non-depository creditors and, hence, the type of risk shifting is other debt-based.

Risk shifting implies that the amount of risk taken by banks may not be backed by sufficient capital. During a crisis, this can have particularly severe effects. The probability of bankruptcy and, hence, the inability to honour debt obligations tend to increase during a crisis, but they would increase even more sharply if the risk-capital balance were disproportionate due to risk shifting (Kroszner and Strahan 1996; Hovakimian and Kane 2000). Accordingly, to analyse whether there is any observable change in risk shifting as a result of the 2007 financial crisis, we split the US sample into pre-crisis, crisis, and post-crisis periods, and the EU15 sample into pre-crisis and crisis periods.[11] As a result of separating the samples this way, our main findings are that US and EU15 banks apparently engaged in other debt-based risk shifting during the pre-crisis and crisis periods. However, in the post-crisis period, the US banking system does not appear to show empirical evidence of risk shifting.[12]

Therefore, risk shifting seems to have been a regular practice of US and EU15 risk-increasing banks before and during the 2007 crisis. Given that risk shifting (especially in a downturn) may increase the instability of the banking system, this practice is likely to bear part of the responsibility for the severity of the effects of the 2007 crisis. Indeed, as the Basel Committee on Banking Supervision (2011) points out, undercapitalization (to which risk shifting contributes) has been one of

---

[11] Following the Business Cycle Dating Committee of the National Bureau of Economic Research, the crisis period in the US is 2008–2009, so the pre-crisis and post-crisis periods are 1998–2007 and 2010–2011, respectively. For EU15, the pre-crisis and crisis periods are 2002–2006 and 2007–2009, respectively.

[12] Results from this analysis are available upon request.

the main weaknesses of the banking system in successfully facing the crisis. Our results, nevertheless, suggest that the crisis could have put an end to risk shifting—at least in the US.

With regard to the variables that strengthen or weaken the incentives to shift risk, according to Table 2, *PROF* and *BUF* seem to disincentivise risk shifting in the US sample. This conclusion is based on the coefficients in Panel II of Table 3; specifically, the effects of these variables on ΔCR are positive and significant (i.e., β^C_{PROF} and β^C_{BUF} are 0.3241 and 0.1372, respectively), whereas their effects on ΔDR and ΔNDR are negative and significant (i.e., β^D_{PROF} and β^D_{BUF} are -0.3135 and -0.0308, respectively, and β^{ND}_{PROF} and β^{ND}_{BUF} are -0.0339 and -0.0595, respectively). The other two explanatory variables used in the analysis of the US banking system, *SIZ* and *DI*, have unclear effects on incentives to shift risk.

To take advantage of the variability in the regulatory and supervisory frameworks of the European countries, the number of explanatory variables included in the analysis of the EU15 is larger; in particular, this analysis also includes the strictness of the restrictions on bank activity, *REST*, and three variables that capture the pillars of Basel II, *CAP*, *SUPERV*, and *MKDISC*. In contrast to the US banking system, Panel II of Table 3 suggests that *PROF* strengthens the incentives of EU15 banks to shift risk, in particular to non-depository creditors. This conclusion is drawn from the fact that β^C_{PROF} and β^D_{PROF} are negative and significant (-2.1658 and -0.8801), and β^{ND}_{PROF} is positive and significant (2.8907). The generosity of the deposit insurance, *DI*, seems to incentivise EU15 bank shareholders to transfer risk, although the group of creditors to which risk is shifted remains unclear ($\beta^C_{DI} = -0.0079$ and β^D_{DI} and β^{ND}_{DI} are insignificant). On the contrary, the empirical evidence suggests that *BUF* and *REST* weaken the incentives to shift risk (β^C_{BUF} and β^C_{REST} are positive and significant (6.4032 and 0.0143), whereas β^D_{BUF}, β^D_{REST}, β^{ND}_{BUF}, and β^{ND}_{REST} are not significant). Surprisingly, none of the variables capturing the three pillars of Basel II disincentivise risk shifting. Moreover, the sign and significance of the coefficients of *MKDISC* in Panel II of Table 3 imply that a stricter market discipline seems to incentivise other debt-based risk shifting, as if strict private monitoring rules were a signal of strength, allowing banks to shift risk to non-depository creditors.

Despite the poor results for Basel II variables, capital buffers are taken into consideration by Basel III and we have already underlined that having these buffers above legal requirements seems to weaken incentives to shift risk in both the US and EU15 banking systems. This result suggests that incentives to hold capital buffers and not to shift risk are related. That is, prudent banks seem to be prudent in more than one sense, for instance, in maintaining more capital than required and in not unbalancing the risk–capital relation through risk shifting. This statement may seem obvious, but it supports the Basel III rules that require banks to maintain conservative buffers.

4 Conclusions

Ultimately, risk shifting implies that risk might not be backed by an adequate amount of capital; thus, it has potentially destabilizing effects over the banking system. This paper discusses a method to empirically study this moral hazard problem. Our method attempts to answer three questions: Do banks engage in risk shifting? If any, what is the type of risk shifting present in a banking system? What are the variables that incentivise or disincentivise risk shifting? We apply this method to the US and EU15 banking systems. Among our findings, we determine that banks in both systems seem to have shifted risk to non-depository creditors before and during the 2007 crisis, although this practice seems to have ended in the US following the crisis.

Acknowledgement The authors gratefully acknowledge the financial support from the Spanish Ministry of Economy and Competitiveness [project ECO2011-26996].

Appendix. Definitions of Variables

- Capital-to-assets ratio (CR): $\frac{C}{A}$.
- Deposits-to-assets ratio (DR): $\frac{D}{A}$.
- Ratio of non-depository debt to assets (NDR): $\frac{ND}{A}$.
- Risk-weighted assets to total assets ratio (RWAR): $\frac{RWA}{A}$.
- Additive inverse of Z-Score (ZS): $-\frac{CR+ROA}{\sigma^{ROA}}$.
- Size (SIZ): $\ln A$.
- Profitability (PROF): $ROA = \frac{NI}{A}$.
- Capital buffer (BUF): $CR - RCR$.[13]
- Generosity of deposit insurance scheme (DI): To build this index, we follow Demirgüç-Kunt and Detragiache (2002). See also Duran and Lozano-Vivas (2014, 2015). The index is increasing in the generosity of the deposit insurance scheme.
- Strictness of restrictions on bank activities (REST): To build this index, we follow Barth et al. (2001, 2008). The index is increasing in the strictness of the restrictions on bank activities.
- Strictness of capital requirements (CAP): As regards the method to build this index and its properties, see REST above.

---

[13] To calculate the capital buffer in the US sample, *CR* is the capital to risk-weighted-assets ratio.

- Strictness of supervision (SUPERV): As regards the method to build this index and its properties, see REST above.
- Strictness of market discipline (MKDISC): As regards the method to build this index and its properties, see REST above.

Legend

A   Total assets
C   Equity
D   Deposits
ND   Non-depository debt
NI   Net income
RCR   Regulatory capital-to-assets ratio
ROA   See profitability above
RWA   Risk-weighted assets
σ^{ROA} Standard deviation of *ROA*

References

Aggarwal R, Jacques KT (2001) The impact of FDICIA and prompt corrective action on bank capital and risk: estimates using a simultaneous equations model. J Bank Finance 25(6): 1139–1160

Barth JR, Caprio G Jr, Levine R (2001) The regulation and supervision of banks around the world—a new database. Working paper, World Bank. Available via http://www-wds. worldbank.org/external/default/WDSContentServer/IW3P/IB/2001/06/01/000094946_01052204005474/Rendered/PDF/multi0page.pdf

Barth JR, Caprio G Jr, Levine R (2004) Bank regulation and supervision: what works best? J Financ Intermed 13(2):205–248

Barth JR, Caprio G Jr, Levine R (2008) Bank regulation are changing. For better or worse? Working paper, World Bank. Available via http://papers.ssrn.com/sol3/papers.cfm?abstract_id=1149579

Basel Committee on Banking Supervision (2011) Basel III: a global regulatory framework for more resilient banks and banking systems. Available via http://www.bis.org/publ/bcbs189.pdf

Berger AN, Herring RJ, Szegö GP (1995) The role of capital in financial institutions. J Bank Finance 19(3–4):393–430

Bichsel R, Blum J (2004) The relationship between risk and capital in Swiss commercial banks: a panel study. Appl Financ Econ 14(8):591–597

Demirgüç-Kunt A, Detragiache E (2002) Does deposit insurance increase banking system stability? An empirical investigation. J Monetary Econ 49(7):1373–1406

Demirgüç-Kunt A, Sobaci T (2001) A new development database: deposit insurance around the world. World Bank Econ Rev 15:481–490

Demirgüç-Kunt A, Karacaovali B, Laeven LA (2005) Deposit insurance around the world: a comprehensive database. Working paper, World Bank. Available via http://www-wds. worldbank.org/external/default/WDSContentServer/IW3P/IB/2005/06/08/000012009_20050608111717/Rendered/PDF/wps36280rev.pdf

Duran MA, Lozano-Vivas A (2014) Risk shifting in the US banking system: an empirical analysis. J Financ Stabil 13:64–74

Duran MA, Lozano-Vivas A (2015) Moral hazard and the financial structure of banks. J Int Financ Market Inst Money 34:28–40

Freixas X, Rochet JC (2008) Microeconomics of banking. MIT Press, Cambridge

Heid F, Porath D, Stolz S (2004) Does capital regulation matter for bank behavior? Evidence for German savings banks. Discussion paper, Deutsche Bundesbank

Hovakimian A, Kane EJ (2000) Effectiveness of capital regulation at U.S. commercial banks, 1985 to 1994. J Finance 55(1):451–468

Jacques K, Nigro P (1997) Risk-based capital, portfolio risk, and bank capital: a simultaneous equation approach. J Econ Bus 49(6):533–547

Jensen MC, Meckling W (1976) Theory of the firm: managerial behavior, agency costs, and capital structure. J Financ Econ 3(4):305–360

Jokipii T, Milne A (2011) Bank capital buffer and risk adjustment decisions. J Financ Stabil 7(3): 165–178

Kroszner RS, Strahan PE (1996) Regulatory incentives and the thrift crisis: dividends, mutual-to-stock conversions, and financial distress. J Finance 51(4):1285–1319

Rime B (2001) Capital requirements and bank behavior: empirical evidence for Switzerland. J Bank Finance 25(4):789–805

Shrieves RE, Dahl D (1992) The relationship between risk and capital in commercial banks. J Bank Finance 16(2):439–457

VanHoose D (2007) Theories of bank behavior under capital regulation. J Bank Finance 31(12): 3680–3697

Structural Reform, Too-Big-To Fail and Banks as Public Utilities in Europe

Philip Molyneux

Abstract Since the global banking crisis in 2007 and 2008 and the more recent euro sovereign debt crisis there have been growing calls to rethink the way banks are monitored and governed. Banks have been forced to take on more capital and liquidity, remove riskier types of activity and also shrink their balance sheets. Numerous new rules have been put in place to constrain their risk-taking business including moves to remove executive excesses by curtailing their remuneration packages. All these new rules place a straightjacket around banker's activities and as a consequence inhibit their freedom and this new environment has led various commentators to talk about banks being no more private free-wheeling profit-maximising firms, but more like public utilities that provide a service to society that should be regulated more heavily, namely limiting prices and profits. These arguments stem from the similarity that banks have with public utilities and the problems associated with current banking size and structures. This chapter outlines various features of European banking along with a brief analysis of proposed structural regulatory reforms aimed at reducing the likelihood of systemic bank failure, too-big-to-fail guarantees and other forms of taxpayer support for troubled banking systems. We finish off by looking at why banks are maybe turning into public utilities.

1 Introduction

Europe's banking system has been subject to major shocks over the preceding decade, including the global financial crisis of 2007–8 and the more recent euro sovereign debt crisis. The former led to large losses and the failure and closure of many banks. It also forced the intervention of both central banks and governments in domestic banking systems. The scale of government intervention has been unprecedented and included four types of intervention: (1) guarantees for bank liabilities; (2) recapitalisations; (3) asset support (measures to provide relief for

P. Molyneux (✉)
Bangor University, Bangor, Gwynedd, UK
e-mail: p.molyneux@bangor.ac.uk

© Springer International Publishing Switzerland 2016
S.P.S. Rossi, R. Malavasi (eds.), *Financial Crisis, Bank Behaviour and Credit Crunch*, Contributions to Economics, DOI 10.1007/978-3-319-17413-6_5

troubled assets) and (4) various liquidity measures. According to Koopman (2011) state support in the EU amounted to 0.5 % of GDP. However, between 1st October 2001 and 1st October 2011 the European Commission approved 4.5 trillion € (approx 37 % of EU GDP) in government support to the banking sector. Most was authorized in 2008, when 3.5 trillion € (28 % of EU GDP) was approved mainly in the form of guarantees, after 2008 approved state support shifted to recapitalization of banks and impaired asset relief. It should be noted that Member States did not take up their full quota of approved aid. The amount of state support actually used between 2008 and 2010 stood at 1.6 trillion € (just over 13 % of EU GDP—the equivalent of 2 % of EU banking sector assets). Around 1.2 trillion € were for guarantees and other liquidity measures, and the remainder went to recapitalisation and supporting impaired assets (around 410 billion €). Between October 2008 and October 2011, around 250 decisions regarding state support of banking systems were made and the only countries where no support was provided were in: Bulgaria, the Czech Republic, Estonia, Malta and Romania. The significant injection of state funds, coupled with an array of regulatory reforms aimed at bolstering bank capital and liquidity, and curtailing excessive bank risk-taking has been relatively successful in avoiding banking system collapse, but then came another crisis! During 2010 and 2011, various European economies (particularly Greece, Ireland, Portugal, Italy and Spain) were hit by the sovereign debt crisis. A spiralling of government debt and deficits led to a crisis of confidence that resulted in widening bond yield spreads and risk insurance on credit default swaps between these countries and other EU members, most notably Germany. In May 2010, the Eurozone countries and the International Monetary Fund agreed a 110 billion € loan for Greece, conditional on the implementation of tough austerity measures. Later in May, Europe's Finance Ministers established the European Financial Stability Facility (comprising a broad rescue package amounting to $1 trillion) aimed at ensuring financial stability across the Euro zone. After the Greek bailout, Ireland had to be supported to the tune of 85 billion € in November 2010, followed by a 78 billion € support program for Portugal in May 2011. This helped many European banks (that are large holders of sovereign debt) although in many countries large banks still have had to raise significant amounts of new capital and are continuing to struggle to achieve returns in excess of the cost of capital. By 2014 banks throughout Europe are still looking to boost their capital by shrinking risk-adjusted assets—by scaling down their lending and (for the big universal banks) investment banking activities. There is a race to be the most strongly capitalised and most liquid. The largest most internationally active banks are also subject to increased capital and liquidity requirements under Basel III (ECB 2012) and have just had to go through the ECB's Asset Quality Review and stress tests (in October 2014) before the ECB took up European Banking Union Supervisory responsibilities. It is against this background, that this paper discusses some features of European banking. The chapter is structured as follows with Sect. 2 providing a brief overview of the structural and performance features of major European banking markets. Section 3 compares the proposed structural reforms set out in the US Dodd Frank Act 2010, the UK's Vickers Report of 2011 (incorporated into the UK' Banking Reform Act of December 2013) and the EU's Liikanen Report of 2012 (that the EC announced in April 2014 will be incorporated into law and implemented in Member States by 2019). Section 4 looks at the case for regarding banks as public utilities and Sect. 5 is the conclusion.

2   Recent Structure and Performance of European Banks[1]

European banking was transformed over the two decades preceding the 2007–8 financial crises by an array of developments including: globalization, deregulation, technological change, integration and harmonization through the creation of a European single market in banking (Goddard et al. 2010). These factors have impacted substantially on the industrial organization of the banking industry. For example, Table 1 reports structural indicators for the banking sectors of the major European countries. The table shows that between 1985 and 2011, the total number of banks operating in all major economies declined substantially. In France, Germany, Italy, Spain and the UK combined the increase in nominal total assets over this period was in excess of 400 %.

In France, Greece, Italy and Spain the number of bank branches increased substantially between 1985 and 2011, while the numbers fell dramatically in the UK. Much of the increase was a result of the de-liberalisation of branching restrictions that encouraged expansion, whereas consolidation and closure was the trend elsewhere. Table 1 also illustrates that banking sector concentration ratios for markets defined by national boundaries have also increased in the majority of EU countries and the long-term trend has clearly been upward.

Europe clearly has a diverse and dynamic banking sector. This is neatly highlighted by the Final Report of the High-level Expert Group on Reforming the Structure of the EU Banking Sector that states:

> The EU banking sector is diverse, which is valuable. Banking sectors differ substantially across Member States, in terms of size, market concentration, foreign ownership, asset and liability structure, supervision, credit cycle, and public involvement. Diversity strengthens the resilience of the banking system as it mitigates vulnerability to systemic interconnections and promotes effective competition. Diversity is explicitly protected by the EU treaty (Liikanen 2012).

European commercial banks from the 1950s onwards pretty much depended on interest margins as the main driver of bank performance. This meant that profits depended on banks maintaining a sizeable gap between interest income and costs, while at the same time trying to reduce operational efficiency. As systems liberalized and cartels broke down, competition in loan and deposit markets intensified driving down margins. This was a clear trend from the early 1980s to early 2000s in many banking systems. The reduction in margins encouraged banks to supplement

---

[1] Parts of Sect. 2 come from Chapter 10 Performance in European Banking: Productivity, Profitability and Employment Trends, in the text to commemorate SUERF 50th Anniversary in 2013.

Table 1 Structural indicators for France, Germany, Italy, Spain and the UK banking sectors

Country	1985	1995	2005	2011
Number of banks				
France	1,952	1,895	1,577	1,147
Germany	4,739	3,785	2,089	1,956
Italy	1,101	970	792	785
Spain	364	506	348	415
UK	772	564	400	405
Assets (billion euros)				
France	1,348.8	2,513.7	5,090.1	8,391.5
Germany	1,495.1	3,584.1	6,826.6	8,393.5
Italy	546.8	1,070.5	2,509.4	4,065.0
Spain	311.3	696.3	2,150.7	3,643.0
UK	1,293.6	1,999.5	8,320.2	9,708.2
Employment (000s)				
France	449	408	430	379
Germany	591	724	705	664
Italy	319	337	336	316
Spain	244	249	253	246
Concentration (Assets CR$_5$)				
France	46.0	41.3	53.5	48.3
Germany	–	16.7	21.6	33.5
Italy	–	32.4	26.7	39.5
Spain	35.1	47.3	42.0	48.1

Source: Central Bank Reports (various); ECB (2006, 2007, 2010) and also from ECB Consolidated Banking Data (online resource)

their income (where possible) by diversifying into non-interest income (or non-traditional) areas such as insurance and securities underwriting. Following the EU's Second Banking Directive of 1989, for instance, noninterest income as a proportion of total income increased from 26 % in 1989 to 41 % in 1998 (ECB 2000) and has remained around this level (experiencing various swings) by mid-2012.[2]

The shift towards a greater emphasis on non-interest income may help maintain profits but it is more volatile than revenue from traditional sources (Stiroh and Rumble 2006) and there is evidence to suggest that low-risk traditional banking activity will subsidize the more volatile non-interest income activity (Boot and Schmeits 2000). Most work in the area confirms the findings of Stiroh (2004) on US banks that non interest income does not tend to boost returns but adversely impacts on return volatility (and trading income is also the most volatile). An extensive

[2] According to ECB (2013) Consolidated Banking Data for June 2012 the non-interest income as a % of total income amounted to 42 %.
See http://www.ecb.int/stats/money/consolidated/html/index.en.html.

literature highlights that agency problems derived from product service diversifi-cation outweigh the benefits from economies of scope (Laeven and Levine 2007). A study of European banks by Lepetit et al. (2008) over 1996–2002 shows that those earning higher commission and fee income have lower interest margins suggesting an under-pricing of loans to boost fee-based services. Banks, expanding into noninterest income activities, may lose their focus on traditional lending activity and this may encourage managers to be less conservative in their lending activities that may boost credit risk. An argument that may well have had resonance during the securitization boom where credit growth expanded rapidly with little monitor-ing as the risk were sold-on by the banks to investors in the form of mortgage-backed and other asset-backed securities. More recently, Brunnermeier et al. (2012), find that banks with higher non-interest income (from securities trading, venture capital and investment banking activity) tend to contribute more to systemic risk than those that focus more on traditional commercial banking business.

There have also been substantial variations in the average profitability of banks located in different EU countries. Table 2 highlights the relatively low profitability of German banks during the early and mid-2000s, when banks in UK enjoyed relatively high average profitability. Differences in average profitability between countries have been attributed to the following: variation in accounting and tax systems; structural factors such as the intensity of competition in specific product segments; the extent of product and geographic diversification; and business cycle effects (Carbo and Rodriguez 2007; Goddard et al. 2007, 2013).

As one would expect, the European banking system was severely impacted by the ensuing credit crisis. From 2007 to 2010, the largest European banks reported huge credit losses, and received massive capital injections with major UK banks being the biggest casualties. Heavy write downs have been matched, as noted earlier, by massive capital-raising and state support. In response to the crisis, every European government has announced a combination of loan guarantee

Table 2 Return on equity (%) of France, Germany, Italy, Spain and the UK banking sectors

Country	1990–94	1995–99	2000	2001	2002	2003	2004
France	6.18	7.36	12.08	10.94	9.38	9.85	13.43
Germany	12.97	12.48	7.86	0.84	−1.71	−2.70	2.26
Italy	11.14	9.29	17.58	8.42	6.44	7.59	11.45
Spain	9.73	10.40	10.37	12.30	12.65	13.35	14.60
UK	15.40	27.88	21.49	13.47	11.59	14.43	19.90
	2005	2006	2007	2008	2009	2010	2011
France	9.54	14.77	9.47	5.80	8.36	8.35	5.59
Germany	8.33	11.02	4.79	2.87	3.57	15.20	2.13
Italy	8.17	10.50	8.74	6.75	3.47	3.68	−12.99
Spain	8.94	15.22	11.53	8.65	1.74	8.04	0.09
UK	9.84	16.10	12.59	10.38	4.37	4.37	4.24

Source: Constructed from Bankscope and ECB Consolidated Banking Data

Table 3 Performance of large and complex banking groups in the Euro area

Year	Return on equity (%)		Impaired loans/total assets (%)		Cost-income ratio (%)	
	Median	Average	Median	Average	Median	Average
2005	10.04	11.93	0.08	0.11	60.69	58.87
2006	14.81	14.61	0.07	0.11	55.95	56.40
2007	11.97	11.65	0.05	0.10	63.00	62.95
2008	2.26	−14.65	0.27	0.31	73.36	160.96
2009	2.97	0.34	0.45	0.55	60.35	62.47
2010	7.68	6.76	0.24	0.32	60.40	62.01

Year	Tier 1 ratio (%)		Solvency ratio (%)	
	Median	Average	Median	Average
2005	7.89	8.20	11.05	11.23
2006	7.75	8.07	11.01	11.16
2007	7.40	7.72	10.60	10.72
2008	8.59	8.58	11.70	11.37
2009	10.15	10.33	13.60	13.37
2010	11.20	11.38	14.10	14.38

Source: Adapted from ECB, Financial Stability Review, June 2011, Table S5, page S30–S31

schemes, bank rescue plans and fiscal stimulus packages in an attempt to preserve their banking systems and avert the potentially damaging recessionary consequences (Stolz and Wedow 2010; ECB 2011).

Since the banking crisis there has been much discussion as to what type of bank or business model will yield the safest and most profitable banking systems. Liikanen (2012) finds that although different bank business models (retail v investment banking) were adversely affected by the crisis it seems that the 'less resilient' were those that depended more on: short-term wholesale funding; excessive leverage; excessive trading/derivative/market activity; poor lending due to aggressive credit growth; and weak corporate governance.

Table 3 illustrates the ECB's estimates of the performance of large and complex banking groups in the Euro Area between 2005 and 2010 highlighting the disastrous losses made in 2008 and small pick-up in ROE thereafter. Note the colossal increase in cost-income ratios in 2008 due to a collapse in income. Also witness the substantial increase in Tier 1 capital and solvency ratios in 2009 and 2010.

3 Structural Reform of Banking Systems

Given the general recognition that banks focused too heavily on high risk non-interest revenue generation—particularly through securities trading and investment banking activity—this has led to a series of major structural regulatory reforms aimed at reducing bank risk and minimising the likelihood of taxpayer financed bank bailouts. These include: the passing of the U.S. Dodd-Frank Wall Street Reform and Consumer Protection Act in July 2010 (the biggest financial reform in the U.S since the Great Depression); implementation of the September 2011 Independent Commission on Banking (known as the Vickers Commission after its Chair Sir John Vickers) into the UK's Banking Reform Act of 2013; and recommendations made by October 2012 EU High-level Expert Group on Reforming the Structure of the EU Banking Sector chaired by Erkki Liikanen (otherwise known as the Liikanen Report) to be incorporated into EU legislation by 2015 and implemented by 2019. In fact all these proposals wont become fully operational until 2019—the target date for the introduction of Basl III and the related EU Capital Requirements Directive (IV). In general, the proposals are similar although differ in details. In the UK, the Vickers Report proposes to ring-fence retail and various investment banking activities (these proposals were supported by the UK Government in late 2012); recommendations of the U.S Dodd Frank Act of 2010 do not allow banks to undertake proprietary trading and limit their hedge fund and private equity activity; and the EU proposal aims to legally separate various 'risky financial activities from deposit-taking banks within a banking group' (Liikanen 2012).

However, the reform process (by late-2014) is still ongoing in the US with full implementation of Dodd-Frank yet to occur (lawyers guesstimate that only 40 % of the legislation has been introduced), and the recommendations made by Liikanen and Vickers being gradually incorporated into law. Clearly, the legislation is at different stages of development and has various features. It is apparent that the US rules stem from a long-standing legal regime and the provisions in Dodd-Frank, are unlikely to be amended. In contrast recommendation by Vickers lack details and leaves room for substantial arbitrage especially with regards to defining what parts of the business specifically need to be ring-fenced. And it could be argued that the Liikanen Report is even more limited as it is simply advice from a high-level expert group to an EU Commissioner—although to be fair, the EU has said it will introduce all its recommendations.

It is interesting to compare the main recommendations of the Vickers recommendations with Liikanen. The Vickers proposals stipulated that:

- Retail banking activity is to be ring-fenced from wholesale and investment banking.
- Different arms of the same bank should have separate legal entities with their own boards of directors.
- Systemically important banks and large UK retail banking operations should have a minimum 10 % equity to assets ratio;
- Contingent capital and debt should be available to improve loss absorbency in the future;
- Risk management should become a self-contained, less complex business for retail banking, but remain complex for wholesale/investment banking.

The cost of these reforms to the UK economy are estimated to range between £1 billion and £3 billion per annum, which compares favourably with the estimated annual cost (of £40 billion) of lost output that follows financial crises. As we noted, the reforms will be implemented by 2019. Key recommendations of the EU's Liikanen Report are:

- Proprietary trading and other significant trading activities should be assigned to a separate legal entity if the activities to be separated amount to a significant share of a bank's business.
- Banks need to draw up and maintain effective and realistic recovery and resolution plans as proposed by the Recovery and Resolution Directive. The resolution authority should request wider separation than considered mandatory above if deemed necessary.
- Banks should build up a sufficiently large layer of bail-inable debt and such debt should be held outside the banking system.
- There should be application of more robust risk weights in the determination of minimum capital standards and more consistent treatment of risk in internal models.
- There should be an augmentation of existing corporate governance reforms by specific measures to (1) strengthen boards and management; (2) promote the risk management function; (3) rein in compensation for bank management and staff; (4) improve risk disclosure and (5) strengthen sanctioning powers.

If we compare the Vickers, Liikanen and Dodd Frank proposals one can see that all recommend either legal separation or ring-fencing the deposit bank from the investment bank or trading arm with slight variation in detail. All insured banks have to separate deposit and investment banking activity in the US; Liikanen recommends separation only if the activities form a major share of banks activities or pose a systemic stability threat; and the White Paper following Vickers says that ring-fencing should occur only for banks with retail deposits greater than £25 billion. Trading and investment banking activity can be undertaken by a company in the same corporate group as the deposit bank—so long as it does not pose resolution problems (in the case of Vickers and Liikanen), although under the Volcker rule this prohibits propriety trading in any group that contains a deposit bank (and the parent of the bank must be a financial holding company if it is to conduct any investment banking/trading). Deposit banks are also prohibited from an array of securities activities—in the US for instance deposit-taking banks are precluded from investing in most securities and entirely from securities dealing (including market-making) and underwriting. Under Dodd Frank they will also have to move out of some derivatives and credit default swap (CDS) activities that are currently done in the deposit-taking bank. In the UK legislation there is a long list of proposed prohibited securities activities (including propriety trading, securities lending, trading, origination, securitisation originated outside the ring-fence and so on)—but these can be conducted if they are regarded as 'ancillary' to the main business; Liikanen refers to similar things as well as prohibition of deposit bank's credit exposure to hedge funds and investments in private equity. The legislation is tougher and more restrictive in the US on the (legal) relationships between deposit banks and investment banks in the same corporate entity, and go far beyond large intra group exposure rules (this is because of big US corporate finance interest in conflicts and problems that can be caused by things like tunnelling).

In contrast Liikanen and Vickers are some what vague on these issues—the UK have some tentative proposals relating to reducing intra group guarantees—but it's all rather unclear. The UK and EC proposals (the latter linked to other legislation) both propose detailed bank resolution regimes, whereas Dodd Frank asks banks themselves to develop their own resolution plans (living wills). Also the UK and EC legislation propose the use of bail-in debt whereas this is not the case in the US (although Dodd Frank may encourage the Fed to ask the biggest banks—systemically important financial institutions, SIFIs) to hold more contingent capital. On capital requirements the EC (and therefore UK) banks are subject to the Capital Requirements Directive 4 (CRD IV) and Capital Requirements Regulation (of 2011). Liikanen has recommended that more capital should be held against trading book exposures and real estate lending; and the UK White Paper suggests more tier 1 capital needs to be held by systemically important banks, US also has buffers for SIFIs. And on top of all this, for Eurozone banks comes the obligations set under the European Banking Union to have to deal/accommodate the new three tiers including the Single Supervisory Mechanism (SSM), coupled with European resolution and deposit insurance schemes.

4 Problems with Banking

Returning to structural issues, despite the aforementioned reforms, it is still the case that many countries banking systems will remain very large relative to country size. Liikanen (2012) estimated that the UK banking system was more than five times domestic GDP, the French four times and German three times larger. And the biggest banks have over the last decade or so been getting bigger with the top five banks accounting for an average of around 55 % of EU banking sector assets—although there are big variations across countries (in the Netherlands the top five banks have an 85 % assets share). Big banks in Europe and the U.S are nowadays roughly the same assets size but the Europeans are much bigger relative to the size of individual European economies as shown in Table 4 where four individual banks are bigger than their domestic economies—HSBC, Barclays, RBS and Santander.

So the problem with banking is that systems are very big and individual banks are large relative to the size of their banking systems. Big banks have also become increasingly complex organizations, with large numbers of subsidiaries operating in many jurisdictions. The top US banks provides a glowing example of this—the biggest, JP Morgan Chase has 3391 subsidiaries, of which 451 are foreign, Goldman Sachs has over 3000, Morgan Stanley 2800+ and Bank of America 2000+. JP Morgan Chase is based in over 80 countries whereas in 1990 it operated in 60 jurisdictions as shown in Table 5. Evidence suggests that only the top ten US banks have any significant overseas presence, and this has increased for all these banks over the last few decades. A similar picture can be drawn for the top

Table 4 Top European banks—big as economies!

Bank	Country	Total assets (million €)	Total assets/ national GDP (%)	Total assets/national EU GDP (%)
Deutsche Bank	DE	2,164,103	84.8	17.4
HSBC	UK	1,967,796	119.8	15.8
BNP Paribas	FR	1,965,283	99.8	15.8
Crédit Agricole Group	FR	1,879,536	95.4	15.1
Barclays	UK	1,871,469	113.9	15.0
RBS	UK	1,803,649	109.8	14.5
Santander	ES	1,251,525	118.2	10.1
Sociètèè Gènèrale	FR	1,181,372	60.0	9.5
Lloyds Banking Group	UK	1,161,698	70.7	9.3

Bank	Country	FTE employees 2011	No. of European branches	Δ in total assets/% change 2007–11)
Deutsche Bank	DE	100,996	2,735	12.4
HSBC	UK	288,316	1,984	22.2
BNP Paribas	FR	198,423	6,816	16.0
Crédit Agricole Group	FR	162,090	9,924	22.0
Barclays	UK	141,100	2,602	12.0
RBS	UK	146,800	2,477	−28.0
Santander	ES	193,349	7,467	37.1
Sociètèè Gènèrale	FR	159,616	6,456	10.2
Lloyds Banking Group	UK	98,538	2,956	141.5

Source: Liikanen Report (2012), p. 39

European banks as well with complex organisational webs spanning hundreds (if not thousands) of subsidiaries and many jurisdictions.

Size and complexity provides big banks with advantage—they are 'too big to be allowed to fail' or 'too systemically important to be allowed to fail'. This means that they get better credit ratings (as they are deemed safer) so they can raise funds more cheaply than smaller banks that do not have this government safety net. Also, these safety net benefits encourage big banks to increase leverage (lower their capital) to take on more risk, as they believe if things go bad the state will bail them out and (most) depositors will be protected via deposit insurance. The more leverage, the greater the risk but potentially greater returns—so shareholders will be happy for big banks to take on more risks if they are rewarded appropriately. There is strong evidence that prior to the 2007–2008 crises CEOs aligned their strategies (and pay) directly in-line with the demands of shareholders to maximise returns. So size and complexity and the government safety net create strong incentives for bankers to gamble.

And when the banks go BOOM—the consequences of failure, as we have already noted, are enormous. So given the features of banking and the enormous cost of failure, and the big push to re-regulate and constrain them an increasingly strong case can be made to treat banks as public utilities (Saunders 2014) and regulate their pricing and profitability further.

Table 5 Top US banks—complex organisations

Bank holding company rank	Name	Number of subsidiaries				Asset value	
		Domestic				Domestic commercial bank (percentage of Y-9C assets)	Consolidated total assets (Y-9C) (billions of U.S. dollars)
		Comm. bank	Other	Foreign	Total		
1	JP Morgan Chase & Company	4	2,936	451	3,391	86.1	2,265.8
2	Bank of America Corporation	5	1,541	473	2,019	77.9	2,136.6
3	Citigroup Incorporated	2	935	708	1,645	68.8	1,873.9
4	Wells Fargo & Company	5	1,270	91	1,366	92.5	1,313.9
5	Goldman Sachs Group, Incorporated	1	1,444	1,670	3,115	11.2	923.7
6	MetLife, Inc.	1	39	123	163	3.2	799.6
7	Morgan Stanley	2	1,593	1,289	2,884	10.5	749.9
10	The Bank of New York Mellon Corporation	3	211	146	360	83.2	325.8
20	Regions Financial Corporation	1	35	4	40	97.1	127.0
30	Comerica Incorporated	2	72	2	76	99.8	61.1
40	First Horizon National Corporation	1	35	1	37	99.1	24.8
50	Webster Financial Corporation	1	21	–	22	99.8	18.7
Total		86	13,670	5,847	19,603	70.4	14,359.1

Source: Avraham et al. (2012), p. 71

5   Why Banks Are Like Public Utilities

Public utilities (like gas, electricity and water companies) have certain economic features that explain why they are regulated differently to private companies. Typically these industries have a common network structure—they have extensive distribution systems (think of piping for gas or cabling for electricity) that involve significant investment (known as large sunk costs) that can be government or privately owned. Quite often utilities are granted legally enforced monopolies over service territories. Activity of utilities can be characterised into production, transmission and distribution. In the case of natural gas (say), production relates to the gas well, transmission (is via the web of pipelines) and distribution (are the local gas distribution firms—who households and firms buy their gas from). These three stages can be owned by public or private firms, but usually (even in North America) production is privately owned whereas transmission or distribution can be either government or private. Banking has similar features—to be a bank and undertake production you need a banking licence, then capital and deposits, transmission is via the payments system (you cannot undertake transactions without means of payment/transfer) and finally distribution is through the branch network and subsidiaries. These stages are typically all privately owned although in some countries (Brazil and China) state ownership remains important.

There are similarities between the production, transmission and distribution features of public utilities and banks. So perhaps we should regulate banks the same as utilities? The rationale for regulating utilities is threefold:

– Public utilities are natural monopolies which means that they realise scale economies indefinitely, ultimately leading to one firm in the industry. In natural monopoly, productive efficiency is achieved with one firm. Because utilities tend to be natural monopolies, consumers need to be protected against price gouging and other bad treatment, hence the justification for regulating utilities, particularly on their pricing. Banks have a tendency to get very big with a handful dominating over time. They have features very similar to natural monopolies—that is why so many countries have highly concentrated domestic banking systems;
– To stop regulators from being captured by producers. The aim here is to protect all producers and not just the biggest by making sure utilities do not capture the regulators and write their own rules. One could argue that in banking this is too late! Big banks for years have helped write the rules for Basel, EU and domestic regulators. The big banks dominate all areas of retail and wholesale activity— they know more than regulators (hence the emergence of shadow banking). Banks also gain from (implicit) safety net benefits that also provide benefits that regulators (unwittingly) provide;
– Other rationale for regulating utilities relate to the evidence on the economic behaviour of utilities that shows that: lowest cost operators are likely to be biggest rent gainers—or to put another way, they can extract monopoly profits; cost-based cross-subsidization is typically widespread; and quasi monopoly

rents are likely to be spread among various groups. In banking it's easy to point to examples of previously found monopoly pricing behaviour (SME lending, payments, credit cards); cross-subsidization is widespread (we have seen retail subsidize investment banking in the 1990s at RBS, and the opposite recently at Barclays); and benefits have accrued (some argue) to a few—senior management and shareholders primarily.

In banking there is a definite trend toward natural monopoly, strong evidence of regulatory capture (or at least barriers to capture are low) and rent-seeking by low cost producers and other parties and cross-subsidization is also widespread. All these factors justify the regulation of public utilities.

6 Conclusions

European banking remains fragile and has to undertake major reform. Pressure from structural regulatory reforms, also Basel 3, and the related EUs Capital Requirements Directive (IV) is forcing banks to restrict their business, and boost their regulatory capital and liquidity. Banks are shrinking their risk assets, curtailing lending and selling off non-core activities. The major structural reforms are similar in various respects—they restrict banks trading activities, ring-fence/separate investment banking from retail banking (in various forms), suggest different resolution procedures and so on. This will make banks safe but it will cripple bank profitability. The regulatory constraints under Basel 3 and the proposed structural reforms are, as Saunders (2014) argues, so restrictive that over the next few years, '....bank ROE's can be expected to be reduced to the 8–10 % range, a range common among "safe" public utilities such as gas and electric companies'. And as we have just noted, banking business shows a global trend toward natural monopoly, evidence of regulatory capture (or at least barriers to capture are low) and rent-seeking by low cost producers and other parties as well as cross-subsidization. These are features that characterise public utilities. Maybe it is time to regard and treat banks as public utilities and regulate their pricing and profitability accordingly?

References

Avraham D, Selvaggi P, Vickery J (2012) A structural view of U.S. bank holding companies. Federal Reserve Bank of New York Economic Policy Review, July

Boot AWA, Schmeits A (2000) Market discipline and incentive problems in conglomerate firms with applications to banking. J Financ Intermediation 9:240–273

Brunnermeier M, Dong G, Palia D (2012) Banks' non-interest income and systemic risk. Working paper, January. Available via SSRN. http://papers.ssrn.com/sol3/papers.cfm?abstract_id=1786738

Carbo S, Rodriguez F (2007) The determinants of bank margins in European banking. J Bank Finance 31:2043–2063

European Central Bank (2000) EU banks' income structure. Banking Supervision Committee. ECB, Frankfurt, April

European Central Bank (2006) EU banking structures. ECB, Frankfurt, September

European Central Bank (2007) EU banking structures. ECB, Frankfurt, September

European Central Bank (2010) EU banking structures. ECB, Frankfurt, September

European Central Bank (2011) Financial stability review. ECB, Frankfurt, June

European Central Bank (2012) Financial stability review. ECB, Frankfurt, June

European Central Bank (2013) Financial stability review. ECB, Frankfurt, November

Goddard J, Molyneux P, Wilson JOS et al (2007) European banking: an overview. J Bank Finance 31:1911–1936

Goddard J, Molyneux P, Wilson JOS (2010) Banking in the European Union. In: Berger AN, Molyneux P, Wilson JOS (eds) Oxford handbook of banking. OUP, Oxford, pp 777–806

Goddard J, Molyneux P, Wilson JOS (2013) Do bank profits converge? Eur Financ Manag 19:345–365

Koopman GJ (2011) Stability and competition in EU banking during the financial crisis: the role of state aid control. Compet Policy Int 7:8–21

Laeven L, Levine R (2007) Is there a diversification discount in financial conglomerates? J Finance Econ 85:331–367

Lepetit L, Nys E, Rous P, Tarazi A (2008) Bank income structure and risk: an empirical analysis of European banks. J Bank Finance 32:1452–1467

Liikanen E (2012) High-level expert group on reforming the structure of the EU banking sector, Brussels, Oct 2. Available via http://ec.europa.eu/internal_market/bank/docs/high-level_expert_group/report_en.pdf

Saunders A (2014) Is Basel turning banks into public utilities? Available at SSRN: http://ssrn.com/abstract=2475627 or http://dx.doi.org/10.2139/ssrn.2475627

Stiroh K (2004) Diversification in banking: is non-interest income the answer? J Money Credit Bank 36:853–882

Stiroh K, Rumble A (2006) The dark side of diversification: the case of US financial holding companies. J Bank Finance 30:2131–2161

Stolz SH, Wedow M (2010) Extraordinary measures in extraordinary times—public measures in support of the financial sector in the EU and the United States. ECB occasional paper series, no 117, ECB, Frankfurt

Vickers J (2011) Independent commission on banking. Final report, Sept 12

Part III
Bank Regulation, Credit Access and Bank Performance

Did Basel II Affect Credit Growth to Corporate Borrowers During the Crisis?

Danilo V. Mascia, Kevin Keasey, and Francesco Vallascas

Abstract The introduction of the risk-sensitive capital Accord, commonly known as Basel II, raised concerns among practitioners about possible increases in the procyclicality of capital charges during downturns. Based on a sample consisting of yearly observations for the period 2007–2012 and related to 76 countries, we test whether—throughout this period of financial distress—banks implementing Basel II reduce corporate lending growth more than banks adopting the first of the Basel Accords. Furthermore, we also test whether Basel II differently affects the growth of corporate loans according to bank size. Our analysis shows that banks, in general, that have complied with Basel II have not apparently reduced the growth of corporate loans. Interestingly, however, we find that the very largest banks decreased corporate lending growth by more than 3 % during the observed period, thus providing evidence of the above mentioned procyclicality issue affecting larger banks.

1 Introduction

This paper investigates whether the implementation of the Basel II Accord affected corporate credit growth during the recent global crisis. Across time, risk-based capital regulation has been revised and become progressively more elaborate. Starting from its first version (Basel I) in 1988, a new capital Accord (Basel II) was agreed in 2004. This new regulatory framework introduces more risk sensitivity in assessing risk-weighted assets compared to the previous regime in order to improve banks' solvency. Nevertheless, the increase in the risk-sensitivity might amplify procyclicality and generate a credit crunch in periods of systemic distress (Repullo and Suarez 2008). This is because the increase in the default risk of

D.V. Mascia (✉)
Department of Economics and Business, University of Cagliari, Cagliari, Italy
e-mail: danilo.mascia@unica.it

K. Keasey • F. Vallascas
Leeds University Business School, Leeds, UK
e-mail: kk@lubs.leeds.ac.uk; fv@lubs.leeds.ac.uk

© Springer International Publishing Switzerland 2016
S.P.S. Rossi, R. Malavasi (eds.), *Financial Crisis, Bank Behaviour and Credit Crunch*, Contributions to Economics, DOI 10.1007/978-3-319-17413-6_6

corporate borrowers during period of financial turmoil, and the consequent increasing effects on capital requirements under the Basel II regime, might lead to problems in respecting the minimum regulatory capital ratio.

We analyse this possibility by using the recent global crisis as a laboratory. Essentially, we test whether banks that have complied with the Basel II rules reduce their corporate lending growth more than banks that have to comply with the original Basel Accord. We conduct our analysis on a sample of 4697 bank-year observations related to banks chartered in 76 countries.

We start our analysis by showing that banks that have complied with Basel II have not apparently reduced the growth of corporate loans. This implies that, at a general level, compared to the Basel I framework, the adoption of a risk-sensitive capital regime (Basel II) has not impacted the growth of corporate loans. However, further tests allow us to show that—depending on the bank size that we use as a proxy for bank investment opportunity set and the sophistication in risk-management practices—Basel II exerts a meaningful impact on corporate lending growth. In particular, we find that larger banks significantly decrease lending to corporate borrowers. This demonstrates that Basel II might amplify the negative phases of the economy, as during downturns banks retract credit growth. Our study highlights the importance of regulatory interventions that soften the procyclicality of capital requirements—such as the countercyclical capital buffer introduced by Basel III; furthermore, these rules should be especially addressed towards large banking firms.

The remainder of the paper is structured as follows. Section 2 describes the sample, the data, the variables and the methodology used. Section 3 reports the results of our analysis and Sect. 4 offers conclusions.

2 Sample, Data, Variables and Methodology

2.1 The Sample

We construct our sample relying on bank-level data provided by Bankscope; this dataset is assembled by Bureau van Dijk with standard criteria thus allowing reliable cross-country research. In particular, our dataset contains yearly information on banks' balance sheets and income statements for the period 2007–2012, focusing on banks whose main activity is lending (i.e., commercial, cooperative, savings, and real estate & mortgage banks). We remove duplications related to banks presenting both consolidated and unconsolidated statements by keeping observations coming from the latter, as the consolidated data might be the result of bank supranational activity. However, we utilize consolidated statements when unconsolidated ones are not available (as in Beck et al. 2013).

Furthermore, we select only banks that appear among the top 50 largest banks in a given country at least once in every single year of our time series coverage. This

Table 1 Sample distribution

	Banks		Observations	
	Number	Percentage	Number	Percentage
Panel A Sample distribution by country				
Algeria	6	0.43	9	0.19
Argentina	54	3.91	214	4.56
Australia	8	0.58	22	0.47
Austria	46	3.33	142	3.02
Bahamas	6	0.43	21	0.45
Bahrain	3	0.22	8	0.17
Belgium	4	0.29	8	0.17
Botswana	1	0.07	3	0.06
Brazil	42	3.04	149	3.17
Bulgaria	20	1.45	84	1.79
Canada	52	3.77	173	3.68
Chile	26	1.88	112	2.38
China	66	4.78	224	4.77
Colombia	27	1.96	87	1.85
Costa Rica	8	0.58	12	0.26
Croatia	26	1.88	104	2.21
Cyprus	5	0.36	12	0.26
Czech Republic	4	0.29	19	0.4
Denmark	51	3.7	190	4.05
Dominican Republic	17	1.23	42	0.89
Ecuador	23	1.67	88	1.87
Egypt	13	0.94	24	0.51
Ethiopia	1	0.07	1	0.02
Finland	3	0.22	7	0.15
France	47	3.41	201	4.28
Germany	54	3.91	200	4.26
Ghana	11	0.8	30	0.64
Greece	14	1.01	44	0.94
Guatemala	16	1.16	68	1.45
Hong Kong	10	0.72	41	0.87
Hungary	5	0.36	18	0.38
Iceland	3	0.22	8	0.17
India	20	1.45	47	1
Indonesia	9	0.65	26	0.55
Ireland	5	0.36	9	0.19
Israel	9	0.65	35	0.75
Japan	11	0.8	13	0.28
Jordan	10	0.72	30	0.64
Kenya	20	1.45	67	1.43
Kuwait	3	0.22	12	0.26

(continued)

Table 1 (continued)

	Banks		Observations	
	Number	Percentage	Number	Percentage
Lebanon	26	1.88	56	1.19
Luxembourg	42	3.04	139	2.96
Mauritius	12	0.87	39	0.83
Mexico	31	2.25	121	2.58
Morocco	4	0.29	14	0.3
Namibia	1	0.07	5	0.11
Netherlands	5	0.36	17	0.36
New Zealand	5	0.36	17	0.36
Norway	30	2.17	117	2.49
Oman	5	0.36	19	0.4
Panama	39	2.83	123	2.62
Peru	12	0.87	48	1.02
Philippines	21	1.52	54	1.15
Poland	26	1.88	82	1.75
Portugal	8	0.58	18	0.38
Republic of Korea	16	1.16	56	1.19
Russian Federation	102	7.39	437	9.3
Saudi Arabia	9	0.65	43	0.92
Singapore	1	0.07	4	0.09
Slovakia	11	0.8	38	0.81
Slovenia	8	0.58	34	0.72
South Africa	8	0.58	31	0.66
Spain	11	0.8	19	0.4
Sri Lanka	3	0.22	3	0.06
Sweden	5	0.36	13	0.28
Switzerland	38	2.75	87	1.85
Thailand	7	0.51	17	0.36
Tunisia	1	0.07	2	0.04
Turkey	11	0.8	38	0.81
United Arab Emirates	9	0.65	32	0.68
United Kingdom	30	2.17	84	1.79
USA	47	3.41	201	4.28
Uruguay	3	0.22	7	0.15
Venezuela	13	0.94	33	0.7
Viet Nam	11	0.8	23	0.49
Zambia	10	0.72	22	0.47
Total	1,380	100.00	4,697	100.00
Panel B *Sample distribution by capital requirements*				
Basel I			1,555	33.11
Basel II			3,142	66.89
Total			4,697	100.00

criterion allows us to remove the excessive concentration of the sample in a limited number of countries. Finally, we control for mergers and acquisitions by removing observations where the growth in total earning assets exceeds 75 %, as in De Haas and Van Lelyveld (2014).

The application of these selection criteria leads us to a final sample of 4697 bank-year observations pertaining to 1380 banks chartered in 76 countries. Panel A of Table 1 provides the detail of the total observations and the number of banks by country.

2.2 The Capital Regulation Database

In order to study the effect of the implementation of Basel II on the lending behaviour of banks, we compile our capital regulation database by collecting information on the implementation of Basel I and Basel II from various sources. Gathering information on Basel I allows us to make sure that by 2007 (our starting year) all the countries in our sample had already implemented at least the first capital regime. Initially, we collect data on the implementation of Basel I from Barajas et al. (2005) and Vallascas and Hagendorff (2013). We then enrich these sources by relying on data publicly available at Central Banks' websites, as well as utilizing information disclosed in the notes to the Annual Reports of the largest banks. With regards to Basel II, our main source of information is the Financial Stability Institute (FSI) Survey on "Basel II, 2.5 and III implementation" released by the Bank of International Settlements (FSI 2013). Again, when unavailable from this survey, data have been manually gathered from Central Banks' or local Monetary Authorities' websites, as well as from bank annual reports.

The collected information allows us to generate our Basel II-dummy variable. This dummy accounts for the period in which only Basel II is being adopted. Hence, it takes values of 1 from the first year of implementation of Basel II onwards, and zero otherwise.

Panel B of Table 1 shows the sample distribution according to the capital adequacy regime. We note that approximately 67 % of our sample belongs to the Basel II period, corresponding to a total number of 3142 observations. The remaining 33 % is formed by 1555 observations within the Basel I era which account for a reasonable control period preceding the adoption of the Basel II regime.

2.3 Dependent Variable

We study the impact of the implementation of Basel II on the growth of lending to corporate borrowers. In particular, following Dinç (2005), we define the growth in corporate lending as the increase of corporate loans that year normalized by gross

Table 2 Variable definitions and summary statistics

		N	Mean	Median	St. dev	1 Pc	99 Pc
Δ Corporate Loans/ Gross Earn. Assets$_{t-1}$	Growth rate of corporate lending over lagged gross earning assets (real LCU)	4,697	0.021	0.010	0.108	−0.320	0.364
Basel II	A dummy variable equal to 1, for the countries involved, during the years of implementation of Basel II. It takes values of zero before the implementation and if the country did not switch to Basel II	4,697	0.669	1.000	0.471	0.000	1.000
Equity Ratio	Equity over total assets	4,697	0.091	0.091	0.773	0.013	0.511
Size	Log transformation of bank total assets	4,697	15.257	15.123	2.185	10.353	20.501
Deposit Ratio	Customer deposits over total assets	4,697	0.556	0.618	0.268	0.007	0.920
ROA	Profit before taxes over total assets	4,697	0.012	0.010	0.024	−0.050	0.076
Real GDP Growth Rate	Annual real growth rate of the domestic GDP	4,697	0.025	0.025	0.041	−0.078	0.108
Ln (GDP per capita)	Log transformation of domestic GDP per capita	4,697	9.702	9.534	1.114	6.723	11.641
Bank Claims	Domestic bank claims on private sector as % of GDP	4,697	0.852	0.742	0.573	0.131	2.165
Public Debt	Domestic Public Debt as % of GDP	4,697	0.485	0.441	0.304	0.055	1.456
Financial Freedom	The overall score ranges from 0 to 1 with higher values denoting higher financial freedom (source: Heritage Foundation)	4,697	0.593	0.600	0.171	0.300	0.900
Private Ownership	The higher the value of the index, the higher the private ownership and, on the other hand, the lower the government ownership of banks (source: Free the World)	4,674	0.763	0.800	0.253	0.200	1.000

earning assets from the previous year, i.e., (*Corporate Loans*(t) − *Corporate Loans* (t − 1))/*Gross Earning Assets*(t − 1)). In order to calculate this growth rate, we adopt variables in real values at year 2012, thus corrected for inflation through the national GDP deflator, and in local currency. This allows our results to actually reflect bank business choices rather than being driven by fluctuations in exchange rates.

Table 2 shows the summary statistics of the variables utilized in our models. With regards to the dependent variable, we note that during our sample period corporate lending grows by 2.1 %. We also observe this variable steadily increasing, given a standard deviation of 11 %. Moreover, we note about 39 % of our bank-year observations related to our dependent variable are negative.

2.4 Control Variables

We control for a number of bank characteristics to isolate the effect of capital regulation on the growth of credit to corporate borrowers. In particular, we include size, the equity ratio, the deposit ratio, and a measure of bank profitability. For sake of clarity, we compute bank size as the log transformation of bank total assets calculated in real US dollars at year 2012. We expect larger banks to show a lower inclination to lend, given the larger investment opportunity set and the related attitude to invest in a wide range of business lines. The equity ratio is given by equity over total assets. It represents a measure of bank soundness and should lead credit institutions to increase their propensity to lend, since well-capitalized banks face lower funding costs due to lower bankruptcy probabilities. The deposit ratio is computed as deposits over total assets. We suppose banks with greater shares of deposits to show a more stable lending. Finally, we measure bank profitability through our ROA index—profit before taxes over total assets. Since banks with greater profitability have greater opportunities to increase capital (through adequate retaining earning policies), they should be more inclined to provide lending, that is, to be involved in activities that lead to larger capital requirements.

We also control for a series of country characteristics by collecting information from different sources, i.e. Euromonitor, the World Bank, the Heritage Foundation and the Fraser Institute. In particular, we utilize the real GDP growth rate (that is the growth rate of GDP in real values) to control for credit demand (see, in this regard, De Haas and Van Lelyveld 2014), and for the procyclicality in bank lending. In general, the growth rate of real GDP should positively affect corporate credit growth as banks should be more prone to lend during economic booms. We also employ the natural logarithm of GDP per capita, as in Dinç (2005), to account for economic development. Again, this variable should be positively linked to credit growth, meaning that banks in more developed countries are (more) inclined to expand their business accordingly. Furthermore, we add domestic bank claims on the private sector over GDP to account for the degree of development of the credit industry; as well as public debt as a percentage of GDP to control for the public debt load.

Finally, we add two indexes of the global institutional environment, namely financial freedom and private ownership. In particular, we obtain financial freedom data through the Heritage Foundation website. It consists of an overall measure of an economy's financial freedom, derived after scoring for the degree of government regulation of financial services, the degree of state intervention in financial firms, the level of financial market development, the government influence in the credit allocation process, as well as the degree of openness to foreign competition. Higher levels of this index indicate higher financial freedom for the given country. We expect financial freedom to negatively impact our credit growth variables, as banks chartered in more financially free countries should be less inclined to provide credit compared to banks located in more state-controlled territories. From "Freedom of the World" (that is a dataset compiled by the Fraser Institute) we download our private ownership variable. This index basically accounts for the percentage of bank deposits held in privately owned banks. This implies that countries with greater shares of deposits held by private institutions are assigned higher scores. Hence, higher values of the index are associated with higher degrees of private ownership.

2.5 Methodology

We estimate the impact of the implementation of Basel II—in a world already compliant to risk-based capital regulation—on the growth of corporate lending via a *difference-in-difference* approach. To do so, we assess panel data models through the within-estimator in order to control for bank heterogeneity. Furthermore, to reduce simultaneity and endogeneity bias, we lag our bank controls by 1 year. Finally, to remove any estimation bias induced by within-group correlation, our standard errors are corrected for heteroscedasticity and clustered at the bank level.

Hence, we assess our models utilizing the following specification:

$$y_{it} = \alpha_i + \beta X_{i,t-1} + \gamma Z_{k,t} + \delta BaselII_{k,t} + \varepsilon_{it} \tag{1}$$

where:

- y is our dependent variable, as defined above;
- α_i is the bank-specific intercept, β, γ and δ are coefficients;
- $X_{i,t-1}$ is a vector of lagged bank-control variables;
- $Z_{k,t}$ is a vector of macroeconomic and country control variables;
- *Basel II*$_{k,t}$ is our dummy that accounts for the Basel II regulatory regime;
- ε_{it} is an idiosyncratic error $\varepsilon_{it} \sim \text{IID}(0, \sigma_\varepsilon^2)$;
- $i = 1, \ldots, N$, where N is the number of banks in the sample;
- $t = 1, \ldots, T_i$, where T_i is the number of years in the sample for bank i.

We, therefore, deduce the impact of the New Basel Accord via the significance of the coefficient related to the Basel II dummy. For sake of clarity, the introduction of Basel II should be negatively linked to credit growth, thus signalling banks reducing lending upon Basel II implementation.

3   The Impact of Basel II on Corporate Lending Growth

In this section we present the results of our analysis on the effect exerted by Basel II on the growth of corporate lending. More precisely, our analysis starts in column 1 of Table 3 where we report a baseline specification that includes the bank size, the equity ratio, the deposit ratio, the ROA (note that all the bank controls are lagged by 1 year), and three country control variables (the real growth rate of GDP, the natural logarithm of GDP per capita and a variable that controls for total country bank claims). In the following column we add three additional country controls to our baseline specification presented in column 1, namely financial freedom, private ownership and public debt.

With regards to our Basel II dummy, we observe in columns 1 and 2 that the introduction of the more risk-sensitive capital framework does not appear to exert a significant impact on the growth of corporate lending compared to the previous Basel I regime. Essentially, we do not find support for the hypothesis that the increase in risk-sensitivity of capital requirements due to Basel II amplifies procyclicality. In terms of control variables, we observe that corporate lending growth increases when banks realize greater levels of profitability, in periods of economic growth, in more developed countries as well as in more bank-oriented countries. In contrast, they reduce lending in countries more financially free.

Next we extend the specifications in the first two columns by adding an interaction term between the Basel II dummy and bank size. This allows us to evaluate whether the impact of the new regulatory framework on the growth of corporate lending varies with bank size. Different reasons can justify an impact of capital regulation contingent on bank size. First, large banks might have more investment opportunities than smaller banks and can, then, easily move resources from lending activities to other business lines with lower capital requirements. Second, the risk-sensitivity of capital requirements under Basel II crucially depends on the approach employed to measure the credit risk for regulatory purposes. In particular higher risk-sensitivity is attached to the Internal Rating Based (IRB) Approach that, given the higher costs of implementation, is more likely to be adopted by large banking firms.

The results on the interaction between Basel II and bank size, reported in columns 3 and 4, clearly suggest that a significant decline in corporate lending emerges when Basel II banks are also large in size: while under the extended specification the coefficient of the Basel II dummy is positive and highly significant, the interaction terms are negative and significant at customary levels.

Table 3 The impact of Basel II on credit growth to corporate borrowers

	Δ Corporate loans/gross earn. assets$_{t-1}$			
	(1)	(2)	(3)	(4)
Basel II	−0.004	−0.007	0.160***	0.145***
	(0.01)	(0.01)	(0.06)	(0.06)
Size$_{t-1}$	−0.063***	−0.060***	−0.054***	−0.052***
	(0.01)	(0.01)	(0.01)	(0.01)
Size$_{t-1}$ × Basel II			−0.011***	−0.010***
			(0.00)	(0.00)
Equity Ratio$_{t-1}$	0.054	0.066	0.071	0.081
	(0.09)	(0.09)	(0.09)	(0.09)
Deposit Ratio$_{t-1}$	0.037	0.035	0.036	0.035
	(0.03)	(0.03)	(0.03)	(0.03)
ROA$_{t-1}$	0.342*	0.296	0.353**	0.308*
	(0.18)	(0.18)	(0.18)	(0.18)
Real GDP Growth	0.191**	0.162*	0.189**	0.163*
	(0.09)	(0.09)	(0.09)	(0.09)
Ln (GDP per capita)	0.134***	0.143***	0.136***	0.143***
	(0.02)	(0.03)	(0.02)	(0.03)
Bank Claims	0.102***	0.102***	0.105***	0.103***
	(0.03)	(0.03)	(0.03)	(0.03)
Financial Freedom		−0.205***		−0.191***
		(0.06)		(0.06)
Private Ownership		0.082***		0.084***
		(0.03)		(0.03)
Public Debt		0.043		0.039
		(0.03)		(0.03)
Constant	−0.442**	−0.530*	−0.573**	−0.640**
	(0.22)	(0.28)	(0.23)	(0.28)
Observations	4,697	4,674	4,697	4,674
R-squared	0.07	0.07	0.07	0.08
Number of banks	1,380	1,369	1,380	1,369
Bank fixed effects	Yes	Yes	Yes	Yes
Time dummies	Yes	Yes	Yes	Yes

The economic relevance of our results is pointed out by the calculation of marginal effects (applied to the specification in column 4 of Table 3); that is, by the calculation of the first derivatives of Basel II on the growth of corporate lending, for given levels of bank size.

This analysis, whose results are reported in Table 4, indicates that about 40 % of the largest banks significantly decreases corporate credit growth upon Basel II implementation. This contraction in lending exacerbates at an increased bank size. If we take, for instance, banks at the 60th percentile of bank size, we observe them decreasing lending to corporate borrowers by approximately 1.6 %. If we

Table 4 Marginal effects of the implementation of Basel II on credit growth to corporate borrowers, by bank size (based on model 4 of Table 3)

Bank size pct	$\partial Y / \partial$ Basel II$_{SIZE}$	Std. err.	z	P > z	[90 % conf. interval]	
10th	0.019	0.014	1.36	0.174	−0.008	0.046
20th	0.009	0.012	0.82	0.413	−0.013	0.032
30th	0.002	0.010	0.21	0.832	−0.018	0.022
40th	−0.004	0.009	−0.43	0.67	−0.022	0.014
50th	−0.010	0.009	−1.14	0.255	−0.027	0.007
60th	−0.016	0.009	−1.84	0.066	−0.033	0.001
70th	−0.023	0.009	−2.45	0.014	−0.042	−0.005
80th	−0.031	0.011	−2.84	0.005	−0.052	−0.010
90th	−0.040	0.013	−3.07	0.002	−0.065	−0.014
95th	−0.048	0.015	−3.16	0.002	−0.078	−0.018

further compute our marginal effects moving towards the largest banks in our sample, we observe corporate lending exponentially declining by 2.3 %, 3.1 %, 4 %, 4.8 %, at the 70th, 80th, 90th, and 95th percentiles of bank size respectively.

This result shows that Basel II played a crucial role in determining a significant decline in the growth of corporate loans according to bank size. As suggested earlier, one of the possible explanations of this result is due to differences in risk-sensitivity within the Basel II framework, namely, in the method adopted by banks to calculate the regulatory capital—i.e., the Standardized Approach (SA) versus the Internal Rating Based (IRB) method. In fact, banks implementing the IRB approach are usually the largest banks—given that they are the ones more likely to bear the costs arising from the setting up of an internal process to assess borrowers' creditworthiness. Thus, our results are probably highlighting that IRB implementers were the banks actually exerting the deeper contraction in lending that we observe at increased levels of size, probably because of the higher risk-sensitivity that characterizes the IRB approach as compared to the SA method.

4 Conclusions

This paper investigates the impact of the implementation of Basel II on the growth of corporate lending during the years 2007–2012. We run this analysis relying on bank-year observations associated with banks located in 76 countries, adding a series of financial and macroeconomic controls as well.

Our analysis shows that corporate lending growth significantly decreases, upon Basel II implementation, with bank size. In particular, we find that 20 % of the largest banks in our sample decreases the growth of loans to corporate borrowers by more than 3 %. Moreover, as the period we study is characterized by a global financial crisis, our results highlight as well that the implementation of Basel II by the largest banks exacerbated the negative effects induced by the global crisis (procyclicality of capital charges) when corporate borrowers turned to the largest banks.

Hence, since we find that corporate lending decreases more when Basel II banks increase in size, future research should investigate whether the result we obtained is led by differences between the two Basel II approaches, namely the Standardized Approach (SA) and the Internal Rating Basel (IRB) method. As the IRB method requires more capital to be set aside at increased risk exposures and is more likely to be adopted by large banks, the likely outcome is reduced corporate lending by the largest banks. Therefore, our result is probably suggesting that the greater corporate lending contraction experienced by the largest banks is given by differences in risk-sensitivity arising from the different approach utilized in computing risk-weighted assets.

Finally, our analysis shows the importance of the recent regulatory interventions (i.e., Basel III) aimed at softening the procyclicality of capital requirements via the introduction of the countercyclical capital buffer; especially in the case of the largest banking firms.

Acknowledgements We are thankful to Adolfo Barajas, Ralph Chami and Thomas Cosimano for sharing their dataset on Basel I implementation dates. Danilo V. Mascia gratefully acknowledges the Sardinian Regional Government for the financial support of his PhD scholarship (P.O.R. Sardegna F.S.E. Operational Programme of the Autonomous Region of Sardinia, European Social Fund 2007–2013—Axis IV Human Resources, Objective 1.3, Line of Activity 1.3.1.), as well as for the financial support through the research grants from the Autonomous Region of Sardinia, *Legge Regionale 2007, N. 7* [Grant Number CRP-59890, year 2012].

References

Barajas A, Chami R, Cosimano T (2005) Did the Basel accord cause a credit slowdown in Latin America? IMF working paper no. 05/38
Beck T, Demirgüç-Kunt A, Merrouche O (2013) Islamic vs. conventional banking: business model, efficiency and stability. J Bank Finance 37:433–447
De Haas R, Van Lelyveld I (2014) Multinational banks and the global financial crisis: weathering the perfect storm? J Money Credit Bank 46(S1):333–364
Dinç IS (2005) Politicians and banks: political influences on government-owned banks in emerging markets. J Financ Econ 77:453–479
FSI (2013) Basel II, 2.5 and III implementation. Bank for International Settlements, Basel
Repullo R, Suarez J (2008) The pro-cyclical effects of Basel II. CEMFI working paper no. 0809
Vallascas F, Hagendorff J (2013) The risk sensitivity of capital requirements: evidence from an international sample of large banks. Rev Finance 17(6):1947–1988

Bank Profitability and Capital Adequacy in the Post-crisis Context

Marina Brogi and Rosaria Langone

Abstract Bank capital adequacy is the key driver of a resilient banking system that is capable of absorbing shocks. Consequently, Basel III regulation raised the quality and quantity of the regulatory capital base. But are better capitalized banks perceived as less risky by the market? In other words, how do banks' capital bases impact the riskiness of their equity? Does the market also consider leverage, asset quality and profitability? In our work, we aim to address these issues, analysing a sample of large European listed banks (those under ECB supervision) for the 2007–2013 period. We expect to find that bank equity return riskiness is influenced by capital adequacy and, in turn, by how higher capital ratios have been achieved: through profitability, retained earnings, new share issues or deleveraging (i.e., lower total assets and/or risk weighted assets).

1 Introduction

Basel III regulations raised the quality and quantity of the regulatory capital base and introduced the leverage ratio to address the shortcomings that emerged in the financial crisis. The rationale behind the rise in the quantity (total capital ratio increased to 10.5 % of risk weighted assets) and the quality (in Basel III common equity must be 7 % of regulatory capital compared to 2 % in Basel II) of the capital base is that more capitalized, less leveraged banks are more capable of absorbing shocks.

To comply with the new regulation, banks are required to modify the composition of their funding sources, increasing the portion of equity compared to other liabilities.

The topic is particularly relevant because the supervisory approach has been challenged by the banking industry,[1] which warned that because equity is the most

---

[1] See for example Institute of International Finance (2010), Admati et al. (2013) review all the concerns raised by the banking industry.

M. Brogi (✉) • R. Langone
Department of Management, Sapienza University of Rome, Rome, Italy
e-mail: marina.brogi@uniroma1.it; rosaria.langone@uniroma1.it

© Springer International Publishing Switzerland 2016   95
S.P.S. Rossi, R. Malavasi (eds.), *Financial Crisis, Bank Behaviour and Credit Crunch*, Contributions to Economics, DOI 10.1007/978-3-319-17413-6_7

expensive source of funding, banks will be forced to add this additional cost to loans. For an investor, holding equity is riskier than holding debt. Therefore, equity holders are likely to require a higher return on their investment that will in turn generate a higher cost for banks that will be transferred to customers via higher interest rates on loans. Through this mechanism, a recomposition of bank liabilities with a higher portion of equity could negatively affect economic growth.

On the other hand, regulators stress the need to sacrifice economic growth to prevent any future financial crisis (Basel Committee on Banking Supervision 2010). Allen et al. (2012), underlying that this debate is overly simplistic, state that there might not even be any need to trade off the level of output and the safety of the financial system. Admati et al. (2013) conclude that bank equity is not socially expensive, and that high leverage is not necessary for banks to perform all of their socially valuable functions, whereas better capitalized banks suffer fewer distortions in lending decisions and would perform better.

In this paper, we aim to provide empirical evidence of the inverse relationship between expected market equity returns and banks' capital bases to demonstrate that better capitalized banks are perceived as less risky by the market and therefore shareholders will require a lower return on equity. It is thus possible to break the industry paradigm positing that additional capital implies extra costs that will be translated into interest paid by borrowers.

In addition to providing further empirical evidence on this topic, this paper contributes to previous literature by considering how higher capital ratios have been achieved, through profitability, retained earnings and new share issues. Moreover, we test our hypotheses on a sample of large European listed banks (namely the listed banks under ECB supervision as of 4th November 2014) for the 2007–2013 period, an extremely significant sample in terms of total assets in the euro area, still not covered in the previous literature.

We expect to find that the relation between the riskiness of bank equity, proxied by CAPM β, and banks' capital adequacy, expressed by common equity tier 1 ratio is negative because better capitalized banks are recognized as less risky by the market. Moreover, better capitalized banks should show a positive relationship between common equity tier 1 ratio and ROA, capital increases and retained earnings.

The rest of the paper is as follows. In Sect. 2 we review the relevant literature; in Sect. 3 we describe the dataset and methodology; in Sect. 4 we discuss the findings; and in Sect. 5 we conclude.

2   Literature Review

The banking business is opaque and complex and can shift rather quickly. Furthermore banks have many more stakeholders than non-financial firms (Mehran et al. 2011). Financial theory states that commercial banks create value by overcoming adverse selection problems intrinsic to external financing because they are able to gather and evaluate private information to assess firms' capacity to reimburse their debt. Banks also have the resources to control and monitor their debt holders until debt expires. On the other hand, depositors, the main source of funding for banks, are small and dispersed claimholders who lack the resources and incentives to monitor and control banks, given the extensive private information in loan portfolios (Slovin et al. 1999). Banks may incur liquidity problems because depositors can use public information regarding bad financial health of other banks to assess the financial soundness of their own bank. If they claim their deposits back at once, their bank will also face solvency issues because they financed illiquid loans with highly liquid forms of funding such as sight deposits. The default of one bank can spread to the whole banking sector; it is consequently more appropriate to refer to the totality of banks in the economy as the banking system. In the recent financial crisis, governments were required to bail out several banks to prevent this domino effect within the banking system, with the side effect of a public debt explosion (Brogi 2011).

By raising capital requirements, regulators try to preserve banks' socially valuable functions, including lending, deposit taking and issuing money-like instruments as well as prevent the need for further government interventions.

Berger and Bouwman (2013) find that, during banking crises, market crises, and normal times, capital helps to enhance the survival probabilities and market shares of small banks and helps medium and large banks primarily during banking crises. Cosimano and Hakura (2011), investigating the impact of the new capital requirements introduced under Basel III regulation, observe that banks' responses to the new rules depend on cross-country variations in banks' net cost of raising equity and the elasticity of loan demand with respect to changes in loan rates.

This paper is related to the strand of the literature that links cost of bank equity to bank leverage. The theoretical framework for this strand of literature is Modigliani and Miller's (1958) analysis of capital structure (henceforth M&M). M&M—under the strong assumptions of random walk market price process, no taxation, no bankruptcy costs, symmetric information and efficient markets—showed that a firm's value and its cost of capital are not affected by the composition of its funding sources. As we described above, the banking industry claims that because equity is the most expensive source of funding, higher capital requirements will lead to a credit crunch, i.e., fewer loans granted to the economy and higher interest on existing loans. Using data on large U.S. banks, Kashyap et al. (2010) demonstrate that while equity is always more risky than debt, the riskiness of a bank's equity declines as its leverage falls. They find evidence of a negative relationship between a bank's equity risk, measured as CAPM β (henceforth β), and its leverage, given by the book value of equity to book value of assets ratio. They conclude that an increase in equity financing will not significantly affect the cost of bank funding. Miles et al. (2013) and ECB (2011), applying the same methodology used by Kashyap et al. (2010), find further supporting evidence of this effect, considering, respectively a sample of UK banks and a sample composed by banks headquartered in 18 countries.

In this paper, we also follow Kashyap et al. (2010) by using β as a proxy of bank equity risk, but we use both the common equity tier 1 ratio (i.e., common shareholders' equity/risk weighted assets, henceforth CET1 ratio) that we consider as a proxy of the Basel III CET 1 ratio, which is currently being phased in, and the book value of equity to book value of assets ratio used in their paper (henceforth LEVERAGE). In this way, we are able to take into account both more stringent capital requirements introduced by Basel III regulation and to ascertain whether the both of them have an impact on banks' equity risk. We would expect the latter to be affected by capital ratios as investors on the market are aware of the importance of common equity in ensuring bank stability. Moreover, we expand the object of the analysis by considering how higher capital ratios have been achieved: through profitability, retained earnings or share capital increases, through public equity offerings or private placements via accelerated book building. To do so we simultaneously estimate the determined variables that influence β and the CET1 ratio. We expect to find that the relation between β and CET1 and LEVERAGE is negative because better capitalized banks should be considered less risky by the market. Moreover, better capitalized banks should show a positive relation between common equity tier 1 ratio and ROA, capital increases and retained earnings.

3 Dataset and Methodology

3.1 Dataset

The starting point of the sample was the 130 banks submitted to the Asset Quality Review performed by the ECB during the first part of 2014. We then selected only listed banks because our analysis is based on market data. We gathered the dataset containing each bank's annual balance sheet, income statement and market data via Datastream. Data quality checks led us to a final sample of 31 banks, headquartered in 9 European countries. Total assets of the banks in our sample represent 55 % of total assets of the initial 130 banks, corresponding in turn to 43 % of bank assets in the euro area.[2]

---

[2] Source: ECB, Statistical Data Warehouse.

3.2 Methodology

For each bank in the final sample we estimated equity β over a year rolling window, using traded daily stock market returns together with the returns of EURO STOXX® Total Market Index (TMI)[3] from 2007 to 2013. Then, the relationship between banks' equity risk and capital adequacy is tested. We employ the three-Stage Least Squares method (henceforth 3SLS), first introduced by Zellner and Theil (1962) to estimate simultaneous equations by combining two-Stage Least Squares (2SLS) with Seemingly Unrelated Regressions (SUR). Our jointly dependent variables are β and CET 1 ratio. To test our hypotheses, we estimate the following equations:

$$\widehat{\beta}_{it} = a_1 CET1_{it} + a_2 LEVERAGE_{it} + a_3 (RWA_{it}/TOTASS_{it}) + a_4 MKTBK_{it} + u_{it} \tag{1}$$

$$\widehat{CET1}_{it} = b_1 ROA_{it} + b_2 (TOTLOANS_{it}/TOTASS_{it}) + b_3 (RetEar_{it-1}/CE_{it-1}) + (CapIn_{it-1}/CE_{it-1}) + u_{it} \tag{2}$$

for banks $i = 1,\ldots, 31$ and time periods $t = 1,\ldots,7$.

3.3 Definition of Determined Variables

For the estimation of parameter $\hat{\beta}$ in Eq. (1) we use the leverage ratio (LEVERAGE), computed as the book value of common shareholders' equity to total assets ratio, the risk weighted assets to total asset ratio (RWA/TOTASS), and market capitalization to the book value of common shareholders' equity (MKTBK), which is a measure of a the market valuation of the bank.

To test which element influences CET1 we take as variables in Eq. (2) return on assets (ROA), which expresses bank profitability, and the ratio total loans/total assets (TOTLOANS/TOTASS), which is a proxy of the business model adopted by the bank. The higher the ratio the more the bank performs commercial banking activities. We further take two ratios that show how banks increased their common shareholders' equity: internally, through retaining earnings, or externally by capital injections deriving from seasoned equity offerings and accelerated book building

---

[3] As specified in the STOXX Limited website: "The EURO STOXX TMI is a regional subset of the STOXX Europe TMI Index which covers approximately 95 % of the free float market capitalisation of Europe. With a variable number of components, the EURO STOXX TMI Index represents a broad coverage of Eurozone companies. The index includes Austria, Belgium, Finland, France, Germany, Greece, Ireland, Italy, Luxembourg, the Netherlands, Portugal and Spain. The EURO STOXX TMI comprises large, mid and small capitalisation indices: the EURO STOXX TMI Large Index, the EURO STOXX TMI Mid Index and the EURO STOXX TMI Small Index".

Table 1 Descriptive statistics for jointly dependent and determined variables

		2007	2008	2009	2010	2011	2012	2013	2007–2013
β	Average	0.90	0.97	1.29	1.29	1.21	1.47	1.26	1.20
	Std Dev	0.39	0.41	0.61	0.37	0.45	0.61	0.44	0.47
	Coeff. of Var. (%)	43.00	42.61	47.38	28.81	37.63	41.42	35.21	39.44
	Minimum	−0.12	0.13	−0.02	0.24	−0.07	−0.08	0.16	0.03
	Max	1.58	1.74	2.94	1.76	2.12	2.32	1.89	2.05
CET1	Average (%)	9.69	9.40	9.90	10.43	10.16	9.97	12.74	10.32
	Std Dev (%)	2.92	2.45	6.11	2.65	3.31	6.03	3.36	3.83
	Coeff. of Var. (%)	30.13	26.13	61.76	25.44	32.63	60.48	26.40	37.57
	Minimum (%)	1.81	4.65	−7.55	5.90	1.07	−5.69	7.13	1.05
	Max (%)	15.74	13.75	20.01	17.41	15.97	18.50	18.32	17.10
CE	Average	16,768	16,569	19,015	18,823	18,674	17,763	19,212	18,118
	Std Dev	20,324	19,104	23,885	22,282	22,517	22,254	22,035	21,771
	Coeff. of Var. (%)	121.20	115.30	125.61	118.38	120.58	125.28	114.69	120.15
	Minimum	469	1,587	−3,870	1,802	477	−2,463	1,498	−71
	Max	76,414	57,724	87,591	74,654	75,370	85,886	75,018	76,094
TOTADCAP	Average (%)	11.29	11.41	12.10	12.05	12.12	11.73	12.82	11.93
	Std Dev (%)	1.76	1.75	4.31	2.09	2.81	4.91	2.98	2.94
	Coeff. of Var. (%)	15.59	15.34	35.62	17.34	23.18	41.86	23.24	24.60
	Minimum (%)	8.72	8.58	−6.10	8.88	5.50	−5.70	–	3.31
	Max (%)	16.18	15.19	19.20	17.80	19.00	18.91	16.40	17.53
RWA	Average	139,840	132,363	146,220	161,660	158,902	146,584	139,870	146,491
	Std Dev	168,737	159,115	166,029	171,993	170,904	158,711	152,233	163,960
	Coeff. of Var. (%)	120.66	120.21	113.55	106.39	107.55	108.27	108.84	112.21
	Minimum	13,666	16,752	19,286	21,143	21,268	19,885	17,499	18,500
	Max	558,639	535,147	620,714	604,885	613,567	557,030	559,632	578,516

TOTASS	Average	402,637	425,508	387,359	411,467	415,587	421,420	418,185	411,738
	Std Dev	555,440	601,923	507,688	560,693	591,385	587,265	575,615	568,573
	Coeff. of Var. (%)	137.95	141.46	131.06	136.27	142.30	139.35	137.65	138.01
	Minimum	18,922	21,795	26,642	23,412	17,174	24,804	26,704	22,779
	Max	2,015,577	2,193,953	1,792,578	1,988,916	2,155,366	2,004,611	2,047,648	2,028,378
TOTLOANS	Average	172,440	197,488	200,805	211,839	209,229	207,087	198,303	199,599
	Std Dev	185,956	212,480	221,896	231,849	232,070	225,057	215,106	215,566
	Coeff. of Var. (%)	107.84	107.59	110.50	109.45	110.92	108.68	108.47	109.06
	Minimum	14,330	17,304	19,440	22,319	24,642	24,336	22,273	14,330
	Max	618,219	688,284	738,665	750,466	769,340	738,784	739,387	769,340
RWA/TOTASS	Average (%)	54.32	52.62	54.38	59.18	60.73	54.37	48.95	54.94
	Std Dev (%)	24.21	23.42	18.21	20.05	24.69	20.92	17.45	21.28
	Coeff. of Var. (%)	44.57	44.52	33.48	33.87	40.65	38.48	35.66	38.75
	Minimum (%)	14.00	16.00	16.00	21.63	17.69	15.94	15.83	16.73
	Max (%)	87.90	79.98	81.70	93.00	90.00	89.62	83.19	86.49
TOTLOANS/ TOTASS	Average	62.52	66.79	66.06	71.06	74.24	70.47	65.78	68.13
	Std Dev	17.36	18.16	18.95	19.19	25.39	20.48	19.82	20.11
	Coeff. of Var. (%)	27.77	27.19	28.69	27.00	34.20	29.06	30.13	29.52
	Minimum	11.02	15.31	19.24	33.71	19.33	26.02	20.14	11.02
	Max	91.89	90.88	107.11	113.63	143.49	106.07	129.55	143.49
LEVERAGE	Average (%)	5.80	5.29	5.03	5.95	5.76	4.77	5.93	5.50
	Std Dev (%)	2.73	2.11	3.34	1.95	2.18	3.43	1.94	2.53
	Coeff. of Var. (%)	47.10	39.90	66.39	32.73	37.79	71.91	32.76	46.94
	Minimum (%)	1.12	1.40	−4.12	2.45	0.83	−5.10	2.53	−0.13
	Max (%)	13.49	10.51	9.76	10.57	9.32	11.17	10.40	10.74
MKTBK	Average	1.36	0.96	0.61	0.68	0.88	0.50	0.62	0.80
	Std Dev	0.77	0.63	0.39	0.34	0.74	0.72	0.32	0.56
	Coeff. of Var. (%)	56.53	65.58	65.03	50.41	83.52	145.05	51.55	73.95
	Minimum	0.25	0.25	−0.32	0.21	0.19	−2.35	0.19	−0.23
	Max	3.04	2.91	1.38	1.32	3.46	2.31	1.60	2.29

(continued)

Table 1 (continued)

		2007	2008	2009	2010	2011	2012	2013	2007–2013
ROA	Average	1.26	1.00	0.41	0.68	0.71	-0.50	0.55	0.59
	Std Dev	0.80	1.19	0.88	0.60	1.40	3.36	1.22	1.35
	Coeff. of Var. (%)	63.33	118.57	217.03	88.24	196.85	-673.11	220.23	33.02
	Minimum	-0.53	-3.30	-1.81	-0.47	-5.77	-12.42	-1.61	-3.70
	Max	3.88	3.57	1.96	2.40	2.49	2.26	4.99	3.08
RetEar	Average	633	571	481	462	404	562	578	527
	Std Dev	897	944	929	1,026	1,076	1,260	1,313	1,064
	Coeff. of Var. (%)	141.87	165.49	193.25	222.15	266.15	224.16	227.31	205.77
	Minimum	-104	-7	-2	-19	-807	-650	-875	-352
	Max	3,706	4,093	4,327	4,880	4,383	4,826	5,223	4,491
RetEar/CE	Average	4.30	3.45	3.11	2.31	0.55	2.83	4.35	2.99
	Std Dev	3.15	2.99	3.26	2.67	6.04	17.91	8.04	8.07
	Coeff. of Var.	73.35	86.88	104.82	115.59	1,098.59	632.16	184.60	270.33
	Minimum	-2.70	-0.20	-0.04	-0.32	-21.63	-74.14	-1.11	-74.14
	Max	10.66	9.82	11.76	7.09	7.22	55.67	38.92	55.67
RetEar/CE	Average	2.16	8.26	4.12	2.44	3.86	1.79	-44.15	-3.07
	Std Dev	10.92	14.75	9.81	6.16	9.00	10.65	251.52	95.74
	Coeff. of Var.	506.51	178.59	237.97	253.00	232.89	593.62	-569.71	-3114.66
	Minimum	0.00	0.00	0.00	0.00	0.00	-34.34	-1398.51	-1398.51
	Max	60.70	47.53	36.65	27.83	39.46	42.61	21.34	60.70
Number of CapIn	Total	5	12	8	10	13	10	13	10
CapIn	Total sum	2,543	22,581	21,789	18,683	23,223	12,612	18,879	17,187

Data for CE, RWA, TOTASS, RetEar and CapIn are in million euros
Source: Authors' elaboration on Datastream data

operations. In the former case, we take the ratio between retained earnings and common equity in $t - 1$ (RetEar/CE) and in the latter case we use the ratio between capital injections deriving from seasoned equity offerings and accelerated book building operations and common equity in $t - 1$ (CapIn/CE).

In Table 1 descriptive statistics for jointly dependent and determined variables are provided. We can note that, within the period of observation, CET1 ratio rises from 9.69 to 12.74 %, with a sharp increase in 2013. The latter can be related to the effect of the capital increases enacted by banks as a result of the imminent comprehensive assessment to be carried out by the ECB. Despite what we would expect, β rose from 0.90 in 2007 to 1.47 in 2012 and then declined to 1.26 in 2013.

Average common equity increased from 16.8 billion euros in 2007 to 19.2 billion euros in 2013 whereas average RWA increased in the first 4 years and peaked in 2010. It then declined until 2013 with the figure for 2013 almost the same as in 2007 (approximately 139 billion euros).

We can thus impute the improvement in CET1 ratio to the increase in common equity. It may be attributed to the action of supervision (higher Basel III requirements and the imminent comprehensive assessment) which led to the considerable number of new share issues that occurred during the period either with public seasoned equity offerings or with private book building placements. As indicated in Table 1, while in 2007, which may be considered the last year before the crisis, only five seasoned equity offerings occurred with a total capital injection of two billion euros, overall capital raised by the sample surged to almost ten times the amount in 2008 and 2009 and remained strong in subsequent years as testified to by the fact that we count on average almost 11 capital increases per year with an annual capital injection of more than 19 billion euros.

Contrary to the RWA trend, total assets increased from 403 to 418 billion euros, leading the risk weighted assets to total assets ratio to drop from 0.54 to 0.49 and the average level of leverage to rise from 5.80 % in 2007 to 5.93 % in 2013. Both the market valuation of banks expressed by market to book ratio and the banks' profitability, given by return on assets, halved during the period.

Additionally, average loans to customers (TOTLOANS) increased in the period from 172 to 198 billion euros. Concerns raised by banking industry representatives do not seem to have occurred because in our findings higher capital ratios have been achieved through capital increases and retained earnings and not through deleveraging, indeed, both total assets and total loans to customers increased in the period.

Because the coefficient of variation is more than 1 for several variables, we split our sample into bigger and smaller banks in terms of total assets. In Table 2, descriptive statistics of the key variables β, CET1, RWA/TOTASS and LEVERAGE are provided separately for each of the two groups. We classified a bank as bigger if total assets in 2013 are more than 200 billion euros. Following this criterion we split our sample into 12 bigger banks and 19 smaller banks (Table 2).

We can notice that smaller banks have a lower CET1 ratio (it is 9.20 % on average for the period versus the 12.10 % of bigger banks) but they have a higher leverage ratio (5.87 % versus 4.75 %), which stems from the considerably higher

Table 2 Descriptive statistics for β, CET1 and RWA/TOTASS variables

		2007	2008	2009	2010	2011	2012	2013	2007–2013
β Bigger banks	Average	0.94	1.08	1.46	1.31	1.35	1.59	1.25	1.28
	Std Dev	0.44	0.47	0.68	0.53	0.59	0.74	0.54	0.57
	Coeff. of Var. (%)	47.08	43.57	46.39	40.64	43.71	46.50	43.50	44.48
	Minimum	−0.12	0.13	−0.02	0.24	−0.07	−0.08	0.20	0.04
	Max	1.36	1.61	2.48	1.76	1.86	2.32	1.89	1.90
β Smaller banks	Average	0.86	0.87	1.14	1.23	1.08	1.34	1.21	1.11
	Std Dev	0.37	0.39	0.56	0.30	0.35	0.56	0.44	0.42
	Coeff. of Var. (%)	42.90	44.23	49.08	24.20	32.74	41.55	36.52	38.75
	Minimum	0.04	0.29	0.47	0.43	0.46	0.33	0.16	0.31
	Max	1.58	1.74	2.94	1.69	2.12	2.25	1.74	2.01
CET1 Bigger banks	Average (%)	10.10	10.04	12.99	11.67	12.18	13.47	14.24	12.10
	Std Dev (%)	2.53	2.49	2.74	2.25	2.41	2.98	2.05	2.49
	Coeff. of Var. (%)	25.05	24.78	21.07	19.30	19.78	22.14	14.42	20.93
	Minimum (%)	5.69	4.65	9.27	7.92	6.40	8.22	11.79	7.70
	Max (%)	14.84	13.7	20.01	16.1	15.26	18.5	17.95	16.6
CET1 Smaller banks	Average (%)	9.32	8.85	8.06	9.60	8.91	7.89	11.81	9.20
	Std Dev (%)	3.13	2.43	6.71	2.58	3.12	6.32	3.62	3.99
	Coeff. of Var.	33.57	27.49	83.29	26.89	35.07	80.14	30.63	45.30
	Minimum (%)	1.81	5.37	−7.55	5.90	1.07	−5.69	7.13	1.15
	Max (%)	15.74	13.24	17.96	17.41	15.97	15.63	18.32	16.32
RWA/TOTASS Bigger banks	Average (%)	36.27	37.53	40.62	41.81	40.91	37.10	34.51	38.39
	Std Dev (%)	21.44	23.58	17.80	13.53	13.32	15.65	11.34	16.66
	Coeff. of Var. (%)	59.11	62.85	43.81	32.35	32.56	42.19	32.86	43.67
	Minimum (%)	14.00	16.00	16.00	21.63	17.69	15.94	15.83	16.73
	Max (%)	60.81	67.96	63.31	67.66	57.93	66.19	54.72	62.65

RWA/TOTASS Smaller banks	Average (%)	64.75	61.30	62.07	68.79	71.67	63.93	57.11	64.23
	Std Dev (%)	18.51	18.00	12.85	15.97	22.46	16.68	14.49	17.00
	Coeff. of Var. (%)	28.60	29.37	20.70	23.22	31.34	26.09	25.37	26.39
	Minimum (%)	0.00	0.00	36.65	42.80	40.34	38.33	36.74	27.84
	Max (%)	87.90	79.98	81.70	111.12	125.14	89.62	83.19	94.09
LEVERAGE Bigger banks	Average (%)	4.23	4.19	5.43	4.84	4.96	4.74	4.89	4.75
	Std Dev (%)	1.87	1.96	1.84	1.73	1.92	1.67	1.70	1.81
	Coeff. of Var. (%)	44.04	46.85	33.98	35.68	38.82	35.29	34.69	38.48
	Minimum (%)	1.84	1.40	2.88	2.45	2.48	2.16	2.53	2.25
	Max (%)	7.75	8.50	9.03	8.20	7.48	7.77	7.50	8.03
LEVERAGE Smaller banks	Average (%)	6.62	5.83	4.75	6.51	6.15	4.74	6.50	5.87
	Std Dev (%)	2.80	2.02	3.93	1.85	2.22	4.12	1.83	2.68
	Coeff. of Var. (%)	42.25	34.63	82.70	28.48	36.13	86.85	28.12	45.66
	Minimum (%)	1.12	2.77	-4.12	3.52	0.83	-5.10	3.50	0.36
	Max (%)	13.49	10.51	9.76	10.57	9.32	11.17	10.40	10.74

Source: Authors' elaboration on Datastream data

ratio between RWA and total assets (64 % versus 38 %), presumably attributable to a lower use of internal models by smaller banks.

4 Findings

In Table 3 3SLS regression results are reported. CET1 and β are the jointly dependent variables.

We can observe that, in contrast to our hypotheses, CET1 has a positive and significant coefficient. This means that an increase of CET1 amplifies β as well as the equity return required by shareholders. This result is quite surprising so we need to take into account CET1 composition to explain why better capitalized banks are expected to offer higher equity returns.

CET1 is computed as the ratio between common equity and RWA. It can increase either because the bank augments its common equity or decreases its RWA. In Table 4 we report the correlation matrix among CET1, common equity, RWA and TOTAL ASSETS to find out whether the latter variables are positively or negatively correlated. We can observe that the correlation coefficient between common equity and RWA is 93 %, meaning that the two amounts in most cases move together.

Because correlation coefficient between total assets and RWA is 80 %, an increase in banks' total assets corresponds to higher RWA. However, we need to consider also the ratio between RWA and total assets that is on average 0.55, although it varies considerably with respect to bank size measured by total assets. As reported in Table 2, in bigger banks RWA are on average only 0.38 of total assets, whereas in smaller banks the same ratio is on average 0.64. Hence in bigger banks an increase of 100 in total assets corresponds only to an increase of only 38 in RWA. It is possible to attribute this finding to the extensive use of internal models to compute RWA in larger banks.

Table 3 3SLS regression results

Variable	Coefficient	T-statistic	Standard error	P-value
CET1	13.282	2.136	6.218	<0.00001***
LEVERAGE	−14.803	4.196	−3.528	0.0004***
RWA/TOTASS	1.297	0.141	9.210	<0.00001***
MKTBK	−0.059	0.055	−1.088	0.2764
ROA	0.013	0.002	5.834	<0.00001***
TOTLOANS/TOTASS	0.118	0.006	20.222	<0.00001***
RetEar/CE	0.099	0.046	2.149	0.0316**
CapIn/CE	0.004	0.004	0.982	0.3263

Jointly dependent variables are β and CET 1 ratio
Instruments for Eq. (1): ROA, TOTLOANS/TOTASS, RetEar/CE, CapIn/Ce
Instruments for Eq. (2): LEVERAGE, RWA/TOTASS, MKTBK
**significant at the 5 % level; ***significant at the 1 % level

Table 4 Correlation matrix among total assets, book value of common shareholders' equity, CET1 and risk weighted assets

	Total assets	Common equity	CET1	RWA
Total assets	1			
Common equity	87 %	1		
CET1	33 %	45 %	1	
RWA	80 %	93 %	30 %	1

At the end of our analysis we can claim that the positive relationship between CET1 and β is rather clear. This initially unexpected result can be explained by the positive correlation involving common equity and CET1 along with the simultaneous positive correlation obtained between RWA and CET1. At the same time common equity and RWA are positively correlated, and this in turn implies a co-movement in the increase or decrease of these two variables. This evidence can be justified by the less than proportional relationship between RWA and common equity. Consequently an increase of CET1 does not necessarily reflect an enhancement of bank resilience. The positive correlation with β shows that the market perceives this evidence and perhaps requires a direct correlation between common equity and total assets to ask for a lower return on equity. This is confirmed by the coefficient of variable LEVERAGE which is in fact negative and significant at the 1 % level.

Moreover, despite MKTBK ratio and CapIn/CE coefficients are not significant, the coefficients of variables ROA, TOTLOANS/TOTASS and RetEar/CE are positive and significant. It means that a higher value of CET1 ratio correspond to an increase of one of these three variables.

5 Conclusions

In this paper, we analysed the relationship between banks' riskiness of equity returns, proxied by CAPM β, and banks' capital adequacy, measured by the common equity tier 1 ratio and the leverage ratio introduced by Basel III to address the shortcomings that emerged in the financial crisis. The rationale behind the rise of the quantity and the quality of capital base is that less leveraged banks are more capable of absorbing shocks. The banking industry warned that because equity is the most expensive source of funding, banks will be forced to add this additional cost to loans, thus negatively affecting economic growth.

In this paper, we aimed to provide empirical evidence of the inverse relationship between expected market equity returns and banks' capital bases to demonstrate that better capitalized banks are perceived as less risky by the market and shareholders' required return on equity will be lower. We analysed 31 listed banks that were objects of the Asset Quality Review performed by ECB during the first part of 2014 in the 2007–2013 period.

Our results partly confirm our expectations. We took a proxy of Basel III CET1 ratio as capital adequacy measure and we found a positive relationship between CET1 and β. This means that, contrary to what we would have expected, the market requires a higher equity return for better capitalized banks according to Basel III regulation. However, at the same time, we found a negative relationship between β and LEVERAGE.

The positive relationship between CET1 and β shows that the market perceives that RWA do not fully reflect the riskiness of banks' assets because of the use of internal models, and instead relies on the ratio between common equity and total assets to require a lower return on equity. This provides strong evidence to support the introduction by Basel III of an un-risk-weighted leverage ratio for banks.

Industry allegations regarding the credit crunch, which would ensue following higher capital requirements, did not emerge in our analysis that on the contrary found an increase in total loans to customers in the period under observation.

Future research may further investigate the role played in risk weighted assets, looking at their composition and cross-country differences. Another possible extension could be the use of other measures of equity risk premia, such as CDS spreads or bond spreads.

References

Admati AR, De Marzo PM, Hellwig MF et al (2013) Fallacies, irrelevant facts, and myths in the discussion of capital regulation: why bank equity is not socially expensive. Stanford University Graduate School of Business Research Paper No. 13-7

Allen B, Chan KK, Milne A et al (2012) Basel III: is the cure worse than the disease? Int Rev Financ Anal 25:159–166

Basel Committee on Banking Supervision (2010) An assessment of the long-term economic impact of stronger capital and liquidity requirements. Bank for International Settlements, August

Basel Committee on Banking Supervision (2011) Basel III: a global regulatory framework for more resilient banks and banking systems

Berger AN, Bouwman CHS (2013) How does capital affect bank performance during financial crises? J Financ Econ 109:146–176

Brogi M (2011) Capital adequacy, corporate governance and organization in the support of the bank – firm relationship. In: Bracchi G, Masciandaro D, Masciandaro D (eds) XVI Rapporto sul sistema finanziario italiano "L'Europa e oltre. Banche e imprese nella nuova regolamentazione. Fondazione Rosselli, Edibank, Milan, pp 179–210.

Cosimano TF, Hakura D (2011) Bank behavior in response to Basel III: a cross-country analysis. IMF working papers no. 11/119

ECB (2011) Financial stability review. European Central Bank, Frankfurt, pp 125–131

Institute of International Finance (2010) Interim report on the cumulative impact on the global economy of proposed changes in banking regulatory framework

Kashyap A, Stein JC, Hanson S (2010) An analysis of the impact of substantially heightened in capital requirements on large financial institutions. Working paper

Mehran H, Morrison A, Shapiro J (2011) Corporate governance and banks: what have we learned from the financial crisis? Federal Reserve Bank of New York Staff Reports No. 502

Miles D, Yang J, Marcheggiano G (2013) Optimal bank capital. Econ J 123.567:1–37.

Modigliani F, Miller MH (1958) The cost of capital, corporation finance and the theory of investment. Am Econ Rev 48:261–297

Slovin MB, Sushka ME, Polonchek JA (1999) An analysis of contagion and competitive effects at commercial banks. J Financ Econ 54:197–225

Zellner A, Theil H (1962) Three-stage least squares: simultaneous estimation of simultaneous equations. Econometrica 30(1):54–78

Bank Credit Access and Gender Discrimination: Some Stylized Facts

Emma Galli and Stefania P.S. Rossi

Abstract Based on a broad body of literature that investigates the determinants of gender discrimination in the credit market, we provide some descriptive evidence on women's access to credit by employing a set of financial viability and socio-economic data for a sample of 11 European countries after the global financial crisis (2009–2013). From our preliminary analysis it emerges that, on the demand side, female firms apply for bank loans less than male firms, and one of the relevant determinants for their decision not to apply is the fear of rejection. On the supply side, when applying, female firms face a higher rate of rejection or receive less bank financing than male firms. No general patterns seem to emerge when crossing micro and macro data, even though at the country level, we detect some correspondence between banking system characteristics, socio-institutional indicators and gender differences in access to formal credit.

1 Introduction

The role of women entrepreneurs in the social and economic development of industrialized and developing countries has become widely recognized in the literature. Easy access to a broad range of financial services, including credit by women entrepreneurs, can be a decisive factor in the survival of their businesses, a reality that also holds true for the small- and medium-size enterprises. In this respect, two critical issues are (1) whether there is gender discrimination and (2) how the structure of the market, as well as the social and institutional context, affects women's access to credit. Gender discrimination in business has been examined from different perspectives.[1] In a seminal work, Becker (1957) shows that there are three ways to discriminate in formal credit markets: (1) by applying

---

[1] See Aspray and Cohoon (2007) and Cesaroni (2010) for exhaustive literature reviews.

E. Galli
Department of Social and Economic Sciences, Sapienza University of Rome, Rome, Italy
e-mail: emma.galli@uniroma1.it

S.P.S. Rossi (✉)
Department of Economics and Business, University of Cagliari, Cagliari, Italy
e-mail: stefania.rossi@unica.it

© Springer International Publishing Switzerland 2016   111
S.P.S. Rossi, R. Malavasi (eds.), *Financial Crisis, Bank Behaviour and Credit Crunch*, Contributions to Economics, DOI 10.1007/978-3-319-17413-6_8

higher interest rates on loans requested by female firms, (2) by imposing tighter contractual conditions on female firms than on male firms and (3) by requiring female entrepreneurs to demonstrate higher credit worthiness than male counterparts when granting loans. Since then, a growing theoretical and empirical literature has aimed to explain gender differences when accessing credit as due either to demand side and/or to supply side factors. More recently, another strand of literature analysed the effects of social capital on the financial access granted to female and male firms. The issue of credit access in Europe is considered crucial, as demonstrated by a recent initiative of the European Central Bank, which, beginning in the first half of 2009, has conducted a 6-month survey of small- and medium-size enterprises (SMEs) in the Euro area (SAFE survey) regarding their access to finances. The survey asks firms to provide information on several financial-related issues—growth and profitability, internal/external source of financing, credit applications and outcomes, credit availability and conditions—that are then stratified by gender. This unique data set for Europe has been extensively used by Stefani and Vacca (2013) to empirically investigate whether gender affects small firms' financial structure and access to credit in the four largest European countries—Germany, France, Italy and Spain. Their findings indicate that female firms have difficulty accessing bank finance. On the demand side, female firms apply for bank loans less frequently as they anticipate rejection, while on the supply side, they experience a higher rejection rate. However, these patterns seem to be largely explained by the characteristics of female firms, such as business size, age and sector of activity rather than by gender-discrimination.

In our paper, we focus on bank loan access granted to female and male firms using the same dataset as Stefani and Vacca (2013), but for a larger sample—11 European countries that belong to different macro-regions—and for a longer interval—2009 to 2013—to investigate whether a significant degree of gender discrimination emerges. We then complement the credit viability information provided by the survey with data on the characteristics of the banking system and the quality and social capital of the institutions—both of which may play a role in affecting access to credit.

The paper is organized as follows. In Sect. 2, we review two different strands of literature, one which focuses on the determinants of gender discrimination in formal credit access from the demand and/or supply side and the other which addresses the effects of social capital on financial access of female and male firms. In Sect. 3, we present some stylized facts about bank access stratified by gender, together with data about major aspects of the banking system and the social context at the country level. In Sect. 4, we present our conclusions and identify further research avenues.

2   Literature Review

Several studies have emphasized the existence of gender differences in the financial structure of enterprises. Generally, women are more likely to use personal funds, earnings from the business, home equity loans, credit cards, and family loans to finance their businesses rather than go into debt or sell shares (see, among others, Treichel-Zimmerman and Scott 2006; Coleman and Robb 2009). As noted by Cesaroni (2010), women-led enterprises are financially weaker and face greater difficulties than male firms face in accessing credit.

   The economic literature is divided in explaining women's reasons for self-financing and provides mixed evidence with respect to different geographical areas. Part of the literature attributes observed gender-based differences in interest paid, collateral required and credit made available to demand-driven factors, such as differences in risk-aversion and in reliability between men and women. Robust evidence based on both experimental and real data suggests that women generally tend to be more risk-averse and less self-confident than men, especially in the areas of financial investments and that women exhibit a lower propensity toward indebtedness (see, among others, Barber and Odean 2001; Croson and Gneezy 2009). Some studies note that in many cases, gender discrimination is only a perception of female entrepreneurs; in other words, it is the perception that women face more challenges to access bank credit, which may itself explain their lower propensity to use external sources of credit or their tendency to apply for loans in smaller amounts (Coleman 2000; Cole and Mehran 2011). Moreover, women's access to credit could be affected by their choices about firm characteristics, sector of operation, lower education, business management experience, inability or resistance to provide collateral or personal guarantees and smaller firm size (Coleman 2002). A few more recent papers have focused on the lender's gender to investigate whether perceptions of borrowers' creditworthiness significantly differ between male and female loan officers (Wilson et al. 2007) or whether the average default rates on loans handled by female officers are statistically lower (Beck et al. 2009). Another branch of literature focuses on the supply side to verify whether female entrepreneurs face lower credit availability and/or worse cost conditions. While some studies find that female firms have greater difficulties than male firms in obtaining bank loans (Calcagnini and Lenti 2008; Bellucci et al. 2010), others exclude gender discrimination after controlling for credit history, assets, sales, and years in business (Cavalluzzo et al. 2002; Blanchflower et al. 2003; Muravyev et al. 2009).

   Recently, Stefani and Vacca (2013) aver that in the major Euro-area countries, female firms have difficulty accessing bank finance from both the demand side and the supply side, but they find that these patterns are largely explained by the characteristics of female firms, such as business size, age and sector of activity rather than by gender-discrimination. At the country level, weak evidence of gender discrimination appears in the supply of bank loans in Germany, Italy and Spain, while some demand obstacles are evident in France.

From the supply side perspective, a few papers focus on the role that social capital[2] plays in the credit market, specifically on women's access to credit. The presence of social capital in the economy may increase the level of trust and reduce the asymmetric information that characterizes the credit contract, thus facilitating easier access to bank loans (see, among others, Guiso et al. 2004, 2013). This is because the stable functioning of the credit market is based on credibility. Therefore, on the debtor side, social capital affects individual behaviour, thus causing the firm to be less inclined to engage in opportunities that are contrary to moral and social rules. On the creditor side, however, social capital facilitates the collection of soft information, which in turn reduces adverse selection and moral hazard decisions. Moreover, by stimulating peer monitoring and other social collateral, social capital more efficiently allocates resources in the credit market, thereby reducing transaction costs and costs for credit, especially for small firms, and diminishing the use of real guarantees for the mortgage (see, for example, Moro and Fink 2013; Mistrulli and Vacca 2014). In areas where social capital is extremely high, the access to bank credit is easier for people and firms that generally use informal financing channels, such as friends and families (Guiso et al. 2004), and the ability to reimburse the mortgage is higher (Guiso et al. 2013). By controlling for the financial viability before and after an unexpected shock, e.g., the 2008 financial crisis, Mistrulli and Vacca (2014) and Lozzi and Mistrulli (2014) show that social capital, together with business networking, played an important role in increasing thrust and reducing asymmetric information. Indeed, in areas characterized by high social capital, the negative effect of the 2008 financial crisis on credit access was significantly less pronounced. Finally, other studies have found that the role of cooperative banks in credit markets is more relevant and that the quality of the credit supply is greater where social capital is higher, given that the latter positively affects cooperation in credit markets by reducing the free-ride phenomenon (Albertazzi and Marchetti 2010; Catturani et al. 2014).

More specifically, Carter et al. (2003) find that social capital does not increase the likelihood of using external sources of financing even though the nature of social capital affects women's funding behaviour. Alesina et al. (2013) have investigated whether the structure of the bank industry, the degree of competition and the presence of small banks, for which fiduciary and personal relationships with the clients matter, benefit women. They find that women pay higher interest rates within any structure of the banking industry. To further investigate the role of trust and risk, Alesina et al. (2013) consider social capital across different provinces and find that interest rates are lower where social capital is higher. However, when they examine the interaction of the measures of social capital and the gender of the

---

[2] Social capital can be defined as the advantages and opportunities that people obtain through membership to certain communities or resources of individuals that emerge through social ties (for a wide discussion of the different dimensions of social capital see Coleman 1994 and, more recently, De Blasio et al. 2012).

borrower, they find that women benefit from the trust effect of higher social capital less so than men.

3   The Access to Credit by Male and Female Small-Medium Size Firms: Data Description and Stylized Facts

3.1   Financial Viability Information

To describe the access to credit by female and male small- and medium-size firms and to provide information about sources of financing, terms and conditions, applications and results of bank loans, stratified by gender, we use data from the SAFE Survey, which examines access to finance of small- and medium-size enterprises (SMEs) in the Euro area. The survey, which is now conducted by the European Central Bank every 6 months in a large number of European countries, was initially administered in the first half of 2009. We include in our sample countries that belong to different macro-regions—Italy, Greece, Portugal and Spain (southern Europe); Austria, Belgium, France, Germany and the Netherlands (western Europe); and Ireland and Finland (northern Europe).[3] Different waves of the ECB survey from the first half of 2009 to the first half of 2013 are available for these countries.[4]

From this survey, it emerges that, overall, female firms resort to bank loans less frequently than their male counterparts—30 % and 37 %, respectively. This pattern is further confirmed by information regarding the use of other sources of finance as approximately 30 % of male firms use other channels, including internal funds, for finance, while 25 % of female firms seek funds from other sources.

Moreover, when we examine the terms and conditions of loan financing (Table 1), a higher percentage of female firms compared to male firms report that the interest rate and the available amount of credit remained unchanged over the period of the survey—34.4 % versus 30.9 % and 60.1 % versus 57.7 %, respectively. On the other hand, the opposite is reported for non-interest costs of finance—50.9 % for male firms versus 52.7 % for female firms. However, a higher percentage of male firms report a worsening of the terms and conditions of bank financing following the financial crisis, thus suggesting that credit restraints that follow a global financial crisis affect men more so than women, at least from the male perspective. It is further noted that slightly significant gender differences emerge for the collateral requirements and the available maturity of the loan.

---

[3] For the Central-Eastern European countries, the ECB SAFE data are available only for Slovenia and Slovakia, but on two waves.

[4] The total number of interviewed firms is 61,276.

Table 1 Terms and conditions of bank financing, overall sample

	Increased by bank (%)			Unchanged (%)			Decreased by bank (%)		
	Male	Female	t-stat	Male	Female	t-stat	Male	Female	t-stat
Level of interest rate	49.00	46.98	***	30.95	34.40	***	16.62	13.93	***
Cost of financing other than interest rate	50.89	52.69	***	40.59	37.74	***	4.15	3.34	**
Available size of loan or credit line	18.07	16.35	***	57.72	60.14	***	20.11	18.05	***
Available maturity of the loan	8.04	7.11	***	76.23	75.47	**	9.54	8.76	**
Collateral requirements	36.91	36.77	*	55.62	54.62	**	3.06	2.52	**
Other, e.g., loan covenants	32.00	31.06	**	56.89	55.97	**	2.41	2.56	*

Source: Our elaborations are based on data from the ECB SAFE survey, waves from the first half of 2009 to the first half of 2013. Differences are statistically significant at the 1 % (***), 5 % (**) and 10 % (*) levels

We then focus on the demand and supply of bank credit of small-medium firms analysing the applications for bank loans and their outcomes. Information on the financial viability is portrayed in Fig. 1, where the applications for bank loans are disjointed from the results. With respect to the demand side, we notice that (a) female firms seem to apply for bank loans less frequently than male firms (respectively, 22 % and 27 %); (b) the percentage of female firms that do not apply due to fear of rejection (respectively, approximately 8 % and 6 %) or for other reasons (respectively, approximately 24 % and 21 %) is different from that of male firms. From the supply side, data on outcomes of applications indicate that the rate of rejection for female firms is higher than that for male firms (respectively, 14 % and 11 %). Furthermore, the percentage of female firms receiving the full amount requested, approximately 62 %, or the partial amount requested, approximately 8 %, is lower than that of male firms, which is approximately 63 % and 9 %, respectively. Overall, female firms apply for bank loans less often than male firms because they are afraid of being rejected. This fear is legitimized in that when female firms do apply, they face a higher rate of rejection or receive less bank financing than do male firms.

To capture the demand side of the bank loans, in Fig. 2, we report the self-restraint of female firms in bank loan applications as measured by the frequency percent of not applying due to fear of rejection and stratified by country. We find a common pattern across countries, with the exception of Greece and Portugal, that shows that female firms apply significantly less often than male firms because the former fear that their applications will be rejected. The difference in self-restraint due to fear of rejection between female and male firms is more pronounced in France, Germany, Ireland, Italy, the Netherlands and Spain. Finland, Greece and

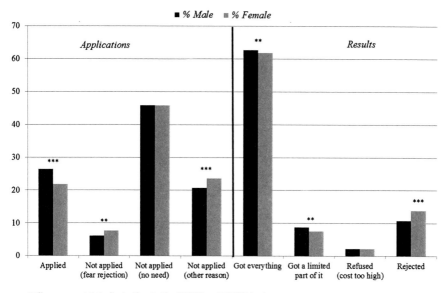

Differences are statistically significant at the 1% (***) and 5% (**) levels.

Source: Our elaborations are based on data from the ECB SAFE survey, waves from the first half of 2009 to the first half of 2013.

Fig. 1 Bank loan applications and results, overall sample (percentage frequencies)

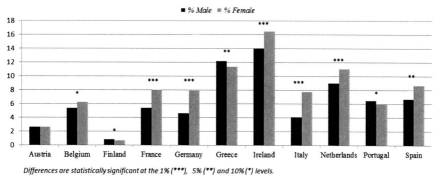

Differences are statistically significant at the 1% (***), 5% (**) and 10% (*) levels.

Source: Our elaborations are based on data from the ECB SAFE survey, waves from the first half of 2009 to the first half of 2013.

Fig. 2 Bank loans: Did not apply due to fear of rejection, by country (percentage frequencies)

Portugal are the only countries where the gender gap regarding access to credit is slightly inverted, while in Austria, the difference is statistically not significant.

On the supply side, in Fig. 3, we report the results of applications, stratified by country. Data show that rejection rates for female firms are significantly higher than those for male firms in most countries, particularly France, Germany, Italy and the Netherlands. Greece and Ireland are the only countries where the opposite is evidenced. This descriptive analysis suggests that at the country level, different degrees of gender restraint in credit access exist.

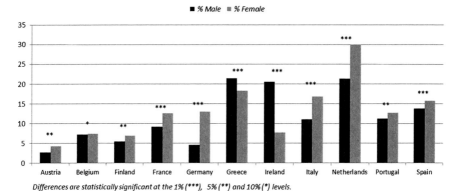

Differences are statistically significant at the 1% (***), 5% (**) and 10% (*) levels.

Source: Our elaborations are based on data from the ECB SAFE survey, waves from the first half of 2009 to the first half of 2013.

Fig. 3 Bank loan rejections, by country (percentage frequencies)

3.2 *Banking System, Social Capital and Quality of Institutions Features*

From the descriptive analysis of the applications for bank loans and the results, significant differences emerge for the 2009 to 2013 period. Stefani and Vacca (2013), who use the same survey for France, Germany, Italy and Spain for the years 2009 to 2011, argue that the existing gap in credit access is due primarily to specific characteristics of the female firms rather than the result of gender discrimination. To further examine this argument, we introduce an additional set of variables that may play a role in credit demand and supply. First, we consider certain characteristics of the banking systems, such as the degree of concentration, the percentage of commercial and cooperative banks and the ratio of non-performing loans to total gross loans. Greater competition in credit supply generally guarantees greater viability and more favourable conditions and therefore, ceteris paribus, female firms may take advantage of this (Alesina et al. 2013). Data on non-performing loans are a proxy of bank credit risk as extant literature has noted their relevance in affecting the pro-cyclic behaviours of banks with respect to lending (see, among others, Bouvatier and Lepetit 2008). According to the theory of discrimination, female firms may be perceived as riskier borrowers; therefore, ceteris paribus, they would be more heavily penalized when accessing formal credit during the slowdown of the economic cycle when compared to male firms. We also consider the percentage of cooperative and commercial banks. In this regard, the literature (Albertazzi and Marchetti 2010; Catturani et al. 2014) has found that cooperative banks increase credit quantity and quality in areas characterised by higher social capital. Therefore, where both the percentage of cooperative banks and the degree of social capital are higher, female firms may have easier access to credit.

Second, we select some measures of social capital and quality of the institutional environment that may affect the differences in credit access between female and male firms. As a proxy of social capital, we use the global gender gap, which assesses the magnitude of gender-based disparities in four areas—political empowerment, educational attainment, economic participation and opportunity, and health and life expectancy. To capture the degree of effectiveness of the legal system and the enforcement of the contract laws in practice, we use the strength of legal rights and women's economic rights (La Porta et al. 1997). The data, stratified by countries, are reported in Table 2.

First, the European countries appear quite diversified with respect to banking systems and socio-institutional features. Countries such as Belgium, Finland, Greece, Ireland, the Netherlands, Portugal and Spain show a high degree of concentration, while Germany and Italy are characterized by a more competitive banking system. With respect to non-performing loans over total loans, Greece, Italy, Portugal and Spain are among the poorest performing countries, with Ireland being the worst. The percentage of cooperative banks in the credit market is high only in Germany and Italy, while it is very low in Finland, Greece, the Netherlands and Portugal. Moreover, Belgium, Finland, Greece, the Netherlands and Portugal are characterized by a low percentage of cooperative banks and a high concentration of banks in the banking system. Conversely, Germany and Italy are noted to have a low level of concentration, but a high presence of cooperative banks.

The global gender gap index shows that Italy, Greece and Portugal are the worst performing countries, while Finland, Germany, Ireland and the Netherlands are among the best. This picture is generally confirmed with respect to the strength of the legal rights and the women's economic rights.

Albeit our investigation remains only descriptive and does not allow to infer any correlation among the variables of interest, crossing financial micro data with the banking and social context data results in some interesting features emerging at the country level.

In some countries, high social capital and good enforcement of legal rights coexist with a low gender difference in bank loan applications and rejections (Austria and Finland). In Italy and Spain, it is determined that low socio-institutional indicators correspond with significant differences between male and female firms with respect to applications and rejections.

Surprisingly, such a correspondence is not detected in Germany or the Netherlands, where a high gender difference in bank loan applications and rejections coexist with a high quality socio-institutional environment.

Upon examining the banking systems indicators in Austria, Finland and the Netherlands, a low level of applications and rejections corresponds with a low level of credit bank risk. It is further noted that France, Ireland, Italy and Spain are consistently characterized by high gender differences in bank loan applications and rejections and in high non-performing loans. Germany exhibits a significant gender gap with respect to access to credit even in the presence of relatively low credit risk. No general patterns are identified between concentration degree and cooperative percentage, on the one hand, and gender differences in credit access, on the other.

Table 2 Banking system, social capital and quality of institutions indicators, by country (2009–2013)

Country	Concentration (%)	Commercial banks (%)	Cooperative banks (%)	Bank nonperforming loans to total gross loans	Global Gender Gap index	Legal rights index	Women's economic rights index
Austria	53.07	23.2	28.6	2.7	0.722	7	2
Belgium	71.83	39.2	8.0	3.4	0.751	6	2
Finland	87.52	49.1	3.5	0.6	0.835	8	3
France	49.82	32.7	16.9	4.1	0.709	7	3
Germany	37.65	7.3	52.0	3.0	0.756	7	3
Greece	87.22	67.4	2.3	17.1	0.680	4	2
Ireland	68.12	26.9	–	17.5	0.777	9	3
Italy	47.88	15.7	63.2	12.0	0.680	3	2
Netherlands	74.65	36.4	1.2	3.0	0.753	5.4	3
Portugal	72.71	54.6	2.6	7.6	0.709	3	2
Spain	55.41	22.5	33.2	6.1	0.740	6	2

Sources: The concentration index of the banking system (calculated as the ratio of total assets of the largest five banks to the total assets of the banking industry in each country), the percentage of commercial banks over total banks, and the percentage of cooperative banks over total banks are our elaborations on data from Bankscope. Data on bank nonperforming loans to total gross loans (%) are obtained from the World Bank. The global gender gap index is retrieved from the World Economic Forum and ranges from 0 (inequality) to 1 (equality). The index of the strength of legal rights is obtained from the World Bank and ranges from 0 (weak) to 10 (strong). The index of women's economic rights is retrieved from the Quality of Institutions dataset, University of Goteborg, and ranges from 0 (no economic rights) to 3 (all or nearly all of women's economic rights are guaranteed by law and the government fully and vigorously enforces these laws in practice). We report the average values calculated for the period 2009 to 2013

4 Conclusions

Following the global financial crisis, liquidity shortage and heavy restrictions worsened the conditions of the credit market. Under such circumstances, access to formal credit by female small- and medium-size firms is crucial to the survival of the businesses. In this paper, we review two different strands of literature on the issue, one which focuses on the determinants of gender discrimination in credit access from the demand and/or supply side, and the other, which addresses the effects of social capital on financial access of female and male firms. Based on the literature, we present descriptive evidence on bank loan access that is stratified by gender using the ECB SAFE survey for a sample of 11 European countries during the period 2009–2013.

The survey indicates that female firms have some difficulty in accessing bank finance. Overall, female firms apply for bank loans less frequently than their male counterparts, and one of the relevant determinants for this is the fear of rejection experienced by female firms. When applying, female firms face a higher rate of rejection or receive less bank financing than male firms. Furthermore, slightly significant gender differences also emerge when we examine the perceived changes in terms and conditions of loan financing. To better understand this issue, we introduce data regarding the characteristics of the banking systems and the socio-institutional context, which the empirical literature on gender discrimination in Europe has not, thus far, fully considered. Our preliminary analysis shows that, although no overall general patterns seem to emerge, at the country level we detect some correspondence among banking system characteristics, socio-institutional indicators and gender differences in formal credit access.

Further investigation on this issue is warranted. A possible research direction would be the integration of the set of factors suggested herein with other relevant macro (GDP, short- and long-term interest rates) and micro (business size, age and sector of activity, etc.) variables, to assess through an empirical framework the determinants of the existing gender differences in credit access in Europe.

Acknowledgments We thank the ECB for the use of data from the ECB SAFE Survey on access to finance of small- and medium-size enterprises (SMEs) in the Euro area. Additionally, we thank Sara Colella for assistance with the data. Stefania P. S. Rossi gratefully acknowledges research grants from the Autonomous Region of Sardinia, *Legge Regionale 2007, N. 7* [Grant Number CRP-59890, year 2012].

References

Albertazzi U, Marchetti DJ (2010) Credit supply, flight to quality and evergreening: an analysis of bank-firm relationships after Lehman. Bank of Italy, Temi di Discussione (Working Paper) No. 756. Available via SSRN. http://ssrn.com/abstract=1670563 or http://dx.doi.org/10.2139/ssrn.1670563

Alesina A, Lotti F, Mistrulli PE (2013) Do women pay more for credit? Evidence from Italy. J Eur Econ Assoc 11(1):45–66

Aspray W, Cohoon J (2007) Access to financial capital: a review of research literature on women's entrepreneurship. Information Technology Field, National Center for Women and Information Technology, Entrepreneurial Report Series 3

Barber BM, Odean T (2001) Boys will be boys: gender, overconfidence, and common stock investment. Q J Econ 116:261–292

Beck T, Behr P, Güttler A (2009) Are women better loan officers? Tilburg University. http://siteresources.worldbank.org/INTFR/Resources/Becketal022409.pdf

Becker G (1957) The economics of discrimination. University of Chicago Press, Chicago, IL

Bellucci A, Borisov A, Zazzaro A (2010) Does gender matter in bank-firm relationships? Evidence from small business lending. J Bank Fin 34(12):2968–2984

Blanchflower DG, Levine PB, Zimmerman DJ (2003) Discrimination in the small-business credit market. Rev Econ Stat 85(4):930–943

Bouvatier V, Lepetit L (2008) Banks' procyclical behavior: does provisioning matter? J Int Fin Mark Inst Money 18:513–528

Calcagnini G, Lenti E (2008) L'accesso al credito per l'imprenditoria femminile. In: Zazzaro A (ed) I vincoli finanziari alla crescita delle imprese. Carocci, Roma

Carter N, Brush C, Greene P et al (2003) Women entrepreneurs who break through to equity financing: the influence of human, social and financial capital. Venture Capital 5(1):1–28

Catturani I, Kalmi P, Stefani ML (2014) Social capital and the credit cooperative banks. Bank of Italy, Mimeo

Cavalluzzo KS, Cavalluzzo LC, Wolken JD (2002) Competition, small business financing, and discrimination: evidence from a new survey. J Bus 75(4):641–679

Cesaroni F (2010) Donne imprenditrici e banche. Le ragioni di un rapporto difficile. In: Calcagnini G, Favaretto I (eds) L'economia della piccola impresa. Franco Angeli, Milan

Cole RA, Mehran H (2011) Gender and the availability of credit to privately held firms: evidence from the surveys of small business finances (March 30, 2011). FRB of New York, Staff Report No. 383. Available via SSRN. http://ssrn.com/abstract=1799649 or http://dx.doi.org/10.2139/ssrn.1799649

Coleman JS (1994) Foundations of social theory. Harvard University Press, Cambridge, MA

Coleman S (2000) Access to capital and terms of credit: a comparison of men and women-owned businesses. J Small Bus Manage 38:37–52

Coleman S (2002) Constraints faced by women small business owners: evidence from the data. J Dev Entrep 7(2):151–174

Coleman S, Robb A (2009) A comparison of new firm financing by gender: evidence from the Kaufman Firm survey data. Small Bus Econ 33:397–411

Croson R, Gneezy U (2009) Gender differences in preferences. J Econ Lit 47:448–474

De Blasio G, Scalise D, Sestito P (2012) Universalism vs. Particularism: a round trip from economics to sociology. Bank of Italy, Questioni di Economia e Finanza No. 212

ECB Survey on the access to finance of enterprises (SAFE). https://www.ecb.europa.eu/stats/money/surveys/sme/html/index.en.html

Guiso L, Sapienza P, Zingales L (2004) The role of social capital in financial development. Am Econ Rev 94(3):526–556

Guiso L, Sapienza P, Zingales L (2013) The determinants of attitudes toward strategic default on mortgages. J Fin 68(4):1473–1515

La Porta R, Lopez De-Silanes F, Shleifer A et al (1997) Legal determinants of external finance. J Fin 7(3):1131–1150

Lozzi M, Mistrulli PE (2014) Loan applications and social capital in the great recession. Bank of Italy, Mimeo

Mistrulli PE, Vacca V (2014) Social capital and the cost of credit in a crisis. Bank of Italy, Mimeo

Moro A, Fink M (2013) Loan managers' trust and credit access for SMEs. J Bank Fin 37:927–36

Muravyev A, Talavera O, Shäfer D (2009) Entrepreneurs' gender and financial constraints: evidence from international data. J Comp Econ 37(2):270–286

Quality of Governance standard dataset, University of Goteborg. http://www.qog.pol.gu.se/data/datadownloads/qogstandarddata/

Stefani ML, Vacca V (2013) Credit access for female firms: evidence from a survey on European SMEs. Bank of Italy, Occasional paper No. 176

Treichel-Zimmerman M, Scott JA (2006) Women-owned businesses and access to bank credit: evidence from three surveys since 1987. Venture Capital 8(1):51–67

Wilson F, Carter S, Tagg S et al (2007) Bank loan officers' perceptions of business owners: the role of gender. Br J Manage 18:154–171

World Economic Forum (Various years) The global gender gap report. World Economic Forum, Cologny

When Do Individual Bank Executives Matter for Bank Performance?

Duc Duy Nguyen, Jens Hagendorff, and Arman Eshraghi

Abstract This chapter seeks to understand how the characteristics of executive directors affect the market performance of US banks. To explore the expected performance effects linked to executive characteristics, we measure changes in the market valuation of banks linked to announcements of executive appointments. We show that age, education and the prior work experience of executives create shareholder wealth while gender is not linked to measureable value effects. Our results are robust to the treatment of selection bias. By illustrating the wealth effects linked to executive appointments, our study contributes to the current debate on whether and how individual executives matter for firm performance and behaviour. The findings also shed light on the value of human capital in the banking industry. This chapter offers important insights to policymakers charged with ensuring the competency of executives in banking. Our findings advocate policies that mandate banks to appoint highly qualified executives with relevant banking experience.

1 Introduction

There is a considerable debate amongst the public, policymakers and academics as to whether individual executives matter for firm performance and behaviour. A growing body of research demonstrates that executive directors are a heterogeneous group and suggests that executive behaviour is governed by more than economic trade-offs. Studies have shown that executives affect the performance of firms (e.g. Bennedsen et al. 2008; Custodio and Metzger 2013; Kaplan et al. 2012) and their policy choices (e.g. Bertrand and Schoar 2003; Malmendier et al. 2011). Other studies argue that individual executives have little impact on firm performance and behaviour because seemingly unique executive-specific 'styles' may in fact be shaped by the board of directors and that new executives are appointed with desired characteristics to take a firm in the direction determined by the board (Fee et al. 2013). This chapter sheds new light on whether and how executives matter

D.D. Nguyen • J. Hagendorff (✉) • A. Eshraghi
University of Edinburgh – Business School, Edinburgh, UK
e-mail: D.Nguyen@sms.ed.ac.uk; Jens.Hagendorff@ed.ac.uk; Arman.Eshraghi@ed.ac.uk

© Springer International Publishing Switzerland 2016
S.P.S. Rossi, R. Malavasi (eds.), *Financial Crisis, Bank Behaviour and Credit Crunch*, Contributions to Economics, DOI 10.1007/978-3-319-17413-6_9

125

by demonstrating that variations in observable demographic and experience characteristics of executives have market valuation effects.

With existing work mostly limited to non-financial firms, there is an inherent lack of analysis concerning the banking sector. Since banks are complex institutions and may require employees with specialised skills (Philippon and Reshef 2012), selecting the right executives could give banks a significant competitive edge as well as contribute to the growth of the economy. Recently, the banking sector has received much criticism for its contribution to the financial crisis that started in 2007. Many blame incompetent banking executives for engaging in activities that endangered the safety and soundness of the financial system and gave rise to unprecedented government support of the banking sector. By the same token, certain bank executives have been credited with steering their organisations successfully through the financial crisis.[1]

In this chapter, we focus on executive directors[2] who are responsible for the day-to-day running of the bank. Since executive directors have substantial discretion over their decisions, their individual characteristics such as prior experience could make an important difference to bank outcomes (e.g. Landier et al. 2013). We argue that executive characteristics such as age, education, and employment history are performance relevant. In our analysis, we examine whether the stock market reaction to the appointment of a new executive is driven by the characteristics of the appointee. Focusing on the appointment of a new executive offers an appropriate setting in which to examine the value of characteristics that the appointee brings to the hiring bank. In an efficient capital market, the market reaction is indicative of the anticipated future performance conditional on relevant information (Warner et al. 1988). Thus, market returns will be higher when an appointee with desirable characteristics is hired because investors believe that this appointee will improve performance.

Our sample consists of 252 executive appointment announcements by 145 US banks. Exploring this dataset, we examine whether the stock market reaction to the appointment announcement is affected by seven characteristics of the appointee: (1) age, (2) gender, (3) the number of prior executive directorships, (4) the number of current non-executive directorships (busyness), (5) the number of non-banking industries (in which the appointee has experience), (6) an Ivy League education and (7) an MBA degree.

Our key findings are as follows. First, announcement returns following appointments are statistically positive, suggesting that the addition of top managers, on average, is valuable for US banks. Second, we examine whether the market reaction to executive appointments is influenced by characteristics of the executive. Overall,

---

[1] For example, John Stumpf from Wells Fargo and Jamie Dimon from JPMorgan are often cited as successful bank executives. See 'Jamie Dimon, the last King of Wall Street', Financial Times, 17 May 2013.

[2] We define top executives as CEO, CFO, COO, CRO, CIO, Chairman, President, Division CEO, Division President, Division Chairman, Head of Division, Regional CEO, Regional President, and Regional Chairman.

our findings suggest that the age, education and prior experience of the executives create shareholder wealth in the US banking sector. In contrast, gender, non-banking experience or an MBA degree do not lead to any measurable market returns. In addition, the appointment of executives who hold non-executive directorships with outside firm at the time of the appointment results in negative returns, consistent with the hypothesis that busy executives have less attention to focus on an individual bank (Fich and Shivdasani 2006).

Overall, this chapter makes several significant contributions to the literature. First, we contribute to a growing literature that uses manager fixed effects to address the question of how important executive 'styles' are to various corporate outcomes (Bertrand and Schoar 2003; Graham et al. 2012). It is empirically challenging to quantify the effects of individual executives on firm performance. Fee et al. (2013) argue that executive turnover, which forms the empirical basis to work out executive styles, may frequently be endogenous (e.g. when they follow a period of underperformance). When focusing on 'exogenous' CEO replacements brought about by CEO retirements and deaths, the authors do not find evidence of manager fixed effects in corporate policy choices. This raises the question whether or not the results of the manager styles literature are biased and that whether, more broadly, executives matter for corporate outcomes.

Our work offers an alternative route to showing that executives indeed matter. Unlike Fee et al. (2013) we do not focus on executive 'styles', but on demographic and experience variables of executives. We show that the majority of executive appointments are linked to value gains around the announcement date. By analysing the variation in short-term returns following executive appointments, we can exclude events other than the appointment causing the observed effect. We thus interpret our results as evidence demonstrating that it matters who bank executives are in a similar way that much of the executive styles literature demonstrates.

Second, we provide direct empirical evidence on the value of top executive characteristics in the US banking sector. We are unaware of any published research that looks at the value of top executives in the banking sector. Since the banking sector is relatively opaque, complex and skill-intensive (Philippon and Reshef 2012), we contribute towards uncovering the 'black box' of desirable characteristics top corporate leaders should possess to affect performance in the banking sector. In addition, our findings add to the current debate on the value of generalist versus specialist managerial experience in banking. While many studies recognise the growing importance of general managerial experience (Custodio et al. 2013), we show that cross-industry experience is not value-relevant to US bank shareholders.

This chapter proceeds as follows. The next section surveys major theoretical and empirical evidence and develops our primary hypotheses, followed by a section describing our sample and empirical strategy. We then present our empirical results and conclude the chapter.

2   Literature Review

2.1   *Theoretical Background*

Much research in both non-financial and financial firms has devoted considerable attention to studying the board of directors (e.g. Adams and Mehran 2012; Coles et al. 2008). However, relatively little attention has been paid to top executives who are responsible for managing the bank on a daily basis. There remains considerable uncertainty around whether or not individual executives matter for corporate outcomes. Thus, neoclassical economics assumes that individuals are homogeneous and different executives are perfect substitutes for each other. Agency theory, while acknowledging that executives may pursue different courses of action to advance their personal interests, sees executive actions shaped by the quality of corporate governance in the organisation.

In contrast, the management literature and Hambrick and Mason's (1984) upper echelons theory suggests that individual characteristics matter. Upper echelons theory argues that executives' idiosyncratic experiences affect their interpretations of strategic decision-making situations and, in turn, affect their strategic choices and performance levels. Upper echelons theory predicts individual differences among executives will be most salient when the decision-making situations are complex and ambiguous as would be the case for banking organisations.

To summarise, existing theories make contradicting predictions regarding whether executives matter for firm outcomes. To shed light on this issue, we use variations in observable demographic and experience characteristics of executives to answer two key empirical questions: (1) *whether* executives matter and (2) *how* executives matter.

2.2   *Executive Characteristics and Bank Performance*

In this section, we explain how demographic and experience characteristics of executives affect the announcement returns.

2.2.1   Age

Compared to younger appointees, older ones have more experience in making decisions when they face complex and ambiguous tasks (Worthy et al. 2011). Furthermore, older appointees face less career uncertainty and have fewer incentives to improve their job security. Thus, they are less likely to engage in value-destroying excessively risky activities. Hence, older appointees could create wealth for bank shareholders.

However, younger appointees have more energy and drive (Roberts and Rosenberg 2006). This could translate into other characteristics such as enthusiasm, decisiveness and ambition. In addition, compared to older appointees, younger ones have more ideas, are quicker in learning new technologies (Grund and Westergaard-Nielsen 2008) and are able to make innovative decisions. With these qualities, younger appointees may create shareholder wealth.

2.2.2 Gender

Female appointees possess unique skills, experience and networks, allowing them to contribute to the functional decision making capability of the bank. In addition, female appointees could counterbalance potentially excessive risk-taking behaviour by male colleagues. For example, Faccio et al. (2014) document that firms run by female CEOs have lower leverage, less volatile earnings, and a higher chance of survival than firms run by male CEOs. Since excessive risk-taking could destroy value, the appointment of a female executive could create wealth for bank shareholders.

However, there is a possibility of conflict between the newly appointed female executive and the existing male executives. It may prove difficult for female executives to be listened to on an equal basis by other members if there are very few females on the board or in the executive suite (Terjesen et al. 2009). This could impose psychic costs on the female executive, which could result in performance losses (Becker 1957).

2.2.3 Prior Executive Directorships Experience

It is possible that there is a unique set of skills and managerial abilities acquired by those with prior executive directorships that sets them apart from other individuals. Hence, holding prior executive directorships in listed firms signals the appointee's proven track record and accomplishments. In addition, experienced appointees also bring their existing social ties and networks to the bank. This places the bank in the networks of other firms, giving it access to various external constituencies such as industry regulators (Hillman et al. 2000).

2.2.4 Current Non-executive Directorships (Busyness)

The appointment of an executive with non-executive directorships could give the bank 'endorsement benefits', allowing it access to corporate elites and external resources (Masulis and Mobbs 2011). However, appointees holding non-executive directorships can be distracted from their responsibilities at the bank (Fich and Shivdasani 2006). They might not have the time and energy to fulfil their duties.

2.2.5 Experience in Non-banking Industries

Several studies suggest that general skills acquired through experience in a diversified set of industries are becoming increasingly important and value-adding (e.g. Custodio et al. 2013). This allows appointees to make a variety of decisions in different contexts. However, as the banking industry is highly specialised, appointees with experience in multiple non-banking industries might have fewer specialist financial skills and thus, might be less capable of making technical decisions.

2.2.6 Ivy League Education

We choose Ivy League institutions[3] as an indicator of highly reputable universities. There is empirical evidence showing that Ivy League graduates perform better than non-Ivy ones. For example, Laderman (1994) finds that during the period from the 1989–1993 period, mutual funds managed by Ivy League graduates generally outperform their non-Ivy counterparts. More recently, Falato et al. (2014) demonstrate that CEOs who study at more selective institutions are paid at a premium and this effect is associated with talent.

However, Ivy League educated appointees might choose to engage only with peers with a similar educational background and refuse to collaborate with other members in the executive team. This could result in an unhealthy corporate culture where different social groups compete for power (Farnum 1990). Since conflicts of social preference can impose psychic costs on team members and lower overall group performance (Becker 1957), the presence of Ivy League educated appointees could destroy shareholder wealth.

2.2.7 MBA Degree

One well-documented benefit of an MBA degree is the extensive social links that the appointees form during their MBA study. Appointing executives with an MBA degree could place the hiring bank in a more central position in the corporate social networks, and this could create value for bank shareholders. However, there is no clear empirical evidence suggesting that MBA executives outperform non-MBA ones. For example, Chevalier and Ellison (1999) find that hedge fund managers with an MBA degree do not perform significantly better than those without one.

Overall, there are arguments for both positive and negative effects linked to the executive characteristics we discuss above. Therefore, it is ultimately an empirical

---

[3] Ivy League institutions are eight North Eastern American higher education institutions, including Brown University, Columbia University, Cornell University, Dartmouth College, Harvard University, Princeton University, University of Pennsylvania and Yale University.

question to see whether the director characteristics have positive or negative effects on shareholder wealth.

3 Data

We examine new appointments of executives to US banks from January 1999 to December 2011. We start by obtaining a list of all banks on *BoardEx*, a leading business intelligence service that provides information on executive characteristics. We then use Factiva to search for newspapers articles containing the search terms related to executives ('officer', 'executive' etc.) and appointments ('appoint', 'name' etc.).

The event date is defined as the earliest trading day when the announcement is made. In the final sample, we impose two exclusion criteria to ensure that the stock market reaction is purely driven by the event of the incoming executive appointment. First, we remove all appointment announcements that are simultaneously announced with other corporate events (e.g. earnings or merger announcements) because the stock market reactions might be confounded by the other news items in these cases. Second, we exclude all appointment announcements that are made simultaneously with announcements of *unplanned* executive departures. We exclude these announcements, because the stock market reaction to this type of event might be driven by the predecessor's unplanned departure rather than by the incoming executive appointment. Planned departures (that is, previously announced executive departures due to retirement) are kept in the sample.

Our final sample consists of 252 single appointment announcements of externally-hired executives to 145 US banks. This enables us to unambiguously measure the marginal value effect linked to the inclusion of new executives.

4 Event Study Methodology and Results

We use event study methodology to examine the stock market reactions to single and externally-hired appointment announcements ($N = 252$). Following prior studies on executive appointments, we concentrate on the time period immediately surrounding the appointment announcement.

Specifically, we estimate the following market model:

$$R_{it} = \alpha_i + \beta_i R_{mt} + \varepsilon_{it} t = -300, \ \ldots, \ -46 \qquad (1)$$

where R_{it} are the daily stock returns for firm i at day t and R_{mt} are equally-weighted CRSP index return for day t. We estimate the model parameters using 255 daily return observations starting from 300 to 46 days before the executive

Table 1 The stock price reaction to appointments

Event window	N	Average CAR (%)	Patell- Z	Median CARs	Sign- ranked	% Positive CARs
−1 to 0 day	252	0.71	1.14	0.18	0.99	52.8
0 to +2 day	252	0.31	0.55	−0.16	0.07	48.0
0 to +3 day	252	0.47	0.74	0.14	0.49	52.0
0 to +4 day	252	0.99	1.96**	0.24	1.65**	53.2

This table shows the stock price reactions to 252 single and externally-hired executive appointment announcements to 145 US banks between 01 January 1999 and 31 December 2011. We report abnormal returns for different event windows surrounding executive appointment announcements
** denote significance at the 1 %, 5 % and 10 % level, respectively

announcement date. We construct abnormal returns as the sum of the prediction errors of the market model.

Table 1 presents the cumulative abnormal returns (CARs) surrounding single and externally-hired executive appointment announcements. The stock market reaction to the appointment news, on average, is positive. For example, over 5-day event window, the market returns are +0.99 % (significant at 5 % level). Thus, the addition of top managers, on average, is valuable for US banks.

4.1 Empirical Strategy

Our main purpose is to investigate how market investors evaluate appointee characteristics using the stock market reactions to executive appointments. We employ the following equation:

$$\text{5-day CAR } (\%) = \alpha + \beta_1 \text{ appointee characteristics} + \beta_2 \text{ control variables} + \varepsilon \qquad (2)$$

The dependent variables are 5-day CAR (%) around the announcement of a single externally-hired executive appointment.

We obtain data on appointee characteristics from *BoardEx*. We first include two basic demographic measures: AGE measures the age of the appointee at the time of the appointment and FEMALE is a dummy that equals 1 if the appointee is a female and 0 otherwise. Second, we include three variables that capture the appointee experience and competitiveness in the external labour market: #EXECUTIVE DIRECTORSHIPS measures the number of executive directorships with listed firms that the appointee has held prior to joining the bank. BUSYNESS measures the number of non-executive directorships the appointee holds at the time of the appointment. #NON-BANKING INDUSTRIES measures the number of non-banking industries (based on 4-digit SIC codes) the appointee has worked in prior to joining the bank. Finally, we include two variables that capture executive

Table 2 Summary statistics

Variable	Definition	N	Mean	SD	P1	P99
Panel A: Executive characteristics						
AGE	The age of the appointee	252	49.47	6.54	35.00	66.00
FEMALE	Dummy equals 1 if the appointee is a female and 0 otherwise	252	0.06	0.24	0.00	1.00
#EXECUTIVE DIRECTORSHIPS	Number of executive director-ships at listed firms that the appointee holds prior to joining the bank	252	0.69	0.86	0.00	4.00
BUSYNESS	Number of non-executive directorships the appointee holds at the time of the appointment	252	0.06	0.32	0.00	2.00
#NON-BANKING INDUSTRIES	Number of non-banking indus-tries the appointee has worked in prior to joining the bank	252	0.25	0.80	0.00	5.00
IVY LEAGUE	Dummy equals 1 if the appointee obtains at least one degree from Ivy League insti-tutions and 0 otherwise	252	0.15	0.35	0.00	1.00
MBA	Dummy equals 1 if the appointee possesses an MBA degree and 0 otherwise	252	0.46	0.50	0.00	1.00
Panel B: Bank characteristics						
ROA	Earnings before interests and taxes (EBIT) divided by book value of total assets	252	1.26	1.27	−2.63	5.63
BANKSIZE	Natural logarithm of total assets	252	22.84	2.06	19.49	28.41
PORTFOLIO RISK	Risk-weighted assets divided by book value of total assets	252	0.76	0.28	0.03	0.93
CHARTER VALUE	Market value of equity divided by book value of equity	252	1.67	1.06	0.13	4.60
LEVERAGE	Book value of liabilities divided the book value of equity	252	9.95	3.50	1.52	19.68
BOARDSIZE	Number of executive and non-executive directors on the board	252	12.10	3.58	6.00	21.00
BOARDIND	The proportion of non-executive directors on the board	252	0.76	0.14	0.25	0.93
DUALITY	Dummy equals 1 if the CEO is also a Chairman and 0 otherwise	252	0.52	0.50	0.00	1.00

(continued)

Table 2 (continued)

Variable	Definition	N	Mean	SD	P1	P99
CEOINNOM	Dummy equals 1 if the CEO sits in the nominating committee and 0 otherwise	252	0.10	0.30	0.00	1.00
CEOPOST	Dummy equals 1 if the appointee is appointed to a CEO position and 0 otherwise	252	0.27	0.43	0.00	1.00

This table reports the descriptive statistics of the variables in our sample. The sample consists of 252 single externally-hired executive appointment announcements to 145 US banks between 01 January 1999 and 31 December 2011

educational background: IVY LEAGUE is a dummy that equals 1 if the appointee obtains at least one degree from Ivy League institutions and 0 otherwise and MBA is a dummy that equals 1 if the appointee possesses an MBA degree and 0 otherwise.

We then control for various bank-specific and corporate governance variables. Table 2 shows variable definitions and summary statistics.

5 Results: Appointee Characteristics and Appointment Announcement Results

Table 3 reports the relationship between the announcement effects and various appointee characteristics. In columns 1, 3, 6 and 8, we show that the stock market returns are positively and significantly related to three appointee characteristics: (1) age, (2) number of executive directorships, and (3) Ivy League education. The magnitude for each of the coefficient estimates is generally consistent across columns. The coefficient estimates indicate that CARs are on average 1.2 % higher when the appointee is 10 years older, 1.4 % higher when the appointee has one prior executive directorships position and 3.5 % higher when the appointee has an Ivy League education.

6 Discussion and Conclusion

This chapter investigates the value of executives to shareholders of US banks by examining the stock market reaction to the appointment of new executives. Our argument is that if executives are valuable to shareholders, announcement returns will be higher when executives with certain desirable characteristics are appointed to a bank. We employ an event study to compute the expected performance gains linked to executive characteristics such as age, education and experience.

Table 3 Regression results

	(1)	(2)	(3)	(4)	(5)	(6)	(7)	(8)
AGE	0.12*							0.13**
	(1.77)							(1.99)
FEMALE		−0.76						1.21
		(−0.44)						(0.79)
#EXEC DIRECTORSHIPS			1.36**					1.53***
			(2.43)					(2.89)
BUSYNESS				−3.27***				−3.91***
				(−2.60)				(−3.46)
#NON-BANK INDUSTRIES					−0.34			–
					(−0.80)			–
IVY LEAGUE						3.52**		2.15*
						(2.12)		(1.65)
MBA							1.83	−1.42
							(1.56)	(−1.62)
ROA	0.60	1.27*	0.43	1.22*	1.24*	1.20*	1.34*	0.58
	(0.93)	(1.85)	(0.67)	(1.78)	(1.81)	(1.72)	(1.92)	(0.86)
BANKSIZE	−0.18	−0.41	−0.17	−0.27	−0.37	−0.54**	−0.43*	−0.20
	(−0.82)	(−1.60)	(−0.88)	(−1.07)	(−1.43)	(−2.01)	(−1.66)	(−0.91)
PORTFOLIO RISK	−0.45	0.01	−0.58	−0.04	−0.10	−0.05	0.08	−0.78
	(−0.45)	(0.01)	(−0.56)	(−0.03)	(−0.07)	(−0.04)	(0.06)	(−0.68)
CHARTERVALUE	−1.11*	−2.07***	−0.86	−2.02***	−2.04***	−2.09***	−2.11***	−0.98
	(−1.66)	(−3.01)	(−1.39)	(−2.90)	(−2.97)	(−3.07)	(−3.03)	(−1.64)
LEVERAGE	0.07	0.02	0.08	0.00	0.02	−0.00	0.02	0.08
	(0.63)	(0.10)	(0.74)	(0.03)	(0.13)	(−0.03)	(0.12)	(0.74)

(continued)

Table 3 (continued)

	(1)	(2)	(3)	(4)	(5)	(6)	(7)	(8)
BOARDSIZE	0.09	−0.01	0.13	0.03	−0.00	−0.01	−0.03	0.19†
	(0.89)	(−0.06)	(1.18)	(0.19)	(−0.03)	(−0.05)	(−0.21)	(1.70)
BOARDIND	5.79	10.60**	3.75	9.95**	10.48**	10.34**	10.35**	4.49
	(1.42)	(2.49)	(0.97)	(2.34)	(2.46)	(2.45)	(2.42)	(1.16)
CEOINNOM	0.36	−0.61	0.43	−0.73	−0.71	−0.80	−0.81	0.33
	(0.43)	(−0.59)	(0.51)	(−0.70)	(−0.67)	(−0.79)	(−0.77)	(0.36)
DUALITY	0.60	1.54	0.25	1.79	1.58	1.67	1.65	0.66
	(0.29)	(0.66)	(0.13)	(0.78)	(0.68)	(0.76)	(0.71)	(0.34)
CEOPOST	−0.68	−4.09**	0.03	−3.81**	−4.03**	−4.42**	−4.48**	−0.12
	(−0.41)	(−2.07)	(0.02)	(−1.97)	(−2.06)	(−2.31)	(−2.21)	(−0.09)
POST_CRISIS	−4.41	−7.74*	−4.69	−7.04*	−7.73*	−7.72*	−7.70*	−4.76
	(−1.21)	(−1.82)	(−1.33)	(−1.67)	(−1.83)	(−1.83)	(−1.81)	(−1.33)
Year dummies	Yes	Yes	Yes	Yes	Yes	Yes	Yes	Yes
Observations	252	252	252	252	252	252	252	252
R-Squared	9.56 %	8.60 %	9.87 %	10.93 %	9.11 %	9.66 %	8.58 %	16.36 %

This table reports the relationship between appointee characteristics and stock market reactions to executive appointments. The dependent variables of all models are 5-day CAR (%). POST_CRISIS equals to 1 if year is 2008–2011 and 0 otherwise. Standard errors are clustered at bank-level. All other variables are defined in Table **2**. t-Statistics are reported in brackets

***, **, * denote significance at the 1 %, 5 % and 10 % level, respectively

Using a hand-collected of 252 executive appointments from 1999 to 2011, we demonstrate that certain executive characteristics create shareholder wealth. In particular, we show that market returns are higher when the appointee is older, has prior experience as an executive director or holds an Ivy League degree. By contrast, the appointment of an executive who holds multiple non-executive directorships results in negative returns. In addition, the gender of the appointee and experience in non-banking industries do not affect stock market returns around the announcement of a new executive.

Overall, this chapter complements existing literature on why and how individual executives matter for firm performance. Our results stress the crucial role of the nominating committee, which is responsible for searching and hiring directors (Shivdasani and Yermack 1999). Our results also have an important policy implication. We echo de Haan and Vlahu (2013) that appointing more executives with expertise to the bank is an important policy concern. Our findings are consistent with calls by policy makers to appoint more executives that are highly qualified and possess relevant industry experience.

References

Adams RB, Mehran H (2012) Bank board structure and performance: evidence from large bank holding companies. J Fin Intermed 21(2):227–248

Becker GS (1957) The economics of discrimination. University of Chicago Press, Chicago

Bennedsen M, Perez-Gonzalez F, Wolfenzon D (2008) Do CEOs matter? Working paper. http://web.stanford.edu/~fperezg/valueceos.pdf

Bertrand M, Schoar A (2003) Managing with style: the effects of managers on firm policies. Q J Econ 118(4):1169–1208

Chevalier J, Ellison G (1999) Are some mutual funds better than others? Cross-sectional patterns in behavior and performance. J Fin 54(3):875–899

Coles J, Daniel N, Naveen L (2008) Boards: does one size fit all? J Fin Econ 87:329–356

Custodio C, Metzger D (2013) How do CEOs matter? The effect of industry expertise on acquisition returns. Rev Fin Stud 26(8):2007–2047

Custodio C, Ferreira MA, Matos P (2013) Generalists vs. specialists: life time work experience and chief executive officer pay. J Fin Econ 108:471–492

de Haan J, Vlahu R (2013) Corporate governance of banks: a survey. DNB Working paper No. 386, July

Faccio M, Marchica M, Mura R (2014) CEO gender, corporate risk-taking, and the efficiency of capital allocation. Working paper. Available via SSRN. http://papers.ssrn.com/sol3/papers.cfm?abstract_id=2021136

Falato A, Li D, Milbourn TT (2014) Which skills matter in the market for CEOs? Evidence from pay for CEO credentials. Manage Sci. doi:10.2139/ssrn.1699384

Farnum R (1990) Prestige in Ivy League: Meritocracy at Columbia, Harvard and Penn: 1870-1940. Dissertation, University of Pennsylvania

Fee CE, Hadlock CJ, Pierce JR (2013) Managers with and without style: evidence using exogenous variation. Rev Fin Stud 26(3):567–601

Fich E, Shivdasani A (2006) Are busy boards effective monitors? J Fin 61(2):689–724

Graham JR, Li S, Qiu J (2012) Managerial attributes and executive compensation. Rev Fin Stud 25:144–86

Grund C, Westergaard-Nielsen N (2008) Age structure of the workforce and firm performance. Int J Manpower 29(5):410–422

Hambrick DC, Mason PA (1984) Upper echelons: the organization as a reflection of its top managers. Acad Manage Rev 9(2):193–206

Hillman AJ, Cannella AA, Paetzold RL (2000) The resource dependence role of corporate directors: strategic adaption of board composition in response to environmental change. J Manage Stud 37(2):235–256

Kaplan S, Klebanov M, Sorensen M (2012) Which CEO characteristics and abilities matter? J Fin 67:973–1003

Laderman JM (1994) Business Week's guide to mutual funds. McGraw-Hill, New York

Landier A, Sauvagnet J, Sraer D et al (2013) Bottom-up governance. Rev Fin 17(1):161–201

Malmendier U, Tate G, Yan J (2011) Overconfidence and early-life experiences: the effects of managerial traits on corporate financial policies. J Fin 66:1687–1733

Masulis RW, Mobbs S (2011) Are all inside directors the same? Evidence from external directorships market. J Fin 66:823–872

Philippon T, Reshef A (2012) Wages and human capital in the US finance industry: 1909–2006. Q J Econ 127(4):1551–1609

Roberts S, Rosenberg I (2006) Nutrition and aging: changes in the regulation of energy metabolism with aging. Physiol Rev 86:651–667

Shivdasani A, Yermack D (1999) CEO involvement in the selection of board members: an empirical analysis. J Fin 54(5):1829–1853

Terjesen S, Sealy R, Singh V (2009) Women directors on corporate boards: a review and research agenda. Corp Gov 17(3):320–337

Warner JB, Watts RL, Wruck KH (1988) Stock prices and top management changes. J Fin Econ 20:461–492

Worthy DA, Gorlick MA, Pacheco JL et al (2011) With age comes wisdom: decision-making in older and younger adults. Psychol Sci 22(11):1375–1380

Part IV
Credit Crunch: Regional Issues

Bottlenecks of the Financial System at the National and Regional Levels: The Cases of Italy and Sardinia

Roberto Malavasi

Abstract Analyses of the financial structure of Italian firms agree on the evidence that compared with other European countries, companies are characterised by a peculiar fragility because of their lower capitalisation and higher leverage. These effects, in terms of the current and potential financial vulnerability, are well known. During crises, the problems related to internal financing capacity and bank debt funding intensify. What are the best solutions to rebalance the financial structure of Italian firms? How should banks refinance firms to provide them with the necessary period to settle finances? This paper provides the reader with some answers to both questions. With regards to the capitalisation processes, we recommend setting up new highly capitalised intermediaries. In particular, they should be created with capital that comes from selling those bank buildings that are no longer useful, given the increasing importance of online services. Later, we analyse the opportunity for and, thus, the effects of banks to securitise their loans. For both alternatives, we obtain relevant findings that can represent suitable solutions for firms and intermediaries to overcome the credit crunch issue.

1 The Financial Structure of Italian Firms

The analysis of the financial structure of Italian firms shows that historically, compared with other European countries, they are characterised by a peculiar fragility due to their lower capitalisation and higher leverage (cfr. Table 1).

This also occurs because there are relatively few non-financial listed companies and their market value is less than half that of firms in countries such as Germany, France and Spain. Moreover, the development of the bond market is quite weak (e.g., bonds cover less than 10 % of corporate financial debt).

Such a gap in the funding structure of firms is explained by both operative conditions (i.e., low business size, higher presence of family businesses, sectorial

R. Malavasi (✉)
Department of Economics and Business, University of Cagliari, Cagliari, Italy
e-mail: malavasi@unica.it

© Springer International Publishing Switzerland 2016   141
S.P.S. Rossi, R. Malavasi (eds.), *Financial Crisis, Bank Behaviour and Credit
Crunch*, Contributions to Economics, DOI 10.1007/978-3-319-17413-6_10

Table 1 Corporate liabilities by country

Countries & years	Percentage composition of liabilities				Financial indicators	
	Bonds	Loans	Shares and other holdings	Commercial debts and other liabilities	Bank debt share	Leverage
Italy						
2005	2.20	31.70	49.20	16.90	67.20	41.40
2007	2.00	31.80	46.90	19.30	66.90	41.80
2012	3.40	33.90	42.70	20.00	66.50	46.70
2013	4.10	31.50	44.70	19.70	64.20	44.40
France						
2007	3.70	20.10	64.30	11.80	40.10	27.00
2012	6.70	22.00	57.70	13.60	38.40	33.20
2013	6.20	20.00	60.90	12.90	38.30	30.20
Germany						
2007	2.50	28.10	47.00	22.50	53.70	39.40
2012	2.70	29.10	44.20	23.90	52.50	41.80
2013	2.70	27.70	47.20	22.40	50.90	39.20
Spain						
2007	0.30	34.00	48.60	17.10	64.50	41.40
2012	0.50	40.90	44.10	14.60	51.50	48.40
2013	0.60	37.00	49.90	12.40	46.20	43.00
Euro area						
2007	2.40	29.10	54.00	14.50	51.60	36.90
2012	3.80	32.00	49.70	14.40	47.00	41.90
2013	3.80	29.80	52.80	13.60	45.50	38.90
UK						
2007	7.50	28.20	59.40	5.00	41.30	37.50
2012	10.40	27.90	56.30	5.40	31.30	40.50
2013	10.30	26.40	58.10	5.20	29.60	38.70
USA						
2007	9.80	15.80	57.40	17.00	37.60	30.80
2012	14.50	14.20	54.40	16.90	29.80	34.50
2013	13.90	12.80	58.90	14.30	29.10	31.20

Source: Bank of Italy (2014a)

specialisation) and institutional factors (e.g., different fiscal treatment concerning interest expenses, lower stock market development, higher protection provided to creditors).

During the recent financial crisis, the evolution of this specific condition has appeared in line with the usually identified weaknesses in such a corporate financial model:

– The particular vulnerability to the negative phases of the cycle and to the shocks that hit the banking system;

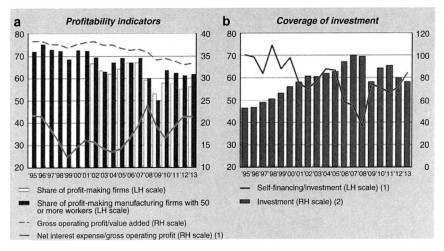

Fig. 1 Profitability and coverage of investment (*per cent; indices*). Source: Bank of Italy (2014a)

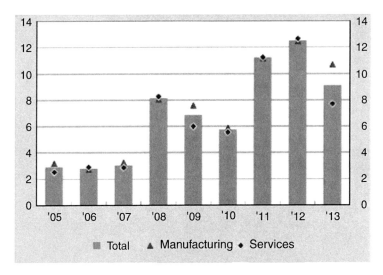

Fig. 2 Share of credit-rationed firms (per cent). Source: Bank of Italy (2014a)

– The lower capability of the financial system to allocate funding to firms managing highly profitable projects, notably to high-tech (Rossi 2013).

As pointed out in Figs. 1, 2, 3, during the crisis the problems intensify:

– Competitiveness worsens;
– Income profitability shrinks, becoming negative for a higher number of firms;
– Self-financing collapses;
– Investments decrease;

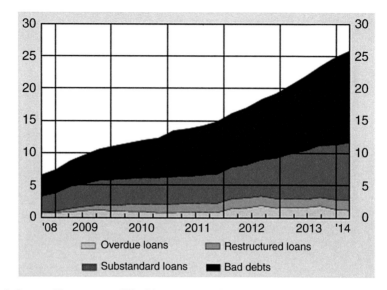

Fig. 3 Loans with repayment difficulties *(per cent of total loans)*. Source: Bank of Italy (2014a)

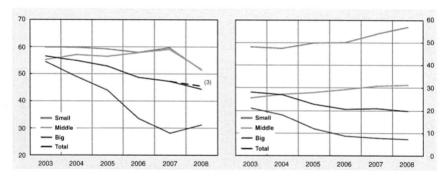

Fig. 4 Degree of indebtedness by size. Leverage *(left)* and financial debt-to-income *(right)*. Source: Bank of Italy (2009)

– Capability to allocate funds to R&D further decreases;
– Selection in the credit allocation process intensifies;
– Loan losses in bank portfolios increase.

The general comparison between the financial structure of Sardinian firms and the average pre-crisis data on Italian companies shows even lower capitalisation ratios and higher leverage justified by excessive bank debt exposure (see Fig. 4). Differences in profitability appear even deeper, on a negative base, especially with regard to operative margins (see Table 2).

Table 2 Balance sheet indicators (%)

	2003	2004	2005	2006	2007	2008
EBITDA/Total Assets	5.9	7.6	8.9	8.4	9.2	5.8
ROA	0.7	2.2	2.2	3.6	4.9	0.7
ROE	2.7	8.7	8.4	12.5	16.1	2.1
Interest expense/EBITDA	37.3	20.6	14.8	16.9	16.6	28.2
Receipts and payments management ratio	9.2	10.2	9.3	10.1	10.8	9.2
Current (liquidity) ratio	106.2	107.6	110.0	116.3	119.9	114.0
Leverage	56.5	54.8	52.8	48.7	47.2	44.3
Financial debt/Value added	181.2	153.6	136.1	135.1	130.9	158.5

Source: Bank of Italy (2014a)

2   The Main Weakness of Our Regional Firms

Understanding the operative conditions of Sardinian firms is critical to the aim of the present study. Given the high contribution in terms of analyses realised, it is essential to briefly list the main weaknesses of the economic system of Sardinia:

2.1   Size, Specialisation and Innovative Propensity

This context is characterised by the pulverisation of corporate activities. During the period 2006–2012, 40 % of corporations have no employees, and 47 % were very small businesses (up to nine employees). Only 11.5 % of firms had a number of employees up to 40 and just 1 % overcame this limit.

Family businesses in particular, which are considered to be poorly implemented management models, are extremely evident in this framework.

With reference to productive specialisation, during the same period, we observe a predominance of commercial and construction firms that account for 50 % of total corporations. At the same time, the manufacturing industry, mostly food, plastic and oil-refining firms, represent only 10 %. In general, except for oil refining, they are traditional productions, as underlined by the Bank of Italy, with low- to medium-technology equipment. This contributes to the growth of a phenomenon that sees a widening gap between the Sardinian and the Italian manufacturing sectors, the latter characterised by opposite trends, i.e., higher technology (see Table 3). The analysis of the ability of the Sardinian firms to innovate (as shown in Table 4) confirms its weaknesses compared with the Italian average situation. Moreover, though improving, they further appear weaker compared with the European average productive capability.

Moreover, as pointed out in Table 5, a further divergence is found with regard to the growth rate of new and innovative businesses, meaning that obsolete and non-competitive sectorial structures were not adapting throughout the years.

Table 3 Units of labour

	Sardinia		Southern Italy		Italy	
	2001	2011	2001	2011	2001	2011
Primary sector activities	5.9	4.2	4.7	3.9	2.9	2.7
Manufacturing industry	5.0	4.6	5.8	5.7	8.4	8.6
of which						
High-tech	7.5	6.0	28.0	22.5	28.5	24.7
Upper medium-tech	16.7	11.4	21.3	19.8	22.8	20.2
Lower medium-tech	5.9	5.3	6.0	5.6	8.0	7.7
Low-tech	3.6	3.7	4.4	4.3	6.2	6.3
Non-manufacturing industry	12.1	16.9	13.5	14.1	13.8	14.4
Construction	3.2	2.8	3.3	3.0	2.9	2.8
Services	2.5	2.6	2.3	2.2	2.8	2.7
of which:						
with high knowledge intensity	2.3	2.2	2.3	2.2	2.8	2.7
of which:						
High-tech	3.9	4.1	4.5	4.3	5.2	5.2
Financials	4.1	3.9	4.0	3.5	5.0	4.8
Other market-oriented services	1.9	1.8	1.7	1.7	2.2	2.1
Other services	2.1	2.1	2.1	2.5	2.2	2.3
with low knowledge intensity	2.6	2.8	2.3	2.7	2.8	3.2
of which:						
Market-oriented	2.6	2.8	2.3	2.7	2.8	3.3
Other services	2.6	2.7	2.4	2.6	2.6	2.8
Total	2.9	2.9	2.9	2.9	3.6	3.6

Source: Bank of Italy (2012)

Table 4 R&D activities in Sardinian firms (year 2012)

	Sardinia	Southern Italy	Italy
Firms that undertook product, process, organisational and marketing innovation	46.0	49.7	56.3
Firms that undertook product and process innovation	26.1	32.0	40.4
Firms that completed product and process innovation	25.3	29.2	38.0
Firms that developed "in-house" innovation	93.3	89.8	92.6
Innovative firms that settled cooperation agreements	18.7	10.4	12.5
Innovative firms that introduced organisational and/or marketing innovation	69.3	68.3	69.8
Innovation expenditures (per worker)	2.0	2.2	4.7
Innovation expenditures (per firm)	156.3	142.7	381.3

Source: Bank of Italy (2013)

Table 5 Percentages and dynamics of the units of labour (manufacture)

	Sardinia			Southern Italy			Italy		
	2001	2011	Δ (2001 = 100)	2001	2011	Δ (2001 = 100)	2001	2011	Δ (2001 = 100)
High-tech	1.0	0.8	64.7	3.6	3.3	73.1	4.3	4.5	84.2
Upper tedium-tech	13.3	8.1	47.1	15.8	17.6	89.0	21.1	25.3	96.5
Lower medium-tech	42.3	45.7	83.4	34.1	34.7	81.2	33.9	31.6	75.0
Low-tech	43.4	45.4	80.7	46.5	44.3	76.0	40.7	38.6	76.3
Total	100.0	100.0	77.2	100.0	100.0	79.7	100.0	100.0	80.5

Source: Bank of Italy (2012)

2.2   Export Capabilities

The limited international openness of Sardinian firms is acknowledged every year
by official statistics (see Figs. 5 and 6). They indicate how the share of regional
firms operating abroad is below the national average and underline a very low
involvement in the formation of the aggregate national data, particularly if we
remove the contribution of oil refining from the analysed variables.

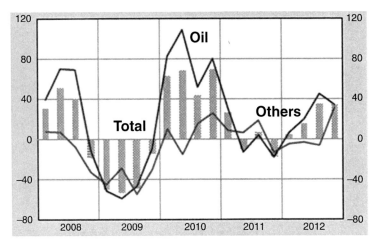

Fig. 5 Export by sector (percentage change). Source: Bank of Italy (2013)

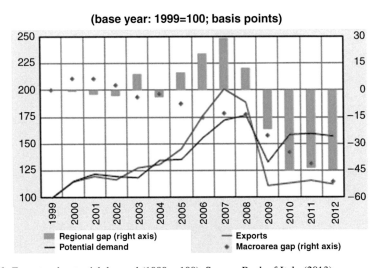

Fig. 6 Export and potential demand (1999 = 100). Source: Bank of Italy (2013)

2.3 The Impact of 2007's Financial Crisis

With regard to profitability, which is computed as operative margin over added value, we observe in Table 6 a decline from 45 % in 2007 to 19 % in 2012 (that represents a reduction of 26 percentage points), whereas in Italy the same variable decreases from 72 to 66 %.

If we move to ROA, we find that this ratio shows an even worse trend: after a steady decline, in 2012 it becomes negative (-0.3 %).

These trends underline the growing issues involving firms, fully synthesised by the interest expenses over operative margin ratio: in Sardinia it grows from 16 % in 2007 to 52 % in 2012 (whereas the Italian one grows from 20 to 22 %). Weaknesses in terms of self-financing and investment capabilities are evident: capital allocated to firms decreases by 2 % in Italy and by 14 % in Sardinia during the period 2008–2012. During the same period, the earnings of Sardinian firms decrease more than the Italian ones. Additionally, fixture and equipment capacity rates decrease to 65 % of the total.

The leverage ratio between 2007 and 2012 increases by 3 %, reaching 53 % in the last year, well above the Italian average of 48 % and the Euro-area level of 42 %.

The impact of bank debts exposure over the company's total debt again indicates the situation described in Table 7.

Table 6 Balance sheet indicators

	2007	2008	2009	2010	2011	2012
Growth of revenues	5.1	11.6	-23.4	20.5	17.1	1.1
EBITDA/EBIT	45.3	36.6	30	22.7	28.1	19.3
EBITDA/Total assets	9.2	6.3	4.7	3.1	3.9	2.4
ROA	7.8	3.6	1.1	0.2	0.4	-0.3
ROE	14.6	2.2	-3	-4.1	-6.2	-6.7
Interest expense/EBITDA	16.3	25.3	25.1	33.4	29.3	52
Leverage	49.7	47.7	39.7	49.8	51.7	52.6
Financial debt/Income	24.6	24.9	34.2	28.7	25.7	26.1
Liquidity	123.1	115.4	116.6	121.4	111.9	113.8
Available liquidity	83.8	80.1	76.8	80.5	72.1	76.5
Cash flow index	13.5	12.8	17.6	16.5	14.2	12.6

Source: Bank of Italy (2013)

Table 7 Debts to banks (percentage of total assets)

Year	Sardinia	Italy	Euro area	Great Britain
2007	72.0	66.9	51.6	41.3
2012	77.0	66.5	47.0	31.3
2013	–	64.2	45.6	29.6

Source: Our elaborations of AIDA (Bureau Van Dijk) and BACH (Banque de France) Data

Again, we find that during the crises, small and very small firms had increased their reliance on this exclusive source of funding.

3 The Banking-Loan Supply

From the point of view of the bank-loan supply, we find in Tables 8 and 9 the results for the periods 2007–2009 and 2010–2013.[1]

We find that, between 2007 and 2009, the funds provided to Sardinian firms grow more than national average, whereas during the last 2 years (2012–2013) the reduction is more consistent than average. At the same time, risk increase determines the growth of the already-high share of collateralised loans and increases the coverage degree with values well above national average: as shown in Table 10, the first one goes from 75.4 % in 2007 to 80 % in 2013 on a regional level, whereas on a national base, we have an increase from 63.5 to 68.8 %; the second grows from 66.5 to 71.7 % for Sardinia, and from 54 to 59 % for Italy.

The analysis (see Table 11, Figs. 7 and 8) of the dynamics related to the credit quality allocated within the region highlights, for the same years, an even more alarming situation: in 2 years (2012–2013), the impaired loans-over-total loans ratio grew from 21 to 25 % for small firms (which represent the largest part of the regional productive structure). Both values are well above the national average. During the same years, impaired loans to firms grew from 16.27 to 22.05 % in Sardinia, whereas in Italy they rose from 13.90 to 17.10 %.

Table 8 Loans to businesses (million Euros). Italy vs. Sardinia

Year	Italy	Sardinia
2007	903,856	10,715
2008	958,549	11,418
2009	939,783	11,515
2010	966,532	13,072
2011	994,753	13,332
2012	962,507	12,469
2013	909,277	11,926

Source: Bank of Italy (2014a)

Table 9 Loans to businesses (Δ). Italy vs. Sardinia

	Italy (%)	Sardinia (%)
2009–2007	3.97	7.47
2013–2010	−5.92	−8.76

Source: Bank of Italy (2014a)

---

[1] Discontinuity in the period of both national and international data gathering has limited our analysis to the two periods taken into account.

Table 10 Guarantees to loans

	Sardinia		Southern Italy		Italy	
	2007	2013	2001	2011	2001	2011
Loan share (a)	75.4	80.0	74.3	78.0	63.5	68.8
of which						
Fully guaranteed	51.2	54.9	50.6	54.1	39.6	24.7
Partially guaranteed	24.3	25.1	23.7	23.9	23.9	24.7
Average guarantee on guaranteed loans (b)	88.2	89.6	88.3	88.0	85.1	85.7
of which on partially guaranteed loans	63.3	66.7	63.5	60.8	60.5	60.2
Coverage degree (a × b)	66.5	71.7				
of which						
Collateral	42.1	42.9	37.2	29.5	32.5	37.6
Personal guarantees	43.7	48.5	44.7	47.1	32.2	34.3

Source: Bank of Italy (2014b)

Table 11 Total loans and impaired loans

	Total loans			Impaired loans			Impaired loans over total loans (%)		
	2011	2012	2013	2011	2012	2013	2011	2012	2013
Firms	13,332	12,469	11,926	2,012	2,029	2,630	15.09	16.27	22.05
Large to medium-sized companies	9,562	8,864	8,487	1,249	1,261	1,757	13.06	14.23	20.70
Small companies	3,770	3,605	3,440	763	768	872	20.24	21.30	25.35
Family households	10,305	10,110	9,878	388	375	469	3.77	3.71	4.75
Total	26,684	25,479	24,597	2,406	2,654	3,112	9.02	10.42	12.65

Source: Bank of Italy (2014b)

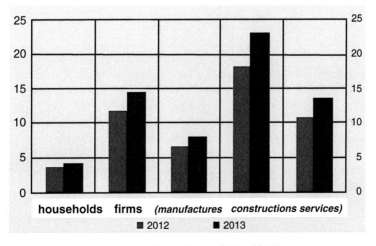

Fig. 7 Impaired loans over total loans. Source: Bank of Italy (2014b)

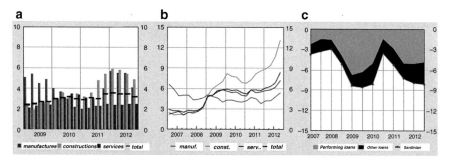

Fig. 8 Quality of credit (per cent). Bad loans on total loans (last 12 months) (**a**). Substandard of loans (**b**). Loans' transitions across different risk classes (**c**). Source: Bank of Italy (2013)

In Sardinia, all structural weaknesses of Italian firms are confirmed, with a decline related to some aspects that on average confirm a national condition of more actual and expected vulnerability.

4 Structural Solutions and Short-Term Interventions

First of all, we need to adopt the necessary corrective measures to overcome the bottlenecks that curb the birth of new business opportunities, in particular of innovative firms, both at national and, even more, at regional level. Public administration inefficiencies and low human capital endowments seem to play a central role in determining a gap that needs to be reduced in the whole country, in general, and in the weaker regions, in particular. These regions, given their low linkages with universities and research centres, are called to operate important substitutive functions in terms of R&D in favour of the firms.

With regard to financial solutions, some of the instruments employed at the national level are: a Development Decree, the Italian FSA rules on equity, innovative start-up crowdfunding and the Italian Investment Funds. The benefits at regional level are still insignificant.

Venture capital investors are still low in number in Italy, and the private equity market still appears underdeveloped (3.4 bn € in Italy in 2012, of which only 3 % are in the South and on the islands, with a prevalence of buy-out operations and a very marginal involvement in the early stage, i.e., 2.4 % of the total). In the EU countries, the involvement in the early stage is higher (10 % in France and 8 % in Germany). This means that an increase of Italian and foreign investors in this sector is desirable, though relying upon new venture capital funds. And this applies despite the fact that the Italian Investment Fund in 2013 decided to invest in private equity funds and venture capital for only 425 mn €.

Firms already in the market, that rely highly upon bank lending, need to stop this excessive dependency encouraging recapitalisation and the development of alternative medium and long-term non-banking sources of funding.

This implies that the focus should be not only on promoting the general recovery of the economy through an increase in lending supply but also on strengthening the bank divisions of certain intermediaries, above all of those closer to firms (reference banks). However, financial intermediaries need an increase in equity to address these changes. New competences and organisational set ups are also required. The funding needed, as observed by Bianchi (2014), could derive from the sale of a relevant share of bank real estate, whose function has lost importance due to the increasing shift from traditional bank activities to online services.

As underlined by the Bank of Italy in 2013, this could produce positive effects on the investment capabilities, on the dimensional growth and on the innovative activities, hence, enabling the financial system to more efficiently face possible credit crunch periods.

Savings from households should be employed—through adequate institutional investors—to fund businesses. This is strongly needed to guarantee the stability of the banking system and the growth and innovation perspectives of the real economy.

Rethinking the current banking intermediation model is needed through the securitisation of those loans related to investments in firms' fixed assets. Following Mottura (2014), "If the bank provides a good consulting service to borrowers, the loan will be of a better quality, will be transferred at better conditions and will constitute good quality material for securitisation" (a.t.). As a consequence, splitting the management of liquid liabilities from a parallel management of risky assets and fewer guaranteed liabilities would be advantageous, "with positive effects on the productivity of the credit intermediation management freed from the need to convert liquid liabilities at par". The buyer of loans, usually an autonomous and independent firm from the bank providing credit, should allocate to the market the related securities characterised by high attractiveness for both private and institutional investors.

This model, made of companies involved in the securitisation process (with features similar to those of investment management companies), could represent a "market solution". In fact, it is in the same market in which the solutions to the problems of funding and undercapitalisation of commercial and savings banks could be found (Mottura 2014). However, for a good functioning of this model, the bank should select and extract the best projects to finance from the real economy. To this end, banks need analysts and administrators endowed with new models for the analysis and evaluation of firms' needs in a changing environment. They should also be able to work in a coordinated way with the aforementioned investment banks.

If banks still find difficulties in selecting credit, even with regard to the best firms, the gap in the development of distinctive capabilities is relevant. A solid and exclusive bond between each bank and each firm could benefit both agents, especially if "there is empirical evidence that a long-term relationship with a bank increases the probability that a firm will run an innovative activity, particularly in terms of R&D" (Mottura 2014).

This finding also means that a local dimension of banking intermediation is needed and would be worthwhile for exploiting the knowledge and competence acquired.

Such capability would benefit the same supply—by banks—of those high-value-added services that prepare and assist firms in allocating securities in the market, thus strengthening the relationships with their customers.

Some authors even observe that "banks seeking dimensional growth and high performance, have progressively modified their behavioural model dismissing a managerial style based on meritocracy and adequacy models, thus favouring an approach based on massive selling with a depletion of knowledge and competence, given the high volumes allocated" (Monferrà and Porzio 2014).

Another criticality is represented by the opacity that characterises the corporate system: "transparency toward the tax agency, the financial security authority and minority shareholders should be restored" (Rossi 2013). This condition appears fundamental not only to tighten bank-firm bonds but also to implement a real and widespread listing of firms and the related creation of markets that specialise in small and medium-sized companies. This should be accompanied by the creation of markets for bonds and mini-bonds, which could help the dimensional growth of those businesses that have technological opportunities. The launch of a fund of funds, specialising in small caps, could eventually appear suitable.

Regulations regarding the ACE (Allowance for Corporate Equity, implemented through the "Salva Italia" Decree) serve this purpose, even if they still appear of modest entity and therefore not determinant of an important change of internal recapitalisation.

The activation of a regional system of ratings could be useful for this purpose. Again, increasing the number of intermediaries is needed together with new financial instruments and new markets, apart from the banking market, with adequate professional capabilities to ensure liquidity in the transaction system. This should be done by guaranteeing a favourable tax regime for investments in equity and in financial instruments aiming at the dimensional growth and the technological development of businesses.

The increased number of alternative fundings compared with traditional banking, and the evolution of intermediary models oriented to separately manage the liquid liabilities of banks, together with the securitisation of long-term loans, all need time and great effort and cannot to be ignored. We thus need to intervene to help SMEs access these new types of funding. This is a way to limit the impairment of loans in the future. An increase in collateralised loans (Fund of guarantees for SMEs, and the Regional Fund of Guarantees) may strengthen bank capital and liquidity adequacy.

However, given the scenario made of insolvencies and an unchanged situation where corporate firm capital equals family business capital (which obstructs any chance to invest in risky projects), there are still lots of adjustments that "Confidi" will have to implement within the region to modify the individual credit assessment of their partners, even through an intensification of business aggregation and reorganisation processes. This is indeed needed if we do not want to transfer risks from the private to the public domain, as has already occurred in the banking industry for state aids.

5   Final Remarks

It is emblematic that, in such an environment that needs new ways to provide companies with credit, most of the support given to firms by the Sardinian regional government takes place through a regional bank, SFIRS, with assisted credit. The selection of the projects to be funded is made through political choices that do not respond to the usual banking process where a good and thorough individual credit assessment is strictly implemented. Moreover, should not this bank, rather than merely allocating funds based on choices made by someone else, do something more important for the regional financial chain, especially now that the need for new growth opportunities to SMEs is required? Should not this bank specialise in the assessment of innovative projects to allow for a plurality of financial participation—even through other banking and non-banking intermediaries—concerning both equity and leverage?

Thus, the Autonomous Region of Sardinia—free of any commitment to finance projects whose outcomes are ambiguous—should focus on administrative simplification, by creating the conditions for a complete and profitable use of its European structural funds, particularly for innovation and internationalisation, given the high number of innovative financial instruments arranged for the period 2014–2020 (i.a.: Horizon 2020 and Cosme programs).

The intensification of the role covered by the University should become a strength for the requalification of the regional productive system and the quality of financial intermediation.

On a regional base, there is no need for further bad financing. We, instead, need modern and efficient infrastructures and, therefore, certainty about when and how to undertake business. This would eventually provide consultancy services aiming to inform and help firms towards better solutions for growth and development, available at both the national and the European level.

References

Bank of Italy (2009) Economie regionali: L'economia della Sardegna. Cagliari, June
Bank of Italy (2012) Economie regionali: L'economia della Sardegna. Cagliari, June
Bank of Italy (2013) Economie regionali: L'economia della Sardegna. Cagliari, June
Bank of Italy (2014a) Annual report for 2013. Rome, May
Bank of Italy (2014b) Economie regionali: L'economia della Sardegna. Cagliari, June
Bianchi T (2014) Vi sono carenze di capitali propri nelle banche? Banche e Banchieri 2:172–179
Monferrà S, Porzio C (2014) I rapporti banca-impresa. Paper presented at the ADEIMF winter workshop, University of Milano-Bicocca, Milan, 13–14 Feb 2014. Available via http://www.

adeimf.it/images/documenti/convegni/febbraio2014/Sessione_1_I_rapporti_banca_impresa_
    Monferr%C2%85_Porzio.pdf
Mottura P (2014) La banca commerciale: sostenibilità del modello di intermediazione. Bancaria
    2:3–15
Rossi S (2013) Finanza e crescita dopo la crisi. Paper presented at Community CIB, SDA Bocconi,
    Milan, 14 Nov 2013. Available via https://www.bancaditalia.it/pubblicazioni/interventi-
    direttorio/int-dir-2013/rossi_141113.pdf

The Potential Evolution of the Supply of Credit to the Productive Chain: A Focus on Italy and the Regional Sardinian Economy

Martino Lo Cascio and Mauro Aliano

Abstract The analysis performed in this chapter aims to define the dynamics of the demand for and supply of credit for the regional Sardinian economy, compared to other Italian regions, during the period from 2002 to 2013. Typical methodologies for the analysis of financial series (velocity and momentum indicators), as well as the methodologies for spatial analysis (principal component analysis, cluster analysis and specialisation indexes), have been employed for this purpose. Based on a sample of macro- and micro-data—the latter being related to 19,000 firms—our analysis highlights the existence of some high-performing industry segments, such as *Lodging, Food and Food Services* (LFFS). Overall, our results show undeniable criticalities with regard to the allocative efficiency of banks. For the most recent years of the sample, banks severely shrank the credit supply towards the most dynamic sectors, exhibiting instead an increasing credit specialisation towards weaker performing sectors, which are characterised by high rates of impaired loans.

1 Introduction

The aim of this chapter is to define a trajectory of the potential demand for credit by some segments of the regional Sardinian economy along with the credit supply strategy of the banking industry. Based on a sample of macroeconomic and microeconomic data during the period 2002–2013, our analysis highlights the existence of some high-performing industry segments, such as *Lodging, Food and Food Services* (LFFS). Overall, our results show undeniable pitfalls in the allocative efficiency of banks. Specifically, on the one hand banks exhibited a significant contraction in the supply of credit towards the most dynamic industry

M. Lo Cascio
University of Tor Vergata, Rome, Italy
e-mail: martino.locascio@uniroma2.it

M. Aliano (✉)
Department of Economics and Business, University of Cagliari, Cagliari, Italy
e-mail: mauro.aliano@unica.it

© Springer International Publishing Switzerland 2016   157
S.P.S. Rossi, R. Malavasi (eds.), *Financial Crisis, Bank Behaviour and Credit Crunch*, Contributions to Economics, DOI 10.1007/978-3-319-17413-6_11

segments, whereas, on the other hand they supplied loans to less-performing sectors, which are characterised by high levels of non-performing loans. The chapter is structured as follows. In Sect. 2, we describe the macroeconomic and financial context for both Italy and the regional Sardinian economy, by employing macro-data variables (Added Value, Investments, and Loans) for the period 2002–2013. The analysis highlights the peculiar position of the regional Sardinian economy compared to the rest of Italy. In Sect. 3, by implementing *Momentum Analysis*, we are able to define a possible trajectory of the credit demand for a potential industry segment. Additionally, through Principal Component and Cluster Analysis, we compare the specific structure of the regional Sardinian economy with other Italian regions. In Sect. 4, we analyse the features and quality of the supply of credit provided by the regional Sardinian banking system. Based on a panel of micro-data on 19,000 firms for the sub-period 2006–2012, we show that firms operating in the productive chain are less dependent on bank credit. Section 5 concludes the chapter by highlighting the pitfalls of the banks' allocative efficiency and the emergence from the credit crunch in the regional Sardinia economy.

2   Recent Trends

We analyse the general macroeconomic environment of the Sardinian economy by focusing on the growth rates of some macro and financial variables: (i) Aggregate Production (measured by the Added Value), (ii) Investment levels, and (iii) Loans. The investigation concerns the years 2002–2013, thus covering both the pre-financial crisis and the post-financial crisis era. Thus, we are able to capture possible changes in the macroeconomic trends that are attributable to the expansion of the recent financial crisis on a regional level.

Overall, the macroeconomic indicators (Added Value and Investments)—which can be viewed as proxies for the credit demand—and the financial variable (Loans)—which can be viewed as the proxy for credit supply—exhibit a negative trend (both for the regional Sardinian economy and for Italy). More specifically, with regard to Aggregate Production (see Fig. 2 in the Appendix), the related growth rates are lower than the average values for Italy. In contrast, the growth rates of the Investments in Sardinia are higher than in Italy (see Fig. 3 in the Appendix). Interestingly, the growth rates trend for Loans in Sardinia appears to anticipate the overall dynamics for Italy (see Fig. 4 in the Appendix). In short, whereas in Sardinia the macroeconomic indicators seem to follow—with some lag—the Italian trends, our financial variable (Loans) appears to anticipate the Italian trend (i.e., Loans *anticipate* the events or the movement of economic variables). This characteristic arises, even more so, in an analysis of the *velocity* of the economic and financial variables. The difference in the *velocity* of the growth rates for the macroeconomic variables approximates the so-called Momentum indicator (see the following section for an extensive definition). Through this indicator, we observe a higher deceleration of the Production and Loans for Italy (compared to

Sardinia); whereas, for the Investments, the loss in the Momentum—i.e., the deceleration—is certainly greater for the Sardinian economy when compared to that of the Italian (primarily during the years 2011–2013; see Table 5 in the Appendix).

Essentially, the Sardinian economy is characterised by particular growth and velocity rates for the economic and financial variables that justify our analyses being performed at a regional basis. Furthermore, the following sections are aimed at understanding the impact of the credit rationing policies on the industrial sectors.

3   Added Value, Investment and Potential Demand for Credit

In this section, we analyse the aforementioned variables considering, as well, the regional and sectorial trends (spatial analysis). We utilise data from NACE 2007 (coming from ISTAT[1] database, Regional Economic Accounts). In particular, we try to investigate the dynamics of the potential demand for credit during the period 1995–2010. The entire period was divided into four sub-periods, and for each sub-period we have calculated the Momentum ($M_{av,n}$) for the Added Value (AV)—to capture the strength or weakness in the variables' movement (Murphy 1999)—as follows:

$$M_{AV,n,i} = \sqrt[t2-t1-1]{\frac{AV_{t2,i}}{AV_{t1,i}}} - 1 \qquad (1)$$

We have also calculated the Momentum for the Investments (inv) as follows:

$$M_{inv,n,i} = \sqrt[t2-t1-1]{\frac{inv_{t2,i}}{inv_{t1,i}}} - 1 \qquad (2)$$

In (1) and (2) "n" indicates the sub-period, whereas "i" represents the territorial's partition (Italy, macro-regions, regions). Essentially, this indicator (i.e., the Momentum) is often used for the analysis of the time series of prices related to financial instruments.

To examine the trajectories related to the Momentum indicator, the expected values of the Momentum for the Added Value and the Investments at time t + 1 are defined as follows:

---

[1] Italian National Institute of Statistics.

$$E(M_{AV,n+1,i}) = M_{AV,n,i} \tag{3}$$

$$E(M_{inv,n+1,i}) = M_{inv,n,i} \tag{4}$$

In few words, the expected value of the Momentum at time $t+1$ is the value of the Momentum at time t. To grasp the dynamics related to each partition (Sardinia, macro-regions, regions) and to the Italian economy, the differences between $M_{AV,n+1,i}$ and $E(M_{AV,n+1,i})$ and between $M_{AV,n+1,i}$ and $E(M_{AV,n+1,italy})$ have been analysed. The first difference indicates the gap from the historical trajectory of growth of the added value, whereas the second difference indicates the gap from the trajectory of growth of Italy as a whole. The same difference has also been computed for the Investments to measure the gaps in the trajectories of growth, both in relation to the past and to the overall Italian situation. With regard to the Added Value, the first difference is defined as follows:

$$diff_{n+1,AV,i} = M_{AV,n+1,i} - E(M_{AV,n+1,i}) \text{ projected on the X-axis} \tag{5}$$

Whereas the second difference is defined as:

$$diff_{n+1,AV,i,italy} = M_{AV,n+1,i} - E(M_{AV,n+1,italy}) \text{ projected on the Y-axis} \tag{6a}$$

Following (5) and (6a), analogous differences have been computed for the Investments:

$$diff_{n+1,inv,i} = M_{inv,n+1,i} - E(M_{inv,n+1,i}) \text{ projected on the X-axis} \tag{6b}$$

$$diff_{n+1,inv,i,italy} = M_{inv,n+1,i} - E(M_{inv,n+1,italy}) \text{ projected on the Y-axis} \tag{7}$$

The projections of the calculated differences above are reported in the figures presented in the Appendix (from Figs. 5, 6, 7, 8, 9, 10, 11, 12, and 13). They represent the positioning and the trajectories of growth of the potential demand for Sardinia compared to the other Italian regions. For the sake of brevity, we only present in the Appendix to this chapter the most significant sectors in terms of "positioning".

The "positioning" on the right side of the x-axis indicates a positive difference between the current and the expected value of the Momentum (i.e., the Momentum of the previous sub-period), which is a higher trend compared to the expected one (based on historical values). A value above zero, with respect to the y-axis, indicates that the value of the Momentum of the analysed territorial partition is greater than the one expected for all of Italy. For example, with regard to the Added Value, Sardinia (for the sub-period 2005–2007) is positioned in the first quadrant; i.e., the estimates related to the Sardinian partition exceed the current and expected values related to the entire Italian territory, thus indicating a potential demand for credit. In the sub-period 2008–2010, on the contrary, the positioning in the third quadrant indicates a negative trajectory, with respect to the current and expected values, related to the entire Italian territory (see Fig. 5 in the Appendix).

The analysis of the differences (5), (6a), (6b) and (7) provide us with some indications that can be summarised according to the variable (Added Value and Investment) and to some industrial sectors. We start by analysing (6a) and (7), which refer to the Added Value, allowing us to infer some characteristics of the demand for credit.

- From the analysis of the entire economy (all industries), we do not find any relevant indication about a possible specific positioning of the Sardinian economy in relation to the other territorial partitions. In fact, during the period 2008–2010, all the values are negative. Hence, there is no geographic characterisation in relation to the potential demand from the real economy (see Fig. 5 in the Appendix).
- In contrast, we find some clear indications from the analysis of the *"food products, beverages and tobacco industries"*. For this segment, in fact, during the years 2008–2010, the Sardinian economy performs better than the other territorial partitions (with respect to the growth differential for all of Italy). Additionally, the distance of the Sardinian partition from the other regions is distinct. This distinctive feature must be dynamically analysed given the performance realised by the same sector during the period 2005–2007. For that period, the performance recorded was in agreement with the average performance of the other regions (see Fig. 6 in the Appendix).
- The distance of the *lodging and food services* industry during the period 2008–2010 is even more significant, although this positive performance could be predicted by the positioning of the Sardinian economy during the period 2005–2007 (see Fig. 7 in the Appendix).
- In contrast, for the *coking plants, refineries, chemical and pharmaceutical* segment, we observe a contraction of the Added Value not only in relation to the expected value for the entire Italian economy but also with respect to Southern Italy. The importance of this segment cannot be underestimated as it accounts (in terms of Added Value) for 12 % of the Sardinian manufacturing industry (see Fig. 8 in the Appendix).
- The same dynamics are observed for the *"manufacturing of basic metals"* segment (which represents 15 % of the manufacturing industry). In this case, this segment exhibits negative values not only for the Sardinian economy— given its positioning in the third quadrant during the period 2008 to 2010—but also for the entire Italian economy (see Fig. 9 in the Appendix).

We can perform a similar analysis with regards to the Momentum indicators for the Investments (6b) and (7).

- Concerning the Added Value, within the *food products, beverages and tobacco industries* segment, we also observe a positive performance in relation to Southern Italy's territorial partition (see Fig. 10 in the Appendix).

– In the *lodging and food services* segment, unlike our findings for Added Value, we do not find a positive performance that enables us to predict an unexpected and potential demand for credit for Investments. This is probably because, unlike the food industries, the need for relevant investments in this segment is lower (see Fig. 11 in the Appendix).
– As for the Added Value, we observe negative values for the Investments in the *coking plants, refineries, chemical, and pharmaceutical* segment (see Fig. 12 in the Appendix). This segment shows the highest decreases in the demand for credit. This feature is shared by the *manufacturing of basic materials* segment, as well (see Fig. 13 in the Appendix).

Overall, from the analysis on the potential demand, we observe a type of dual economy for the Sardinian region. In fact, on the one hand we have found that the *Lodging, Food and Food Services* (LFFS) segment exhibits a better performance if compared to the entire Italian economy. On the other hand, some traditional industry segments appear to be in a stagnant situation, with a corresponding decrease of the potential demand for credit. The positioning of the Sardinian region, from the point of view of potential demand for credit, is even clearer in the following section where we show a strengthening of the peculiar condition of the dual economy.

3.1 Positioning the Sardinian Regional Economy in the National Context

Given the results of the previous section, to underline the "territorial vocation" for each region, we run a Principal Component Analysis (PCA) for i regions and p variables (namely, industry segments). The aim is to identify a potential demand for credit among some characteristic segments of the Sardinian economy. Given the factor scores identified (drawn from the PCA) for all the Italian regions, we then conduct a cluster analysis to understand the positioning of the Sardinian economy compared to the other Italian regions. To better highlight the effects of the productive chains (LFFS) and, in general, of the dual economy identified in previous sections, the PCA has been divided into two parts (PC1 and PC2). PC1 has been performed at a more aggregate sectorial level; whereas PC2, at a less aggregate sectorial level, has been run with the aim of capturing the peculiarities of some specific dynamics—which reflect a possible "implied" demand for credit (e.g., implied demand for oil). In the input matrix $X_{i,p}$[2] of the PCA (where i represents the regions and p the variables used in the factor analysis), the following six variables (i.e., industry segments) have been used:

---

[2] To make the approach in the analysis of the input data clear, see Jobson (1992).

- *public administration*: difference between actual and expected Momentum for the same partition
- *public administration_it*: difference between the actual Momentum (of a specific partition) and the expected Momentum for Italy
- *trade:* difference between actual and expected Momentum for the same partition
- *trade_it*: difference between the actual Momentum (of a specific partition) and the expected Momentum for Italy
- *building and infrastructure*: difference between actual and expected Momentum for the same partition
- *building and infrastructure_it*: difference between the actual Momentum (of a specific partition) and the expected Momentum for Italy

After having run a PCA—computed using the "ordinary correlations" criterion, through the Rotation Method Oblique Varimax[3]—we obtained the coefficients of communalities, as shown in Table 1.

The PC1 has been conducted over the period 2008–2010. The columns F1, F2 and F3 in Table 1 indicate the communalities between the old and the new variables (also known as latent factors). The factor F1 in the new vector space is a summary of the differences between the actual and expected Momentum, both of which are within the same geographic partition and within the partition compared to the entire Italian economy. Through the use of these latent factors, we do not find any "geographical" evidence (see Figs. 14, 15, 16 in the Appendix): both Sardinia as well as the other regions appear to randomly cluster, without any logic of territorial proximity or affinity to macro areas. In fact, after analysing the clusters according to the Ward Criterion,[4] we do not find any logical spatial/territorial clustering.

To more specifically qualify the latent diversities at a regional level, we now perform a further Principal Component Analysis, i.e., PC2, where we utilise data on the following five sectors:

Table 1 Communalities, PC1

	F1	F2	F3
Public administration	0.062433	−0.084	0.679522
Public administration_it	−0.07247	0.065771	0.703934
Trade	−0.00109	0.703587	−0.00818
Trade_it	0.008944	0.700829	−0.00088
Building and infrastructure	0.7468	−0.02387	−0.12308
Building and infrastructure_it	0.658167	0.044118	0.166248

Source: Our elaborations on Istat data

---

[3] See Lebart et al. (1984).
[4] See Johnson and Wichern (2007).

- *agriculture*: difference between actual and expected Momentum for the same partition
- *agriculture_it*: difference between the actual Momentum (of a specific partition) and the expected Momentum for Italy
- *coke*: difference between actual and expected Momentum for the same partition
- *coke_it*: difference between the actual Momentum (of a specific partition) and the expected Momentum for Italy
- *metallurgic*: difference between the actual and expected Momentum for the same partition
- *metallurgic_it*: difference between the actual Momentum (of a specific partition) and the expected Momentum for Italy
- *food industry*: difference between the actual and expected Momentum for the same partition
- *food industry_it*: difference between the actual Momentum (of a specific partition) and the expected Momentum for Italy
- *Lodging*: difference between the actual and expected Momentum for the same partition
- *Lodging_it*: difference between the actual Momentum (of a specific partition) and the expected Momentum for Italy

The results of the PC2 highlight specific characterisations in particular for the *lodging, catering and food industries*, where the extremely positive result for F2 enables us to conclude that the Sardinian economy is different from the other Italian regions, even without the need to conduct an analysis of the clusters (see Figs. 17 and 18 in the Appendix). The Table 2 shows the communality coefficients for the factors resulting from the PC2.

In line with what we have previously stated, the cluster analysis confirms what emerges from the graph inspections about the positioning of Sardinia compared to other Italian regions. Overall, the Sardinian economy emerges as a dual economy prototype (a high share of basic products in decline, and great performances with

Table 2 Communalities, PC2

	F1	F2	F3
Agriculture	−0.03689	−0.0781	0.509139
Agriculture_it	0.024313	−0.29786	0.407577
Coke	0.437884	0.247407	−0.13078
Coke_it	0.46396	0.339608	−0.10722
Metallurgic	0.309972	0.192481	0.422193
Metallurgic_it	0.402841	0.227346	0.3054
Food industry	−0.27286	0.320766	−0.20268
Food industry_it	−0.09532	0.462772	−0.21774
Lodging	−0.38609	0.388326	0.302528
Lodging_it	−0.31636	0.414794	0.307461

Source: Our elaborations on Istat data

regards to the LFFS's productive chain). This condition provides us with useful insights about the validity of the credit rationing policies implemented in various industry segments.

4 Characteristics of Loans in the Italian Regional Banking System

Whereas in the previous sections we analysed the trajectories and dynamics of the potential demand for credit, we now consider the credit supply. We proxy the supply of credit by the amount of loans provided on a regional level (according to the various types of borrowers), and by the structural trend of the debt across the different industry segments. The first type of investigation is conducted with a parallel analysis of the dynamics of the banks' impairments, thus estimating the effectiveness of the banks' specialisations at a regional level.

Starting from the Bank of Italy matrix (which contains data on the regional economies), where the amount of credit for each territorial partition (rows) and market segmentation (columns) is represented, to capture the geographical and sectorial specialisation we calculate the LB (Lo Cascio et al. 2012) specialisation index as follows:

$$LB_{i,j} = \frac{q(x) - q(a)}{[1 - q(a)]q(x) + [1 - q(x)]q(a)} \tag{8}$$

where

$$q(x) = \frac{x_{i,j}}{\sum_i x_{i,j}} \tag{9}$$

$$q(a) = \frac{\sum_j x_{i,j}}{\sum_i x_{i,j}} \tag{10}$$

$x_{i,j}$ is the value (amount of credit supplied in 2012) for the j-th variable (market segmentation) in the i-th region (territorial partition): for $q(x) = q(a), LB_{i,j} = 0$; for $q(x) < q(a), LB_{i,j} < 0$; for $q(x) > q(a), LB_{i,j} > 0$

$$1 \geq LB_{i,j} \geq -1$$

A positive (negative) value of this index indicates a specialisation ("de-specialisation") for the i-th region in the j-th market segment. The specialisation in the supply of credit in 2007 shows that there are highly specialised regions in the provision of loans to certain market segments. For example, the banking system of the Lombardy Region (i.e., the region whose capital is Milan), not unexpectedly, is

Table 3 Credit specialisations in 2012

	Public administration	Financial and insurance companies	Large and medium-sized companies	Small business	Households
Piedmont	−0.146	−0.379	0.005	0.152	0.138
Aosta Valley	−0.438	−0.594	0.108	0.311	0.061
Bolzano / Bozen	−0.662	−0.616	0.095	0.483	−0.020
Lombardy	−0.778	0.362	0.119	−0.149	−0.066
Veneto	−0.715	−0.182	0.150	0.183	0.038
Friuli-Venezia Giulia	−0.426	−0.367	0.049	0.182	0.153
Liguria	−0.459	−0.688	0.089	0.129	0.203
Emilia-Romagna	−0.722	0.105	0.137	0.086	−0.034
Tuscany	−0.542	−0.215	0.091	0.177	0.093
Umbria	−0.536	−0.958	0.114	0.326	0.127
Marche	−0.524	−0.484	0.095	0.272	0.103
Lazio	0.748	0.182	−0.347	−0.666	−0.361
Abruzzo	−0.482	−0.939	0.095	0.274	0.168
Molise	−0.346	−0.906	−0.036	0.343	0.228
Campania	−0.120	−0.837	0.017	−0.011	0.256
Apulia	−0.361	−0.931	−0.051	0.228	0.309
Calabria	0.078	−0.988	−0.201	0.268	0.280
Sicily	−0.163	−0.948	−0.109	0.188	0.326
Basilicata	−0.143	−0.990	−0.003	0.323	0.157
Sardinia	−0.464	−0.391	−0.077	0.222	0.275

Source: Our elaborations on Bank of Italy data

relatively highly specialised in the supply of loans to financial and insurance companies. In 2007, however, the Sardinian banking system was specialised in the supply of credit especially to small businesses and households. In 2012, this peculiarity for the Sardinian region was even more accentuated (that is, there was a rise in the growth of loans provided by the aforementioned agents); see Table 3. However, this rise in the growth of loans to small businesses and households was not associated to an increase in the total amount of credit supplied; in fact, between 2007 and 2012, the global supply of credit decreased.

Apart from the evidence about the regional specialisation of the banking system, it is interesting to provide some information on the overall quality of credit, summarised by the ratio between impaired loans and total loans. We essentially investigate whether the specialisation of the banking system towards small businesses and households is associated (or not) to an improvement of the evaluation of the borrowers' creditworthiness—to therefore understand if the banks have improved their capabilities in assessing the risks towards the two aforementioned

Table 4 Loans and non-performing loans in Sardinia

Loans							
	2007	2008	2009	2010	2011	2012	var. 2007–2012 (%)
Small business (EUR millions)	3,119	3,195	3,060	3,789	3,829	3,605	15.582
Households (EUR millions)	7,882	7,726	8,247	9,956	10,315	10,110	28.267
Total Loans (EUR millions)	20,023	20,833	21,624	25,132	27,041	25,479	27.249
Non-performing loans							
	2007	2008	2009	2010	2011	2012	var. 2007–2012 (%)
Small business (EUR millions)	372	374	406	681	763	810	117.742
Households (EUR millions)	245	239	281	324	388	415	69.388
Total non-performing loans (EUR millions)	1,331	1,401	1,644	1,920	2,406	2,654	99.399
Ratio non-performing loans/loans (%)							
	2007	2008	2009	2010	2011	2012	
Small business	11.93	11.71	13.27	17.97	19.93	22.47	
Households	3.11	3.09	3.41	3.25	3.76	4.10	
Total sectors	6.65	6.72	7.60	7.64	8.90	10.42	

Source: Our elaborations on Bank of Italy data

favourite borrowers. In this regard, the reports on the regional economies (Bank of Italy 2012) highlight a worsening in the quality of the credit supplied to the two favourite borrowers in Sardinia (see Table 4). If we set at 100, for the year 2007, the level of the impaired loans related to the two types of borrowers, we observe that this level of impaired loans reaches 198.73 in 2012—thus highlighting a 98.73 % increase across the period. However, it is worth noting that the total level of impaired loans, during the same period, "only" increases from 6.65 % to 10.42 %. Nevertheless, the *quasi*-doubling growth of the impaired loans towards small businesses and households is consistent with the national trend (i.e., 202.10, +102.1 %).

We now perform an analysis on the different industry segments. We start by assessing the amount of funds provided by the banks to the businesses located in Sardinia. Hence, we extract a sample of 18,741 Sardinian firms from the AIDA database provided by the Bureau van Dijk. Accordingly, we observe—for given industry segments—the allocative efficiency of the credit supply and examine the related effects. We, therefore, utilise three balance sheet ratios that show the trends of (i) profitability; (ii) dependence from the bank lending channel; and (iii) revenues-to-bank loans ratio.

The link between the three ratios is represented by the following equation:

$$\frac{revenues}{tangible\ and\ untangible\ assets} = \frac{bank\ loans}{tangible\ and\ untangible\ assets} * \frac{revenues}{bank\ loans}$$

where:

$$\frac{revenues}{tangible\ and\ untangible\ assets} = \text{a version of the turnover ratio}$$

$$\frac{bank\ loans}{tangible\ and\ untangible\ assets} = \begin{array}{l}\text{a proxy of the degree of bank intermediation}\\ \text{for medium/long non-financial investment}\end{array}$$

$$\frac{revenues}{bank\ loans} = \text{a proxy of bank loan revenues}$$

For the most significant industry segments, in Fig. 1 three lines are represented: (i) The SBD line (SBD—Sample without the effects of firm Births and Deaths) represents the ratio for the firms that have continuously operated throughout the years since 2006; (ii) The BD line (BD—Sample characterised by firm Births and Deaths) represents the ratio for the new firms and for those firms that ceased their business during the analysed period; (iii) Finally, the AS line (AS—All Sample) represents the ratio for all the companies in the dataset. We have, therefore, developed an analysis of the supply of credit that considers the natality/mortality rate of the firms, trying to capture the peculiarities of both the profitability of and dependence on bank capital.

Overall (considering all the industry segments), we do not observe significant changes throughout the years for the three ratios, except for the new and ceased firms that present a very high level of dependence on the banking sector. In contrast, we find a steady dependence on banks by the businesses continuously operating since 2006 (that is, without considering the effects of firm Births and Deaths).

For the lodging and food services sector, which is a part of the best performing productive chain on the demand side (as outlined in previous sections), there is a clear progressive reduction of dependence on the banking sector since 2011. A progressive reduction (though less pronounced) of "bank dependence" is also observed for firms operating in the food industry.

With regards to gross profitability, the related ratios show a decrease starting in 2007, especially for the food sector when compared to the lodging sector, which does not appear to suffer from the financial crisis, primarily because of the new firms initiated after 2007.

5   Conclusions

The analyses performed throughout this chapter highlight some interesting results. When we analysed the potential demand for credit, we found a peculiar condition of credit rationing towards those businesses operating in the most promising industry segments. In this regard, it is worth noting an issue in terms of the allocative efficiency of the financial resources provided by banks to all the industry segments. Furthermore, the issue regarding the trends of the impaired loans is interesting and

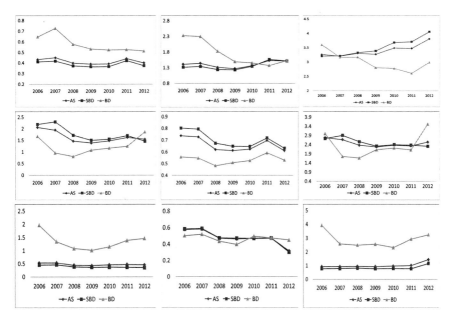

Fig. 1 AS, SBD and BD calculated for commerce as a whole, manufactured food and lodging and food services. *Source*: Our elaborations on AIDA database

alarming. A comprehensive rethinking of the credit rationing policies implemented by banks in Sardinia is required.

Appendix

A.1 Recent Trends

We present here the growth rates of the macroeconomic environment discussed in Sect. 2.

Fig. 2 Rate of growth. Added value. Our elaboration on Istat data. *Source*: Our elaboration on Istat data

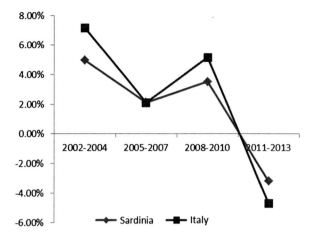

Fig. 3 Rate of growth of investment. *Source*: Our elaboration on Istat data

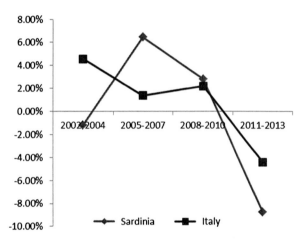

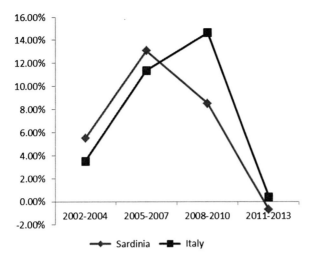

Fig. 4 Rate of growth of loans. *Source*: Our elaboration on Bank of Italy data. Gross loans were considered in the above calculations

Table 5 Momentum gains/losses

	Added value (%)		
	2005–2007	2008–2010	2011–2013
Sardinia	−2.85	1.41	−6.72
Italy	−5.06	3.06	−9.85
	Investment (%)		
	2005–2007	2008–2010	2011–2013
Sardinia	7.65	−3.64	−11.57
Italy	−3.18	0.83	−6.61
	Loans (%)		
	2005–2007	2008–2010	2011–2013
Sardinia	7.58	−4.57	−9.21
Italy	7.86	3.27	−14.24

Source: Our elaboration on Istat and Bank of Italy data

A.2 Added Value, Investment and Potential Demand for Credit

The following figures show the graphic projections of the differences discussed in Sect. 3.

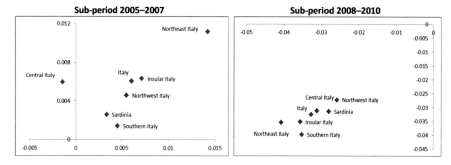

Fig. 5 Added value—all sectors. *Source*: Our elaboration on Istat data

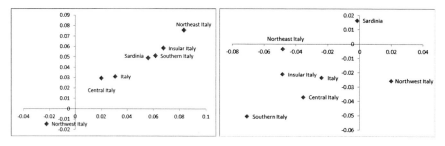

Fig. 6 Added value—food products, beverages and tobacco industries. *Source*: Our elaboration on Istat data

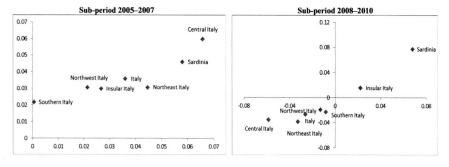

Fig. 7 Added value—lodging and food services. *Source*: Our elaboration on Istat data

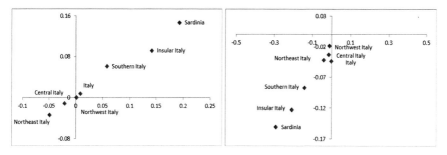

Fig. 8 Added value—coking plants, refineries, chemical and pharmaceutical segment. *Source*: Our elaboration on Istat data

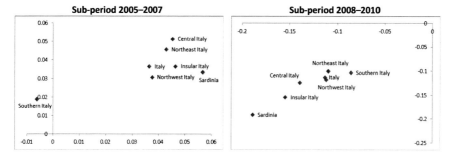

Fig. 9 Added value—manufacture of basic materials. *Source*: Our elaboration on Istat data

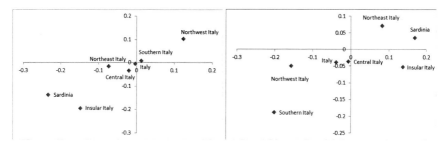

Fig. 10 Investment—food products, beverages and tobacco industries. *Source*: Our elaboration on Istat data

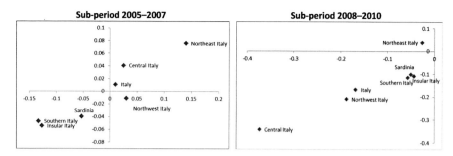

Fig. 11 Investment—lodging and food services. *Source*: Our elaboration on Istat data

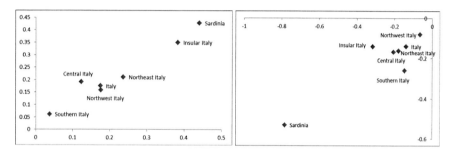

Fig. 12 Investment—coking plants, refineries, chemical and pharmaceutical segments. *Source*: Our elaboration on Istat data

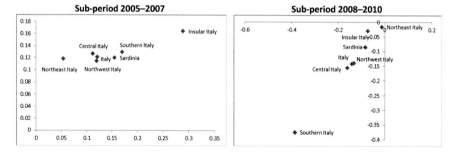

Fig. 13 Investment—manufacture of basic materials. *Source*: Our elaboration on Istat data

A.3 Regional Positioning on Latent Variables

The following figures show the positioning of the Italian regions with respect to the latent variables (factors) that we analysed in Sect. 3.1.

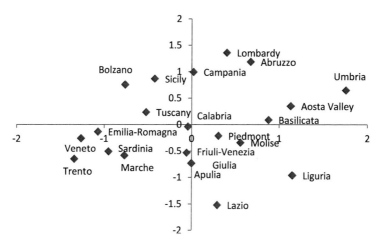

Fig. 14 New latent dimensions. F1 and F2 for PC1. *Source*: Our elaboration on Istat data

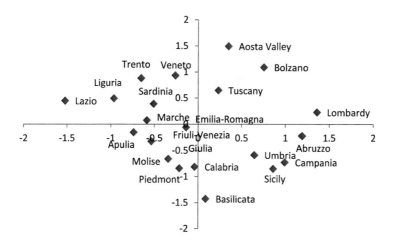

Fig. 15 New latent sectors. F2 and F3 for PC1. *Source*: Our elaboration on Istat data

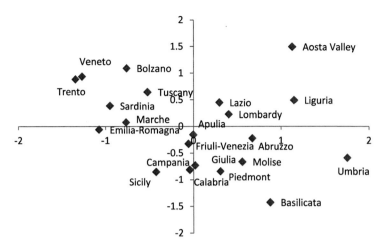

Fig. 16 New latent sectors. F1 and F3 for PC1. *Source*: Our elaboration on Istat data

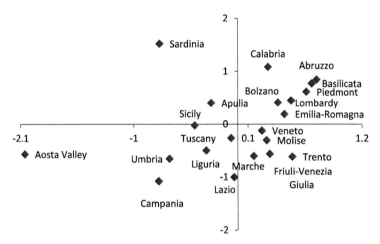

Fig. 17 New latent dimensions. F1 and F2 for PC2. *Source*: Our elaboration on Istat data

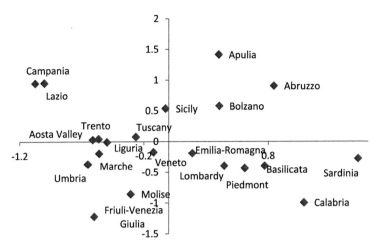

Fig. 18 New latent sectors. F2 and F3 for PC2. *Source*: Our elaboration on Istat data

References

Bank of Italy, Regional economies 2007–2012. Accessed 15 May 2014. http://www.bancaditalia. it/pubblicazioni/economie-regionali/index.html

Jobson JD (1992) Applied multivariate data analysis. Vol II: Categorical and multivariate methods. Springer, New York

Johnson RA, Wichern DW (2007) Applied multivariate statistical analysis. Pearson, New York

Lebart L, Morineau A, Warwick KM (1984) Multivariate descriptive statistical analysis: correspondence analysis and related techniques for large matrices. Wiley, New York

Lo Cascio M, Bagarani M, Zampino S (2012) Economic space trajectory through different regional growth models. In: Bagarani M (ed) Il governo delle Regioni e lo sviluppo economico. Edizioni dell'Orso, Alessandria, pp 41–70

Murphy J (1999) Technical analysis of the financial markets. Prentice Hall Direct, Upper Saddle River, NJ

Direct Access to the Debt Capital Market by Unlisted Companies in Italy and the Effects of Changes in Civil Law: An Empirical Investigation

Giuseppe Riccio

Abstract This paper examines the effects of changes in civil and fiscal law that were made to facilitate direct access to the debt capital market by unlisted companies in Italy to allow them (particularly SMEs) to cope with the persisting credit crunch. This study is based on an empirical investigation of data regarding issues listed in the ExtraMOT Pro market (MTF) of the Italian Stock Exchange from March 2013 to June 2014.

Our results demonstrate that few issues were listed in this period and that approximately one-half of the total outstanding issues were absorbed by issues of the top three companies. This is because companies of medium to large size were also among the first movers; afterwards, issues were primarily launched in smaller amounts. The most frequent sectors are services (Information and Communication Technology, engineering, gaming) and building/real estate sectors.

Despite the slow start, corporate finance regulations have created "work in progress" so that a greater use of direct financing through bonds, in addition to bank credit, is almost at hand.

1 Introduction

This paper uses data regarding issues listed in the ExtraMOT PRO market of the Italian Stock Exchange (the professional segment is only accessible to professional investors) to assess the effects of changes in Italian law that were made to ease direct access to the debt capital market by unlisted companies. The empirical investigation concerns financial instruments issued in the period from March 2013 to July 2014.

G. Riccio (✉)
Department of Economics and Business, University of Cagliari, Cagliari, Italy
e-mail: riccio@unica.it

© Springer International Publishing Switzerland 2016   179
S.P.S. Rossi, R. Malavasi (eds.), *Financial Crisis, Bank Behaviour and Credit Crunch*, Contributions to Economics, DOI 10.1007/978-3-319-17413-6_12

The issue of financing Italian firms is highly topical as a result of the credit crunch caused by the financial crisis and in relation to the regulations issued since 2012 to facilitate SMEs' recourse to debt capital markets. The context of Italian companies, especially SMEs, is traditionally characterized by a historical equity gap and, from the point of view of debt, by the widespread use of bank credit as a form of asset financing (Malavasi 2015). The weakness of firms' financial structures is mostly due to a lack of sources, both internal and external, such as self-financing and bank loans (Gai and Ielasi 2013).

Among the internal sources, in recent years, self-financing has generated modest positive cash flows because of the fall in demand and, consequently, in sales revenue and the extension of the monetary cycle of working capital, particularly the average duration of trade credits. Monetary resources can also be acquired through the sale of financial assets or fixed assets that are not necessary for a company's normal operations or as a result of placing new capital by shareholders. Finally, financial resources may be received by the company through intercompany loans from the parent company or from a financial subsidiary company. In the recent past, these forms of financing have not been able to provide companies with significant liquidity, primarily because the realization of assets is not always a possible source of financing due to a lack of assets, and in any case, it must be seen in the context of extraordinary transactions.

The placing of new risk capital by shareholders does not occur frequently in Italy because past fiscal distortions favoured companies in debt, and this is the cause of the undercapitalization of firms. Recently, fiscal changes regarding allowances for corporate equity have been introduced to stimulate capital contributions by company owners to strengthen a company's financial structure, but they have not yet produced significant results. With regard to intra-group loans, which require a control group, they are utilized only in major firms[1]; while approximately three-quarters of Italian SMEs have individual shareholders.

This paper is structured as follows: Section 2 contains brief introductory remarks on external sources and the evolution of the supply of bank credit in the present context; it also describes the main recent changes in civil and tax laws that were aimed at facilitating direct access to the debt capital market by unlisted companies. Section 3 of the analysis focuses on data concerning issues listed in the ExTraMOT PRO market of the Italian Stock Exchange. This is followed by considerations on the mini-bond market prospects for development, especially with regard to the recent *Decreto Destinazione Italia*. The final section contains conclusions and some considerations on the limitations of the study.

---

[1] It is estimated that a control group is present in only 10 % of small Italian businesses and in approximately 15 % of the medium ones.

2   External Sources, Bank Credit and Access to the Debt Capital Market

The most relevant external sources of capital are public funds, financial markets, venture capital, capital markets debt and bank loans. Direct funding to the economy from public sources is gradually decreasing and is based on increasingly more restrictive criteria, as a result of the cost containment policies imposed by more stringent constraints on public budgets. The decrease in direct funding is balanced by an increase in public guarantee funds for loans granted by the financial system (which enhance the leverage effect).

The financial markets for risk capital are historically low, and only in recent years have we seen a modest increase. The reasons for their minor importance are primarily due to family control over a company: in more than one-half of Italian companies, the majority of members are bound together by ties of kinship, while in about one-quarter of them, control is exercised by a single person.

The fear of losing control causes resistance to opening the company to external subjects, even though it leads to the severe phenomenon of business dwarfism. This fact, together with the lack of transparency in external reporting, does not encourage the entry of private equity and venture capital in companies.

For all of these reasons, the leverage of Italian companies at the end of 2013 (44.4 %) was the highest among euro area countries, 5 percentage points higher than the average value of 38.9 %. In the same period, the role of loans (64.2 %) was much higher than the euro area average (45.5 %), also in the percentage composition of liabilities (Malavasi 2015). Moreover, bank credit, which until the first half of 2007 had experienced a period of expansion lasting almost five years, was characterized by a deceleration phase until mid-2009, when the dynamics of loans turned negative (see Panetta and Signoretti 2010).

Currently, banks are in a deleveraging phase, both because of the need to consolidate their assets to meet the more stringent capital requirements of Basel III and to cope with the increased riskiness of firms. Credit rationing also affects deserving borrowers, who have great difficulty obtaining funds from banks to finance working capital or new investment projects, both in terms of the availability of funds and their increased costs as well as the demand for more guarantees. This has had more stringent effects on SMEs, which have less access to alternative channels to banks. This means that companies with good growth prospects must resort to alternative means of funding to cover their financial requirements.

For this reason, it was necessary to remove one of the causes of reluctance for many companies to open up to the capital market by modifying the legal and tax regulations that discouraged alternative forms of financing to bank credit; among other things, unlisted companies could issue bonds only up to twice the value of their net assets.

The new rules introduced into Italian law in 2012 removed legal and fiscal obstacles to direct recourse to the capital market aimed, on the one hand, to encourage forms of financing alternative to banks in favour of Italian unlisted companies (particularly SMEs)[2] and, on the other hand, to connect them with foreign investors. Concerning the latter question, the harmonization of Italian legislation with that of the most advanced European countries assimilates unlisted companies with listed companies in relation to the issuance of bonds and similar securities. In particular, the intent was to remove restrictions on capital and some administrative formalities, as well as to extend certain tax breaks, which had hampered their use by companies in the name of existing tools.

The regulatory changes that were made at an early stage to civil and fiscal law (Culicchi and Puna 2014) are contained in some Law Decrees issued in 2012 and 2013 (so called *Decreto Sviluppo I*, *Decreto Sviluppo II* and *Decreto Destinazione Italia*).[3] The main changes introduced in the first phase by *Decreto Sviluppo* in favour of companies that "do not issue financial instruments listed on regulated markets or MTFs, other than banks and micro-enterprises" are:

- overcoming quantity limits (equal to twice the net assets) set by previous civil law on bond issues, if "intended to be listed on regulated markets or MTFs, or bonds that give the right to acquire or subscribe to shares";
- changes to the way that bonds and finance bills issued by unlisted companies are treated by taxes; and
- modifying and integrating finance bill regulation (duration, dematerialization, tax benefits, guarantees) to ease its use as a tool for short-term financing.

Because the listing of securities in multilateral trading facilities (MTFs) is a sufficient condition to receive the benefits provided by *Decreti Sviluppo*, Borsa Italiana SpA (The Italian Stock Exchange) established the professional segment ExtraMOT PRO, which is dedicated to debt instruments issued by SMEs (bonds, finance bills, equity instruments and project bonds), that only qualified investors can access. *Decreto Destinazione Italia* introduced a series of further measures to expand the capital market debt (bond issues in particular), given the continuing contraction of credit from the banking system.

The aim of strengthening the facilities for alternative financing has been pursued, on the one hand, with measures to increase the dissemination of mini-bonds and ABS to have them as underlying among institutional investors (that is, insurance companies and pension funds) and, on the other hand, by introducing procedural simplifications and additional tax breaks. There is also the possibility for banks to structure and issue covered bonds that are secured by mini-bonds and other credit assets, primarily loans to SMEs.

With regards to taxation, the new rules extend the exemption on interest and income relative to bonds and finance bills that are payable to investment funds held

---

[2] Even the European Council Recommendation on the National Reform Programme 2014 of Italy, at point 4, suggests that Italy "promote the access of enterprises, especially those of small and medium-size, to non-bank funding".

[3] D.L. n. 83/2012 (Decreto Sviluppo I), D.L. n. 179/2012 (Decreto Sviluppo II) and D.L. n. 145/2013 (Decreto Destinazione Italia). Art. 12 of the latter Decree has further amended: Art. 32 of the Development Decree II, art. 46 of the Banking Law and the Law on securitization.

entirely by qualified investors, which have assets that are invested entirely in mini-bonds, from the withholding tax of 20 %; this could also be used for the aggregation of different issues in a single portfolio, thus facilitating the creation of a real market for mini-bonds. When the first legislative amendments were launched, the Ministry of Economic Development estimated the potential for emissions on the order of 10–12 billion euros in one and a half years as well as a group of more than 600 companies that would be eligible to benefit from the normative changes.

3   Results of the Empirical Investigation and the Reasons for the Slow Start of the Market

On the whole, mini-bonds issued by unlisted companies have contributed to the growth of bond issues. According to data from the Bank of Italy (Annual report 2014, p. 186) from November 2012 to December 2013, 19 companies issued mini-bonds, for a total of 5.9 billion euros or 12 % of the total bonds placed in the same period. Almost all issuers were large-size companies, half of which work in the service sector. In the first quarter of 2014, five issues of small amounts (an average of 16 million) were conducted by SMEs. Some of these issues, made by Italian companies with a recognized brand abroad, have been placed through private placement (primarily at foreign underwriters, as in Italy, a market for private placements is under development); others are listed in foreign markets.

The empirical investigation conducted focuses on data[4] related to listed financial instruments in the Professional Segment of the ExtraMOT market (ExtraMOT PRO[5]) of the Italian Stock Exchange (accessible only to professional investors subject to prudential supervision, while Italian private operators are denied direct access). It should be noted that for the time being, the listing of securities is only a formality because preliminary negotiations are conducted out of the market between the two counterparts. In the period between the first listing (25 March 2013) and 2 July 2014, 54 instruments issued by 39 companies were listed (Table 1), with a nominal value of more than 3.330 billion euros (49 bonds, 4 finance bills and 1 convertible bond).

The average amount of issues is approximately 62 million euros. Moreover, approximately one-half of the total amount was absorbed by the issues of the first three companies, while more than 91 % of the total issues was absorbed by 13 issues of 50 million or more euros (an approximate average of 233 million euros); the residual percentage was covered by the remaining 41 instruments, with an average

---

[4] The calculations reported in this paper relate to issues listed on ExtraMOT PRO until 2 July 2014.

[5] The ExtraMOT falls into the category of MTF (Multilateral Trading Facilities; previously ATS. Alternative Trading Facilities), which are private trading systems that allow for the purchase and sale of securities by bringing trading interest from various parties on the basis of non-discretionary rules.

Table 1 Outstanding allocation on an amount basis

Slot of outstanding	N. of issues	Outstanding (*euro* × *1000*)			
		Min	Max	Average	Total
<2 million euros	10	114.0	1,900.0	1,149.4	11,494.0
>= 2 million euros < 5 million euros	13	2,000.0	4,000.0	3,223.1	41,900.0
>= 5 million euros < 15 million euros	13	5,000.0	14,300.0	10,161.5	132,100.0
>= 15 million euros < 50 million euros	5	15,000.0	28,606.0	22,400.0	112,000.0
>= 50 million euros < 200 million euros	5	100,000.0	198,100.0	175,947.0	879,735.0
200 million euros and more	8	200,000.0	411,600.0	269,179.4	2,153,435.0
Total	*54*	*114.0*	*411,600.0*	*61,679.0*	*3,330,664.0*

Source: Our elaborations of data from *Borsa Italiana*

"outstanding" of approximately 7 million euros. This is because at the start of issuing (until November 2013) among issuers, there were also companies of medium/large size that benefited from the favourable legislation and tax treatment offered by the law to issue assets for significant amounts in other European countries (Luxembourg, Ireland) that also listed on the Italian Stock Exchange. Some of these companies hold large numbers of shares in private equity funds, which are very sophisticated and financially interested in their financial leverage to maximize their return (ROE). Afterwards, issues were launched primarily in smaller amounts; some are so small that their appropriateness in relation to the costs of the operation has been questioned.

In general, the principal declared objective of issues is to fund expansion operations, even abroad, and in some cases, with the intention of reducing the exposure of banks. The polarization of the first issues of mini-bonds followed its own logic with regard to the attitude of the banks; on the one hand are operations and large volumes of a certain risk, which could not be supported by only one bank but required a pool of banks, while on the other hand are small businesses that are willing to pay high rates to access forms of financial funding that could hardly be satisfied by banks on the basis of historical financial statements.

The breakdown of the amounts of issues per sector, grouped in the categories of manufacturing and mining, building and real estate, trade, financial and payment services, and other services (Information and Communication Technology, consulting, tour operators, typographic services, hotels, engineering efforts, logistics, gaming), is reported in Figs. 1 and 2.

Analysis on a local basis shows a concentration of issue in some regions, particularly in Northern Italy. The breakdown of the amount of issues per issuer

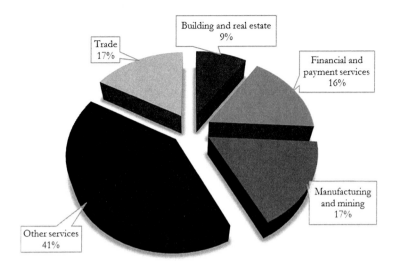

Fig. 1 Outstanding allocation on a sector basis: number of issues. *Source*: Our elaborations of data from *Borsa Italiana*

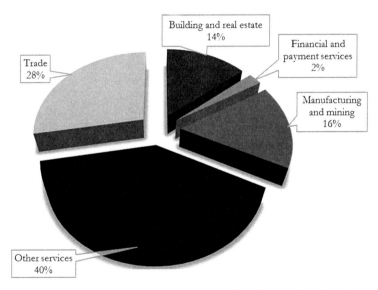

Fig. 2 Outstanding allocation on a sector basis: outstanding. *Source*: Our elaborations of data from *Borsa Italiana*

location is shown in the diagram below (Figs. 3 and 4): the region with the highest volume is Lombardia, followed by Emilia-Romagna, Veneto, Lazio and Marche.[6]

---

[6] 1. Campania; 2. Emilia-Romagna; 3. Lazio; 4. Liguria; 5. Lombardia; 6. Marche, 7. Molise; 8. Piemonte; 9.Puglia; 10. Sicilia; 11. Trentino-Alto Adige; 12. Umbria; 13. Veneto.

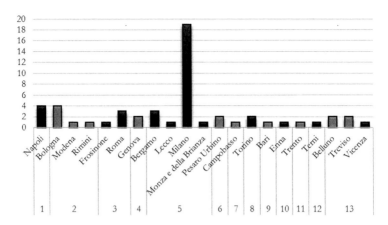

Fig. 3 Outstanding allocation on a geographic range: number of issues. *Source*: Our elaborations of data from *Borsa Italiana*

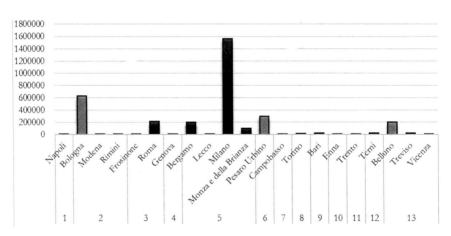

Fig. 4 Outstanding allocation on a geographic range: outstanding. *Source*: Our elaborations of data from *Borsa Italiana*

Most of the bonds, even by value, consider a "bullet" repayment of the entire principal and pay a periodic fixed rate (Table 2). Only seven bonds have variable rates, and the indexation parameter is always the Euribor 3 or 6 months, respectively, for quarterly or semi-annual coupon instruments.

The average maturity of the instruments is in 2018. The annual average fixed rate is approximately 6.8 %, higher than the rates recorded on 31 December 2013 by the Bank of Italy on loan facilities to the productive sector with original maturity between 1 and 5 years, which were included in a range between 3.05 % (for amounts over 25 million euros) and 5.69 % (for amounts up to 250,000 euros).

Table 2 Issue allocation per type of securities and repayment clauses

Type	N. of issues	Outstanding (*euro × 1000*)			
		Min	Max	Average	Total
FINANCE BILLS	4	114.00	10,000.00	2,778.50	11,114.00
BONDS	49	1,000.00	411,600.00	67,582.65	3,311,550.00
Amortizing	10	1,800.00	12,300.00	6,185.00	61,850.00
Fixed rate	9	1,800.00	12,300.00	5,872.22	52,850.00
Floating rate	1	9,000.00	9,000.00	9,000.00	9,000.00
Bullet repayment	39	1,000.00	411,600.00	83,325.64	3,249,700.00
Fixed rate	33	1,000.00	411,600.00	83,242.42	2,747,000.00
Floating rate	6	1,900.00	250,000.00	83,783.33	502,700.00
CONVERTIBLE BONDS (bullet repayment; fixed rate)	1	8,000.00	8,000.00	8,000.00	8,000.00
Total	*54*	*114.00*	*411,600.00*	*61,679.00*	*3,330,664.00*

Source: Our elaborations of data from *Borsa Italiana*

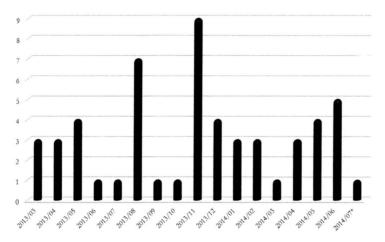

Fig. 5 Issue allocation per month: number of issues. *Source*: Our elaborations of data from *Borsa Italiana*

Among the 39 issuing companies, only 22 had a 2012 turnover exceeding 50 million euros; among them were even very small companies, such as consumer credit companies that were raising funds to finance personal loans, on which rates much higher than those on the issue are applied.

The monthly distribution of the number of issues is rather erratic, with peaks in the months of August and November 2013, while in March 2013, the highest amount was recorded, concentrated in three issues of a single company (Figs. 5 and 6).

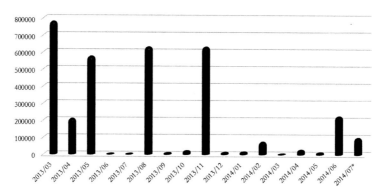

Fig. 6 Issue allocation per month: outstanding. *Source*: Our elaborations of data from *Borsa Italiana*

4 Existing Problems and Possible Developments

As previously discussed, the start was quite slow, and so far, the results have been below expectations. While these data suggest considering the objective limits that have led to a slow start, it must be recognized that to make a turn and promote the development of a dense and efficient mini-bond market, a number of conditions are required involving companies, banks and investors, and particular attention should be paid to the role of guarantees to cover risks and the adequate supervision of risks.

From the point of view of business, it should be preliminarily considered that the structural characteristics of Italian companies, in particular their small dimension (Malavasi 2015), are "per se" an obstacle to the expansion of non-bank financial instruments and make it difficult to find new capital, both debt and risk. This has led some authors to argue that "the crisis of Italian enterprises is the crisis of an industrial system and of its obsolete and non-competitive sector structure. The vulnerability of firms (and banks?) was masked for too long" (Monferrà and Porzio 2014). According to this viewpoint, the effects of the crisis have been exacerbated by existing financial imbalances, although they were not the direct cause of the crisis. That is to say that the structural problems—the dwarfism of businesses and banks farther away from them as the result of concentrations in the sector—have exacerbated the consequences of an endogenous phenomenon and that we must be aware that structural problems cannot be solved only with new finance tools. In a future perspective, sources of company financing should be made more homogenous, in line with the rest of Europe and most developed countries, where bank financing is not dominant, but competes with other channels that provide more capital.

From the point of view of the issuer, the culture of poor transparency, as concerns information, must be overcome with an improvement of information to investors, which should cover both financial statements and the projects that will benefit from financing as well as the results to be achieved; this also requires a revision of the law on "false corporate communication"—which is considered to have had a low deterrent force—and the enforcement of Law 231/2007 on the administrative liability of legal entities.

De facto, all information is now provided directly to investors because preliminary negotiations are carried out between parties that are out of the market and because the quotation of securities is often a subsequent formality.

If the future goal of institutions is to create an efficient and transparent secondary market and companies' goal is to reach a wider clientele of investors, the information in the "Admission Document" required by the Italian Stock Exchange is not sufficient for these purposes; only the risk analysis is reported (activities conducted, actions to be performed) in this document, but the indication of the consequences of the environment, quality of business, commitment to the future and quantitative predictions about the impacts of the flow of resources directed to businesses on the generation of economics are missing.

Actually, the real risk would be the lack of a project, which does not allow for an assessment of the capacity of new funds to generate the development of the company that issues a mini-bond. This calls for the disclosure of a business plan that forecasts the ability to generate future returns in terms of cash. In this regard, it has been noted that for almost all SMEs that have issued bonds listed on the ExtraMOTPRO, the "Admission Document" required by the Italian Stock Exchange is poor in content, as are the strategic directions describing project development to investors (see Zanotti and Martinoli 2014).

Disclosure and the strategic vision are more relevant because the real guarantee that a loan will be repaid is the validity of the industrial project that funds, specifically the ability to generate income and cash flow. It should also be stated that mini-bonds are not a good tool for all businesses, as they are less versatile than bank loans (as they are not extensible), and their issue should have an adequate minimum cut (also in relation to the dimension of the fixed costs) to be attractive for the market, especially for foreign investors.

The loan can be structured to meet the most diverse needs of issuers, for the maturity of the bond (5–7 years) and mode of capital payment (amortizing, bullet, with grace period, convertibility clause at maturity). Based on the characteristics of the issuer, there can be a mini-bond configuration for traditional industrial enterprises and mini-project bonds for utilities that need funding for individual infrastructural projects, which provide cash flow to support debt service.

In any case, to succeed, the company must propose concrete development plans and share these projects with potential investors to involve them in the project, risks and future successes. This is because mini-bonds are essentially illiquid and are placed from the point of view of risk between a medium to long-term bank loan and the involvement of a private equity fund. Compared to these forms, the cost increases as a result of the issue remuneration to compensate for the increased risk (counterparty credit risk and liquidity risk) that is assumed by the investor as well as the fixed costs due to commissions to intermediaries and listing costs.

For the high incidence of fixed costs—which, according to some, makes emissions below 2.5 million euros inadvisable—this market appears to be more suited to companies of a certain size rather than small ones, which could be attracted if the intermediaries adopt standard processes for their evaluation; in any case, it is appropriate for the company to provide itself with a model to compare the costs of different forms of financing as well as of taxes.

In a longer perspective, the problem of dimensional constraint could be overcome with the "mini-bond chain," which combines in one issue the needs of different small businesses that have difficulty accessing the bond market, that also should occur after the introduction of incentives by the Decree for Development. A "cumulative" issue could involve an association of companies in the same sector or geographic area, which may be assisted by a guarantee by trade associations or consortia. At present, however, this proposal is only being discussed; if it advances, it will also call for specific rules to regulate such activities.

As concerns banks, the new laws have also sought to respond to the need to reduce risks as a result of the significant deterioration in the quality of loans (loans to SMEs are more at risk) and the need to align gradually with new rules on capital requirements of the Third Basel Accord.

With the crisis in the model of bank behaviour—leverage used to support financially unbalanced companies, which weakened both—which was not sustainable, they have had to reduce financial flows to SMEs; recourse to the capital market through mini-bonds may represent an alternative channel for bank credit, or rather, a complementary one.[7]

Adding direct access to financial markets to the traditional channel is an opportunity for both banks and businesses; a new relationship between the two entities opens, one that allows companies to have access to other sources of funding with bank support. In fact, when a company contacts a bank to issue a mini-bond, an inquiry is made, as for a new loan application, and the bank evaluates the creditworthiness and feasibility of the project on which to base the issuance of the bonds; if the result is positive, it looks for the availability of specialized funds to be facilitators of the transaction.

The commitment of companies and banks is necessary, but not sufficient: final investors are also necessary because without them, the market does not take off; in this first phase, privately issues placed have prevailed (first movers), while the second phase has already started with the launch of dedicated "closed funds" (over 20 have already been established), which should attract banks (especially those of the territory). In the third phase, foreign institutional investors should step in. In addition to "closed funds" that are reserved for qualified investors, provisions must be made for alternative forms of financing to businesses (in particular SMEs). The role of institutional investors (insurance companies, pension funds, foundations and asset management of securities) must also be considered with regard to bank credit.

The strengthening of the role of mini-bonds and support for the creation of a market for credit funds has been advocated by the Global Financial Stability Report of the International Monetary Fund (2014) because international experience demonstrates the effectiveness of public intervention through the activation of a "fund of funds" that channels available resources and stimulates new entrants. In Italy, the

---

[7] For more details about the role of banks in supporting SMEs in this field, see Malavasi (2015).

project of "fund of funds" of private debt has been launched by the Italian Fund Investment SGR with the sponsorship of *Cassa Depositi e Prestiti*, a joint-stock company under public control, which manages postal saving funds (according to the model of *Kreditanstaltfuer Wiederaufbau-KfW* in Germany, which supports the development of SMEs).

Although the base of investors is potentially large, from the point of view of risk control, funds specialized in mini-bonds are more favoured, with facilities dedicated to the analysis of the risk-return of issuers, which allows for the diversification of risk and ensures the greater liquidity of the investment[8] as well as the distribution of income. Social security institutions deserve special mention: while there is a significant margin to increase the use of pension savings to support the real economy with market-based instruments, such use should be consistent with the mission of social security savings, which is to manage investments with the objective of providing pension benefits.

Considering risk, it is clear that the offer of guarantees (public and mutual)—to be associated with the issue of mini-bonds—plays a key role in dissemination among professional investors and changes the development of the market; in a still "young" market, such guarantees would nullify the danger of a setback caused by defaults among the first issuers. Such initiatives have already been taken in France and the United Kingdom, with public intervention aimed at starting the market and subsequently attracting initially reluctant private capital.

Therefore, the following recent initiatives in this direction in Italy should be welcomed:

- the Central Guarantee Fund of the *Cassa Depositi e Prestiti* will provide its coverage to banks, brokers and asset management companies that subscribe to mini-bonds or minimum bond portfolios.[9]
- the establishment by the S.A.C.E. (the Italian export credit agency) of a closed-end fund that will be dedicated to investing in the private placement of securities issued by Italian companies, listed and unlisted, exporters and customers in the same S.A.C.E.

Moreover, the extent and role of government guarantees and mutual benefits should be assessed for the potential negative effects of the moral hazard that could result. For this reason, the aspect of guarantees has a role, as has been said, in the start-up phase of the market, while in a mature market, more substantial aspects should prevail because the real guarantee of debt repayment—that is, the coverage of risk assumed by investors—is the validity of the industrial project that is financed, namely, its perspective ability to produce income and thus cash-flow.

---

[8] The problem of the illiquidity of securities could be solved by operators who are committed to serving as market-makers for already structured and quoted mini-bonds to develop a liquid secondary market that would also benefit the primary one, as it would stimulate investors to use these relatively new tools.

[9] In perspective, it is planned to extend the warranty even to portfolios of loans already in place, consistent with the intent expressed by the ECB to refinance banks through the ABS.

This suggests allowing "retail" to access the mini-bond market only when it is mature and to carefully consider the transfer of risk from banks to the market, that is, through securitization, in the light of the negative experience of the securitization of "subprime" loans in the United States.

5 Conclusions

The aim of this paper has been to assess direct access to the debt capital market by unlisted companies as a result of the application of new rules that were introduced in Italy starting from 2012. The results achieved are to be considered a rough approximation because they are affected by a short period of observation and are also limited to issues listed on the Italian market.

This study has empirically investigated the listed financial instruments in the Italian Stock Exchange that were issued by unlisted companies in the period from March 2013 to July 2014. We find that the start of mini-bonds has been quite slow; so far, the results have been below expectations. We also underline a polarization of issuers among small businesses and companies of medium large size (which absorbed approximately one half of the total outstanding issues). Generally, the principal declared objective of issues is to fund expansion operations, even abroad, and in some cases, with the intention of reducing the exposure of banks. The main operating sectors are "services" (Information and Communication Technology, engineering, gaming) and building/real estate. Most of the bonds consider a "bullet" repayment of the entire principal and pay a periodic fixed rate. The annual average fixed rate is approximately 6.8 %, higher than the rates recorded on loan facilities to the productive sector with original maturity between 1 and 5 years, which were included at a range between 3.05 % and 5.69 %.

In general, the entire discussion led us to conclude that the changes in the rules on corporate finance have created "works in progress"; therefore, despite the small results that have been achieved, one can see a more widespread use of direct financing to SMEs through bonds and similar securities in the near future.

The full realization of the objective of regulatory changes—namely, the creation of channels for raising alternative funds with respect to the banking system and the opening of the Italian system to foreign channels—entails the expansion of the number of potential investors and the related development of an efficient secondary market. Moreover, the process of developing new forms of financial intermediation should be conducted with prudence and transparency, assessing the contribution and potential risks in terms of liquidity and the stability of the system, adapting best practices and international experience to the Italian reality.[10]

---

[10] This refers, in particular, to the operations of the cornerstone investors of the Business Finance Partnership type in the UK or constraints on portfolios for institutional investors in France.

The conclusions we have come to, even though they only allow a first evaluation of benefits to corporate finance deriving from a market debt alternative to bank credit, suggest further investigations on these topics.

References

Bank of Italy (2014) Annual report for 2013. Bank of Italy, Rome
Culicchi R, Puna J (2014) I nuovi strumenti di finanziamento per le imprese: i c.d. Mini-bonds. Diritto Bancario. http://www.dirittobancario.it/approfondimenti/capital-markets/i-nuovi-strumenti-di-finanziamento-le-imprese-i-cd-mini-bonds
Gai L, Ielasi F (2013) L'impatto dei mini bond sulla gestione finanziaria delle imprese. In: Calugi R, Paglietti G (eds) Mini-bond. Istruzioni per l'uso. CCIAA, Milan
Malavasi R (2015) Bottlenecks of the financial system at national and regional level: the case of Italy and Sardinia. In: Rossi SPS, Malavasi R (eds) The global financial crisis, bank behaviour and the credit crunch (forthcoming)
Monferrà S, Porzio C (2014) I rapporti banca-impresa. In: Paper presented at the ADEIMF winter workshop, University of Milano-Bicocca, Milan, 13–14 Feb 2014. http://www.adeimf.it/images/documenti/convegni/febbraio2014/Sessione_1_I_rapporti_banca_impresa_Monferr%C2%85_Porzio.pdf
Panetta F, Signoretti FM (2010) Domanda e offerta di credito in Italia durante la crisi finanziaria. Bank of Italy, Occasional Paper No. 63
Zanotti F, Martinoli G (2014) "Minibond", strumenti di sviluppo o sopravvivenza? Report by Corporate Strategy Expertise-Crescendo Srl, Milan. http://www.cse-crescendo.it/minibond-strumenti-di-sviluppo-o-sopravvivenza/